A SPOON FULL OF LOVIN'

THIRD EDITION

ROBIN KINDER

Published by Spines
ISBN: 979-8-89691-439-6

A SPOON FULL OF LOVIN'

A CUP OF KINDNESS TO START THE DAY, A HEART FULL OF LOVE TO SHARE, GRATEFULNESS FOR ALL THE BLESSINGS THAT WE RECEIVE, A BIT OF HUMBLENESS THAT STRENGHTENS OUR CHARACTER, A SMILE ALWAYS PEAKING THROUGH THE CLOUDS, AND DON'T FORGET A PINCH OF TENDERNESS AND UNDERSTANDING FOR THOSE LESS FORTUNATE, AND ALWAYS REMEMBER THAT THE CUP IS HALF FULL, AND NOT HALF EMPTY. ALL OF THESE INGREDIENTS COMBINED WITH A GENTLE SPIRIT AND CARRIED WITH US THROUGH EACH DAY, PROVIDES US WITH MUCH MORE THAN JUST A SPOON FULL OF LOVIN TO PASS ON TO THOSE WE TOUCH.

Preface

It is my hope that within these pages, friends and family will find not only tasty treats to bring to the table for their loved ones, but also find small 'pearls of wisdom' and 'sweet thoughts' that will satisfy their soul and spirit, as they have mine through the years. Compiling a cookbook of "comfort" recipes has always been a dream of mine. I have been collecting recipes since I was young girl. I can remember cataloguing recipes in folders on our family front porch deep in the south where food is a way of life. I've kept those folders with me through the years and now, I have the opportunity to share some of them with you. Enjoy the food with family and friends and accept each new day as a gift for us to share with those we love.

Robin Kinder

Contents

1.	APPETIZERS	5
2.	BREADS AND STARCHES	36
3.	SALADS AND GREENS	54
4.	SANDWICHES	74
5.	BEVERAGES	83
6.	DIPS AND SAUCES	88
7.	STEWS AND SOUPS	110
8.	CASSEROLES	137
9.	VEGETABLES	152
10.	BEEF ENTREES	167
11.	PORK ENTREES	185
12.	POULTRY ENTREES	194
13.	SEAFOOD ENTREES	211
14.	PASTA AND RICE	238
15	CAKES AND PIES	251
16.	COOKIES AND TREATS	279
17.	BREAKFAST	316

Appetizers

GRILLED LAMB CHOP
HORS D'OEUVRES

12	SMALL RIB LAMB CHOPS
$\frac{1}{4}$	CUP EXTRA VIRGIN OLIVE OIL
3	TBLS. WORCESTERSHIRE SAUCE
4	PODS GARLIC, FINELY CHOPPED
2	TBLS. FRESH ROSEMARY
1	TSP. OREGANO
	SEVERAL HARDY SHAKES OF
	LEMON PEPPER

HAVE BUTCHER CUT LAMB CHOPS APPROXIMATELY $\frac{1}{2}$" THICK. COMBINE OLIVE OIL, WORCESTERSHIRE SAUCE, GARLIC, ROSEMARY, OREGANO AND LEMON PEPPER IN A SMALL BOWL. POUR OVER LAMB CHOPS IN A RECLOSABLE PLASTIC BAG. MARINATE AT LEAST TWO HOURS AT ROOM TEMPERATURE.

HAVE GRILL AT MEDIUM HEIGHT WITH A HOT FIRE. PLACE LAMB CHOPS ON GRILL. BE CAREFUL AS DRIPPINGS MAY CAUSE FLAME TO JUMP. GRILL FOR APPROXIMATELY ONE TO TWO MINUTES ON EACH SIDE, REMOVING CHOPS WHILE STILL PINK.

SERVE AS HORS D'OEUVRE ON A PLATTER. THERE ARE EASY TO PICK UP WITH YOUR FINGERS. SAME RECIPE MAY BE USED FOR THICKER CHOPS AS A MEAL WITH APPROPRIATE LONGER COOKING TIME FOR DESIRED TASTE.

MAKES 12 SERVINGS. BIG EATERS CAN EAT FIVE
OR SIX, SO GET PLENTY OF CHOPS IF SERVING
FOR A PARTY.

Into every heart, love brings a little heaven.

FRIED COCONUT CURRY SHRIMP
APPETIZER

16/20	COUNT PEELED, DEVEINED SHRIMP
1	8 OZ. CAN COCONUT MILK
1	8 OZ. CAN COCO LOPEZ
$\frac{1}{4}$	CUP + A PINCH OF CURRY POWDER
$1\frac{1}{2}$	CUPS SHREDDED COCONUT (UNSWEETENED)
$1\frac{1}{2}$	CUPS BREAD CRUMBS
1	CUP ALL PURPOSE FLOUR
2	EGGS
$\frac{1}{2}$	CUP MILK
	SALT AND PEPPER
	JALAPENO, FINELY DICED (SEEDS REMOVED)

PREHEAT OVEN TO 350°. TOAST COCONUT.
MARINATE SHRIMP IN COCONUT MILK, COCO
LOPEZ, CURRY POWDER, JALAPENO, SALT AND
PEPPER. COVER AND REFRIGERATE FOR 24
HOURS. MIX TOASTED COCONUT, BREAD
CRUMBS, SALT AND PEPPER. IN A SEPARATE
BOWL, COMBINE EGGS AND MILK. PLACE FLOUR
IN A THIRD BOWL. REMOVE SHRIMP FROM
MARINADE AND DISCARD MARINADE MIXTURE.

BREAD SHRIMP IN FLOUR, THEN EGG WASH
MIXTURE, THEN COCONUT BREAD CRUMBS
MIXTURE. FRY IN 350° OIL. DRAIN ON PAPER
AND SERVE HOT.

I wish you a rainbow and a handful of stars.

PEBBLE SHRIMP

1	LB. COOKED SHRIMP
2	3 OZ. PKGS. CREAM CHEESE, ROOM TEMPERATURE
1	TBL. LEMON JUICE
2	TSPS. HORSERADISH
$\frac{1}{4}$	TSP. TABASCO
1	CUP FINELY CHOPPED FRESH PARSLEY

FINELY CHOP SHRIMP. CREAM THE CREAM
CHEESE, ADD LEMON JUICE, HORSERADISH,
TABASCO AND SHRIMP. MIX THOROUGHLY AND
TASTE FOR SEASONING. SHAPE INTO SMALL
BALLS. ROLL IN CHOPPED PARSLEY. MAKES
ABOUT 40-45 APPETIZERS.

On this journey through time and space.
The heart will find its way.

BOURSIN POTATO GRATIN

2	CUPS WHIPPING CREAM
2/3	CUP BOURSIN CHEESE WITH BLACK PEPPER (RECIPE ON PAGE 21)
2	TBLS. MINCED SHALLOTS
2	CLOVES GARLIC, MINCED
1	TBL. MINCED SHALLOTS
2½	LBS. RED NEW POTATOES, SCRUBBED AND SLICED ¼" THICK (LEAVE SKIN ON) SALT AND FRESHLY GROUND BLACK PEPPER
2	OR MORE TBLS. SNIPPED CHIVES
2	OR MORE TBLS. SNIPPED PARSLEY

GENEROUSLY BUTTER A 13"x9"x2" BAKING DISH. IN A HEAVY 1½ QT. SAUCEPAN, HEAT CREAM, BOURSIN CHEESE, SHALLOTS AND GARLIC OVER MEDIUM HEAT, STIRRING UNTIL CHEESE MELTS.

PREHEAT OVEN TO 400°. ARRANGE HALF OF THE POTATOES IN THE BAKING DISH IN SLIGHTLY OVERLAPPING ROWS. GENEROUSLY SEASON WITH SALT AND PEPPER. POUR HALF OF THE CHEESE MIXTURE OVER THE POTATOES. SPRINKLE WITH THE CHIVES. REPEAT LAYERING WITH THE REMAINING POTATO SLICES, MORE SALT AND PEPPER AND CHEESE MIXTURE.

BAKE UNCOVERED ONE HOUR UNTIL POTATOES
ARE TENDER AND TOP IS GOLDEN BROWN.
SPRINKLE WITH PARSLEY.

The moon must be in love with autumn or it
could never shine down
upon us with such silver splendor.

FRIJOLES MOLIDOS

1	LB. BLACK BEANS, SOAKED OVERNIGHT
1	TBL. VEGETABLE OIL
1	LARGE ONION, CHOPPED
1	GREEN PEPPER, CHOPPED
4	CLOVES GARLIC, MINCED
2	QTS. CHICKEN BROTH
$1\frac{1}{2}$	TBLS. SALT
6	SLICES BACON
1	(4 OZ.) CAN CHOPPED GREEN CHILIES, DRAINED
2	TSPS. TABASCO
1	TSP. GROUND BLACK PEPPER
2	TSPS. GROUND CUMIN
1	TSP. CRUMBLED DRY OREGANO
2	OZS. GRATED ($\frac{1}{2}$ CUP) QUESO ANEJO* (OR SUBSTITUTE GRATED MONTERREY JACK)

DRAIN BEANS. IN A LARGE SAUCEPAN, HEAT
OIL AND SAUTE ONION, GREEN PEPPER AND
GARLIC UNTIL SOFTENED. ADD BEANS AND

CHICKEN BROTH. BRING TO A BOIL. LOWER
HEAT AND SIMMER, COVERED, FOR 2 HOURS, OR
UNTIL BEANS ARE TENDER. DRAIN ANY EXCESS
LIQUID AND MASH BEANS IN SAUCEPAN.
SEASON WITH SALT.

IN LARGE SKILLET, COOK BACON UNTIL CRISP.
CRUMBLE AND SET ASIDE. STIR MASHED BEANS
INTO RESERVED BACON FAT IN SKILLET. STIR
IN BACON, CHILIES, TABASCO, BLACK PEPPER,
CUMIN AND OREGANO.

SERVE HOT OR AT ROOM TEMPERATURE,
SPRINKLE WITH CHEESE JUST BEFORE SERVING.
IF DESIRED, COOL, COVER, REFRIGERATE AND
REHEAT BEFORE SERVING. SERVE WITH
TORTILLA CHIPS AND VEGETABLE DIPPERS.

*AVAILABLE AT MEXICAN MARKETS.
LEFTOVERS FREEZE BEAUTIFULLY. SIMPLY
REFRIGERATE AND WHEN THEY ARE COLD, CUT
INTO INDIVIDUAL SIZE SERVINGS, LIFT OUT
OF CONTAINER WITH SPATULA, AND PUT INTO
SELF-SEALING PLASTIC STORAGE BAGS OR
WRAP IN PLASTIC AND FREEZE UNTIL NEEDED.

*Blessed are those who have the
courage to dream.*

PARMESAN PIZZA POPCORN

3	QTS. POPPED POPCORN
2	TBLS. EXTRA VIRGIN OLIVE OIL
2	TBLS. DRY SPAGHETTI SAUCE MIX
2	TBLS. GRATED PARMESAN CHEESE

PLACE POPCORN IN LARGE BOWL. HEAT OIL IN
SMALL PAN. DRIZZLE OVER POPCORN. ADD
SPAGHETTI SAUCE MIX AND CHEESE.

*Follow your dreams and believe in
the voice of your heart.*

PARROTHEAD PICANTE

4	CUPS WATER SEASONED TO TASTE WITH ZATARAIN'S CRAB BOIL
$1\frac{1}{2}$	LBS. UNPEELED FRESH SHRIMP
2	RIPE AVOCADOS, PEELED AND CUBED
$\frac{1}{4}$	CUP KEY LIME JUICE
6	CUPS CUBED TOMATOES
12	CLOVES GARLIC, MINCED
1	TBL. GROUND CUMIN
2	TSPS. PAPRIKA
3	LARGE ONIONS, CHOPPED
3	JALAPENO PEPPERS, SEEDED AND CHOPPED
1	TSP. SALT
	TORTILLA CHIPS

BRING WATER TO A BOIL. ADD SHRIMP AND
COOK 3 TO 5 MINUTES OR UNTIL SHRIMP TURN
PINK. DRAIN SHRIMP WELL. RINSE WITH COLD
WATER. CHILL. PEEL AND DEVEIN SHRIMP. CUT
SHRIMP INTO QUARTERS AND SET ASIDE.

COMBINE AVOCADOS AND LIME JUICE IN A
SMALL BOWL. SET ASIDE.
COMBINE SHRIMP, TOMATOES, GARLIC, CUMIN,
PAPRIKA, ONIONS, PEPPERS AND SALT IN A
LARGE BOWL. GENTLY STIR IN AVOCADO/LIME
MIXTURE. CHILL AT LEAST ONE HOUR.

RED BELL PEPPER PATE

3	LARGE RED BELL PEPPERS, QUARTERED, SEEDED AND ROASTED
8	CLOVES GARLIC, ROASTED
	DASH OF WHITE WINE
	WORCESTERSHIRE SAUCE
½	(8 OZ.) CARTON CREAM CHEESE AT ROOM TEMPERATURE

PEEL ROASTED BELL PEPPERS. PLACE IN FOOD
PROCESSOR. ADD ROASTED GARLIC AND
WORCESTERSHIRE SAUCE. PROCESS UNTIL
PUREED.

PUT IN SAUCEPAN WITH NO OIL. OVER LOW
HEAT, STIR CONTINUOUSLY UNTIL WATER IS
ALMOST COMPLETELY EVAPORATED. COOK AND

STIR IN CREAM CHEESE. STIR UNTIL SMOOTH.
A SMALL WHISK HELPS WITH THIS.

LINE A ROUND, COVERED BOWL WITH PLASTIC
WRAP. PUT MIXTURE IN BOWL. COVER AND
REFRIGERATE UNTIL READY TO SERVE. TURN
OUT ON SERVING PLATE AND SURROUND WITH
FAVORITE CRACKERS.

*Wisdom may be conceived in knowledge, but it is
born when mankind believes in mankind.*

SAVORY STUFFED MUSHROOMS

24	MEDIUM SIZED FRESH MUSHROOMS (ABOUT 1 LB.)
6	TBLS. UNSALTED BUTTER
$\frac{1}{4}$	CUP CHOPPED ONION
4	CLOVES GARLIC, MINCED
1	CUP PEPPERIDGE FARM HERB SEASONED STUFFING
1	3 OZ. PKG. CREAM CHEESE, SOFTENED
3	TBLS. GRATED PARMESAN CHEESE
2	TBLS. CHOPPED FRESH PARSLEY OR 2 TSPS. DRIED PARSLEY FLAKES

REMOVE STEMS FROM MUSHROOMS. CHOP
ENOUGH STEMS TO MAKE 1 CUP AND SET ASIDE.
IN MEDIUM SAUCEPAN OVER MEDIUM HEAT,
HEAT 2 TBLS. BUTTER. BRUSH MUSHROOM CAPS
WITH BUTTER AND PLACE TOP SIDE DOWN IN
SHALLOW BAKING PAN. HEAT REMAINING

BUTTER. ADD CHOPPED MUSHROOM STEMS,
ONION AND MINCED GARLIC AND COOK UNTIL
TENDER. ADD STUFFING, CREAM CHEESE,
PARMESAN CHEESE AND PARSLEY. MIX LIGHTLY.
SPOON ABOUT 1 TBL. STUFFING MIXTURE INTO
EACH MUSHROOM CAP.

BAKE AT 425° FOR 10 MINUTES OR UNTIL
MUSHROOMS ARE HEATED THROUGH. IF
DESIRED, GARNISH WITH SWEET PEPPER
STRIPS. MAKES 24 APPETIZERS

*Perhaps in destiny's grand design,
there are no chance meetings.*

TORTILLA ROLL UPS

2	8 OZ. PKGS. CREAM CHEESE, SOFTENED
1	4 OZ. CAN WHOLE CHILIES, SEEDED AND CHOPPED
1	6 OZ. CAN PITTED BLACK OLIVES, SLICED
10	FLOUR TORTILLAS
8	OZS. CHOPPED PECANS
½	CUP MEDIUM PACE PICANTE SAUCE
1	TBL. MINCED ONION
1	TSP. LEMON JUICE
¼	TSP. CAYENNE PEPPER
2	TSPS. TABASCO

BEAT CREAM CHEESE, PICANTE SAUCE, ONION,
LEMON JUICE, CAYENNE AND TABASCO UNTIL
SOFT. FOLD IN CHILIES, OLIVES, PECANS AND

SPREAD ON TORTILLA AND ROLL UP AS A "JELLY ROLL". PLACE IN DISH AND COVER WITH SEMI-DAMP PAPER TOWEL AND SEAL WITH PLASTIC WRAP. REFRIGERATE OVERNIGHT. SLICE $\frac{1}{4}$" THICK AND SERVE WITH PICANTE SAUCE.

Love is seen in the embrace of family for in the presence of those who share our story, we are free to be our finest selves.

TORTILLA TIDBITS WITH LATIN ROAST PORK

1	LB. BONELESS PORK LOIN
5	TBLS. LATIN RUB (RECIPE FOLLOWS)
1	8 OZ. PACKAGE SPREADABLE CREAM CHEESE WITH PINEAPPLE
3	TBLS. PREPARED HORSERADISH
8	10" FLOUR TORTILLAS
1	8 OZ. JAR ROASTED RED PEPPERS, DRAINED
1	8 OZ. CONTAINER ALFALFA SPROUTS

COAT ALL SURFACES OF PORK LOIN WITH RUB. PLACE PORK IN SHALLOW PAN AND ROAST IN A 350° OVEN FOR 45 MINUTES, UNTIL INTERNAL TEMPERATURE REGISTERS 155°. REMOVE ROAST FROM OVEN, LET COOL, WRAP AND REFRIGERATE.

MEANWHILE, IN A SMALL BOWL, STIR
TOGETHER THE HORSERADISH AND CREAM
CHEESE. SPREAD A TBL. OF CREAM CHEESE
MIXTURE ON ONE SIDE OF EACH TORTILLA. TOP
CREAM CHEESE LAYER WITH SOME OF THE RED
PEPPER AND ALFALFA SPROUTS.

VERY THINLY SLICE THE PORK LOIN AND TOP
ALFALFA SPROUTS WITH A THIN LAYER OF
SLICED PORK.

ROLL UP TORTILLA TIGHTLY, WRAP SECURELY IN
FOIL AND REFRIGERATE OVERNIGHT. TO SERVE,
SLICE TORTILLA ROLLS INTO 1 TO $1\frac{1}{2}$" SERVING
PIECES AND ARRANGE ON A SERVING TRAY.
MAKES ABOUT 48 TIDBITS

Take a leap of faith to receive love's bounty.

LATIN RUB

3	TBLS. GROUND CUMIN
2	TBLS. CHILI POWDER
2	TBLS. GROUND CORIANDER
1	TBL. CINNAMON
1	TBL. BROWN SUGAR
2	TBLS. SALT
1	TBL. RED PEPPER FLAKES
2	TBLS. GROUND BLACK PEPPER

MAKES ABOUT 1 CUP. USE FOR SEASONING PORK
CHOPS, RIBS OR ROASTS BEFORE GRILLING.
STORE AT ROOM TEMPERATURE IN A
CONTAINER WITH A TIGHT FITTING LID.

*If I could sit across the porch from God, I'd
thank Him for lending me you.*

SEASONED SALT

1	CUP KOSHER SALT
$\frac{1}{2}$	CUP GARLIC POWDER
3	TBLS. CAYENNE PEPPER
1	TBL. WHITE PEPPER
1	TBL. BLACK PEPPER
1	TSP. ONION POWDER

*Of all the moments we gather in our lives,
the ones we cherish most are the moments shared.*

CAJUN SEASONING

1	26 OZ. BOX SALT
3	TBLS. BLACK PEPPER
2	TBLS. GARLIC POWDER
1	TSP. ONION POWDER
1	TSP. NUTMEG
2	TBLS. ACCENT
2	TBLS. DRIED PARSLEY FLAKES
4	TBLS. CAYENNE PEPPER

3   TBLS. CHILI POWDER

MIX ALL IN LARGE BOWL. FILL A SHAKER FOR
DAILY USE. STORE REMAINDER IN A TIGHTLY
COVERED CONTAINER.

*If you love life dearly, harvest your thoughts
and humbly express your feelings in a way that
others might hear the music you hear.*

BLACK BEAN TACO SALAD

6	6" FLOUR TORTILLAS
1	TBL. SAFFLOWER OIL
$\frac{1}{2}$	LB. BONELESS, SKINLESS CHICKEN, CUT INTO THIN STRIPS
3	CLOVES GARLIC, MINCED
1	15 OZ. CAN BLACK BEANS, RINSED AND DRAINED
1	4 OZ. CAN DICED GREEN CHILIES
$\frac{1}{4}$	CUP BOTTLED STIR-FRY SAUCE
$\frac{1}{8}$	TSP. CAYENNE PEPPER
2	FRESH RIPE TOMATOES, DICED
3	CUPS FIELD GREENS OR ROMAINE
1	LIME, CUT INTO WEDGES

CUT TORTILLAS INTO QUARTERS AND PLACE IN
SINGLE LAYER ON LARGE BAKING SHEET. BAKE
IN 400° OVEN 8 TO 10 MINUTES, OR UNTIL
CRISP.

MEANWHILE, HEAT OIL IN LARGE SKILLET OVER
MEDIUM HIGH HEAT. ADD CHICKEN AND
GARLIC. STIR FRY 2 MINUTES. REDUCE HEAT TO
MEDIUM. GENTLY STIR BEANS, CHILIES, STIR-
FRY SAUCE AND RED PEPPER INTO SKILLET.
SIMMER 1 MINUTE OR UNTIL BEANS ARE
HEATED THROUGH. REMOVE FROM HEAT. STIR
IN TOMATOES. FOR EACH SERVING, SPOON
CHICKEN MIXTURE OVER LETTUCE. SERVE WITH
TORTILLA "CHIPS" AND LIME WEDGES. SERVES 4

There is no wisdom greater than kindness.

BLACK-EYED PEA SALSA

1	16 OZ. CAN BLACK-EYED PEAS, DRAINED
2	TOMATOES, CHOPPED
2	BUNCHES GREEN ONIONS, SLICED
2	TBL. CHOPPED FRESH CILANTRO
4	TBLS. FRESH LIME JUICE
1	10 OZ. CAN RO-TEL TOMATOES, PARTIALLY DRAINED
1	TBL. EXTRA VIRGIN OLIVE OIL
4	CLOVES GARLIC, MINCED
$\frac{1}{2}$	TSP. GROUND CUMIN
$\frac{1}{4}$	TSP. SALT
	RED PEPPER TO TASTE
	LEAF LETTUCE

PLACE PEAS IN COLANDER, RINSE WITH COLD
WATER. DRAIN. COMBINE TOMATOES AND

REMAINING INGREDIENTS EXCEPT LETTUCE IN
MEDIUM BOWL. STIR IN PEAS. COVER AND
REFRIGERATE AT LEAST FOUR HOURS. PLACE IN
A LETTUCE-LINED BOWL. SERVE WITH
TORTILLA CHIPS

The things that the child in us loved,
remain in our hearts forever.

BOURSIN CHEESE WITH BLACK PEPPER

6	CLOVES GARLIC, MINCED
$\frac{1}{2}$	TSP. SALT
8	OZ. CREAM CHEESE (ROOM TEMPERATURE)
$\frac{1}{4}$	CUP BUTTER (ROOM TEMPERATURE)
2	TBLS. FINELY SNIPPED PARSLEY
2	TBLS. COARSELY GROUND BLACK PEPPER

IN A SMALL BOWL, MAKE A PASTE WITH THE
GARLIC AND SALT AND COMBINE WITH THE
CREAM CHEESE, BUTTER, PARSLEY AND PEPPER
UNTIL SMOOTH. COVER AND STORE UP TO TWO
WEEKS IN THE REFRIGERATOR. MAKES ABOUT 1
AND 1/3 CUPS

There is always room in the garden
for one more rose.

CHEESE LOGS

½	LB. SHREDDED WHITE CHEDDAR CHEESE
½	LB. GRATED FETA CHEESE
1	BUNCH CHOPPED PARSLEY
1	SMALL CHOPPED YELLOW ONION
½	TSP. CAYENNE PEPPER
½	TSP. CRUSHED OREGANO
1	EGG
1	BOX PHYLLO DOUGH
	MELTED BUTTER

ADD CHEESE, PARSLEY, ONION, PEPPER, OREGANO AND EGG AND MIX WELL IN A MIXING BOWL.

USING 2 LAYERS OF PHYLLO DOUGH, BRUSH TOP LAYER WITH MELTED BUTTER THEN SPREAD CHEESE MIXTURE ACROSS PHYLLO DOUGH LENGTHWISE. THE CHEESE MIXTURE SHOULD BE ABOUT THE THICKNESS OF A FINGER.

ROLL PHYLLO DOUGH TIGHTLY AND CUT TO DESIRED LENGTH BEFORE BAKING. AFTER CUTTING, BRUSH TOP WITH BUTTER AND BAKE IN OVEN FOR 20 MINUTES AT 400°. THIS CAN ALSO BE EATEN COLD.

EASY CRABMEAT APPETIZERS

6	ENGLISH MUFFINS, SPLIT IN HALF
1	STICK BUTTER
1	5 OZ. GLASS JAR OLD ENGLISH SHARP PASTEURIZED CHEESE SPREAD
1	TBL. MAYONNAISE
1	TSP. GARLIC SALT
1	LB. WHITE CRABMEAT, DRAINED AND PICKED FOR SHELL FRAGMENTS

MELT BUTTER AND CHEESE IN HEAVY SKILLET OVER LOW HEAT. ADD MAYONNAISE AND GARLIC SALT. WHISK UNTIL INGREDIENTS ARE BLENDED. LIGHTLY FOLD IN CRABMEAT. SPREAD CRABMEAT MIXTURE OVER EACH ENGLISH MUFFIN HALF. PLACE ON BAKING SHEET, COVER WITH WAXED PAPER AND FREEZE. USING AN ELECTRIC KNIFE, CUT EACH MUFFIN HALF INTO FOURTHS AND PLACE IN PLASTIC BAGS.

WHEN READY TO SERVE, REMOVE FROM FREEZER AND ALLOW TO THAW FOR ABOUT 8 TO 10 MINUTES. BROIL UNTIL TOPS ARE BUBBLY AND HEATED THROUGH. MAKES ABOUT 48 TO 50 APPETIZERS

JALAPENO CHEESE SQUARES

	NON-STICK COOKING SPRAY
4	EGGS
2	CUPS SHREDDED SHARP CHEDDAR CHEESE
1	4 OZ. JAR SLICED PIMENTOS, DRAINED
1	4 OZ. JAR SLICED JALAPENOS, DRAINED

PREHEAT OVEN TO 400°. COAT AN 8"x8" BAKING PAN WITH NONSTICK COOKING SPRAY. SET ASIDE. BEAT EGGS WITH FORK IN MEDIUM MIXING BOWL. ADD CHEESE, PIMENTOS AND JALAPENOS AND BLEND THOROUGHLY, MIXING BY HAND WITH A WOODEN SPOON.

POUR INTO PREPARED BAKING PAN AND BAKE UNTIL SET. LET COOL SLIGHTLY AND CUT INTO SQUARES. SERVE HOT OR COLD. SERVES 8

LAYERED SHRIMP

2	8 OZ. PACKAGES CREAM CHEESE
½	TSP. GARLIC POWDER
2	TSPS. WORCESTERSHIRE SAUCE
1½	TSPS. HOT SAUCE
1	LB. SHRIMP, BOILED AND CHOPPED
8	GREEN ONIONS, CHOPPED
8	OZ. MOZZARELLA CHEESE, SHREDDED
1	BELL PEPPER, CHOPPED
2	TOMATOES, CHOPPED
1	OZ. PARMESAN CHEESE, SHREDDED

BRING CREAM CHEESE TO ROOM TEMPERATURE.
MIX CREAM CHEESE, GARLIC POWDER,
WORCESTERSHIRE SAUCE AND HOT SAUCE.
SPREAD ON A 12" PIE PLATE. LAYER REMAINING
INGREDIENTS IN ORDER GIVEN. SERVE WITH
CRACKERS. SERVES 16

If days offered dreams for sale,
what would you buy?

SPICY CRANBERRY CHEESE

½	CUP WHOLE BERRY CRANBERRY SAUCE
½	CUP JALAPENO PEPPER JELLY
1	8 OZ. PKG. CREAM CHEESE, SOFTENED

COMBINE CRANBERRY SAUCE AND JELLY. SPOON
OVER BLOCK OF CREAM CHEESE.

*We can't feel sad over the loss
of those we love, without first remembering that
the real and true sadness would have been never
having had them in our lives at all.*

SUMMER SAUSAGE

5	LBS. GROUND BEEF
2½	TSPS. MUSTARD SEED
1½	TSPS. GARLIC POWDER
4	TBLS. TENDER QUICK
2½	TBLS. LIQUID SMOKE
2½	TBLS. COARSE GROUND BLACK PEPPER
1	TBL. CRUSHED RED PEPPER

COMBINE ALL INGREDIENTS WELL. COVER AND
REFRIGERATE 24 HOURS. SHAPE INTO LOGS.

BAKE AT 200° UNTIL DONE. THESE MAY BE
FROZEN.

TENDER QUICK IS A CURING SALT MADE BY
MORTON.

SAUSAGE AND HAMBURGER
RYE SNACKS

1	LB. LEAN GROUND MEAT
1	LB. SAUSAGE (MEDIUM TO HOT)
1	LB. VELVEETA CHEESE
1	TBL. OREGANO
1	TSP. GARLIC POWDER
1	TSP. WORCESTERSHIRE SAUCE
2	LOAVES PARTY RYE BREAD

SAUTE GROUND MEAT AND SAUSAGE UNTIL
SLIGHTLY BROWN. DRAIN OFF ANY FAT. BREAK
UP VELVEETA CHEESE INTO SMALL CHUNKS AND
ADD TO MEAT MIXTURE. ADD OREGANO, GARLIC
POWDER AND WORCESTERSHIRE SAUCE. COOK
UNTIL MIXED WELL. SKIM OFF ANY REMAINING
FAT. PLACE RYE BREAD ON COOKIE SHEETS AND
PUT A TSP. OF MIXTURE ON EACH SLICE. PLACE
COOKIE SHEETS IN FREEZER. ONCE FROZEN,
PUT RYE BREAD IN EITHER CONTAINERS OR
FREEZER BAGS.

WHEN COMPANY GETS HUNGRY, JUST PULL OUT
THE APPETIZERS, PLACE THEM ON A COOKIE

SHEET AND BAKE AT 350° FOR ABOUT 15
MINUTES. SERVE HOT

COCKTAIL BALLS

4   CUPS BISQUICK MIX
1   LB. HOT SAUSAGE
1   LB. SHARP CHEESE

KNEAD INGREDIENTS TOGETHER AND FORM
INTO BITE-SIZE BALLS. BAKE AT 350° FOR
ABOUT 12 MINUTES (IF FROZEN). MAY BE
PREPARED IN ADVANCE AND FROZEN.

CHEESE BALLS

3   OZ. PHILADELPHIA CREAM CHEESE
1   STICK BUTTER
1   CUP FLOUR
½   TSP. SALT
1   SMALL CAN DEVILED HAM

BLEND CHEESE AND BUTTER. ADD FLOUR, SALT
AND DEVILED HAM. ROLL THIN (BUT NOT "PAPER
THIN") AND CUT WITH A SMALL BISCUIT
CUTTER. SPREAD HALF OF EACH CIRCLE WITH

MIXTURE AND FOLD OVER. BAKE IN 400° FOR 10
MINUTES.

*When we hurt, our pain can become a bridge to a
deeper awakening.*

BROCCOLI DIP

1   LARGE ONION, CHOPPED OR GRATED
2   STICKS BUTTER
2   PACKAGES CHOPPED BROCCOLI
1   CUP CREAM OF MUSHROOM SOUP
1   PACKAGE GARLIC CHEESE

SAUTE ONION IN BUTTER. ADD BROCCOLI AND
COOK UNTIL TENDER. ADD SOUP AND CHEESE.
CONTINUE COOKING OVER MEDIUM HEAT UNTIL
SMOOTH.

*Every day is a new beginning
made richer by all that has come before.*

PATE

$1\frac{1}{2}$ CUPS CHICKEN LIVERS
        BUTTER
1   TSP. GRATED ONION
1   HARD BOILED EGG, GROUND
3   TBL. HELLMAN'S MAYONNAISE
1   TBL. WORCESTERSHIRE SAUCE
        SALT AND PEPPER

TABASCO

LIGHTLY BROIL CHICKEN LIVERS IN BUTTER
UNTIL DONE. COOL AND PUREE IN FOOD
PROCESSOR. ADD REMAINING INGREDIENTS IN
FOOD PROCESSOR UNTIL MIXTURE HAS
REACHED A GOOD SPREADING CONSISTENCY
(STIFFER THAN PEANUT BUTTER). OIL A MOLD
WITH BUTTER. FILL WITH MIXTURE AND LET
STAND UNTIL FIRM. UNMOLD AND GARNISH
WITH PARSLEY AND SERVE WITH CRACKERS.

There is a magic that comes from loving life with a passion. The only way to find it is to see it with your heart.

SEASONED DIP
WITH RAW VEGETABLES

1	CUP HELLMAN'S MAYONNAISE
2	TBL. DURKEE SAUCE
1	TSP. CELERY SEED
$\frac{1}{2}$	TSP. WORCESTERSHIRE SAUCE
$\frac{1}{4}$	GARLIC CLOVE, GRATED
1	TBL. HORSERADISH
1	TSP. CURRY POWDER
1	TSP. SEASONED SALT
	DASH OF PEPPER
	DASH OF TABASCO SAUCE

MIX WELL AND CHILL. GOOD AS A DIP WITH
CUCUMBERS, CAULIFLOWER, RADISHES, BELL
PEPPER, COCKTAIL TOMATOES, ADVOCADO,
CELERY, CARROTS AND GREEN ONIONS. YIELDS
$1\frac{1}{4}$ CUPS OF DIP

Hope, like love,
transcends all time and distance.

DIP A LA SHRIMP

1	CAN SHRIMP, DRAINED
8	OZ. PACKAGE CREAM CHEESE
1	PACKAGE CHIVE CHEESE
	WORCESTERSHIRE SAUCE, SALT, PEPPER
	AND ONION JUICE TO TASTE

HEAT ALL INGREDIENTS IN DOUBLE BOILER.
SERVE HOT IN CHAFING DISH WITH TOAST
POINTS OR CRACKERS. SERVES 24

Today is the tomorrow we worried about
yesterday.

CHICKEN ALMOND SPREAD

1	SMALL PACKAGE CREAM CHEESE (3 OZ.)
$\frac{1}{2}$	TSP. CELERY SALT
$\frac{1}{2}$	TSP. ONION SALT
1	TSP. SEASONED SALT

1	TSP. WORCESTERSHIRE SAUCE
	DASH OF TABASCO
1/3	CUP SOUR CREAM
1/4	CUP CHOPPED, TOASTED ALMONDS
1	CUP COOKED CHICKEN, FINELY CHOPPED
1	3 OZ. CAN MUSHROOMS, FINELY CHOPPED
	PAPRIKA

SEVERAL HOURS BEFORE SERVING, BLEND
SOFTENED CREAM CHEESE WITH CELERY, ONION
AND SEASONED SALTS, WORCESTERSHIRE,
TABASCO, PARSLEY, AND SOUR CREAM. STIR IN
FINELY CHOPPED ALMONDS, CHICKEN AND
MUSHROOMS. MOLD IN A SERVING DISH.
REFRIGERATE UNTIL CHILLED. SPRINKLE
SPREAD WITH PAPRIKA. SERVE WITH MELBA
TOAST OR CRISP CRACKERS. SURROUND MOLD
WITH FRESH WATERCRESS. SERVES 12 to 14

It is the sweet smelling rain that bathes our city
streets and country roads,
and gives birth to new blossoms, and new
beginnings.

ANDY'S "COLLEGE INN" OYSTERS

SALT AND PEPPER 24 OR MORE OYSTERS.
DREDGE IN FLOUR AND GRILL ON A SLIGHTLY
BUTTERED GRIDDLE ON THE RANGE UNTIL CRISP
AND BROWN. DO NOT BROIL IN THE OVEN. USE

A HEAVY SKILLET. SPRINKLE OYSTERS WITH
BUTTER WHILE GRILLING.

DRESS WITH THE FOLLOWING SAUCE AFTER
THE OYSTERS ARE BROWN AND ARE ON A HOT
SERVING PLATE.

1	TBL. MELTED BUTTER
$\frac{1}{4}$	CUP FRESH LEMON JUICE
1	CUP A-1 STEAK SAUCE
2	TBL. WORCESTERSHIRE SAUCE
1	JIGGER OF SHERRY OR MADERA WINE

CORRECT SEASONING TO TASTE. ADD MORE A-1
STEAK SAUCE IF TOO THIN. ADD MORE SHERRY
IF TOO THICK. SERVE ON A HOT PLATE OR HOT
CHAFING DISH WITH TOOTHPICKS.

*Every day is a time to love and to care about
the earth so that we can give back some of the
wonder the world has given to us.*

CHEESE STRAWS

1	CUP SIFTED FLOUR
1	STICK BUTTER
1	LB. SHARP CHEESE, GRATED
$\frac{1}{4}$	TSP. SALT
$\frac{1}{2}$	TSP. CAYENNE PEPPER

MIX ALL INGREDIENTS WITH A PASTRY
BLENDER. MAKE INTO STRAWS OR BALLS

(MASHED DOWN WITH A FORK). BAKE AT 350°
FOR ABOUT 10 MINUTES.

STUFFED SHRIMP

1   DOZEN CLEANED, COOKED SHRIMP
1   4 OZ. CARTON WHIPPING CREAM
          SOFTENED CREAM CHEESE
          WITH BLUE CHEESE
          DASH GARLIC SALT
½   CUP FINELY SNIPPED PARSLEY

SLIT EACH SHRIMP PART WAY DOWN ON THE
VEIN SIDE. BLEND TOGETHER CREAM CHEESE
AND GARLIC SALT. USING A PASTRY TUBE, FILL
EACH SHRIMP ALONG CUT WITH CHEESE
MIXTURE OR ROLL SHRIMP CAREFULLY IN
CHEESE MIXTURE. CHILL AND SERVE WITH
TOOTHPICKS. I USE SNIPPED PARSLEY IN
CHEESE, IF I ROLL IT IN THE MIXTURE RATHER
THAN STUFFING THEM.

PICANTE TABLESIDE GUACAMOLE

2	TBLS. TOMATOES, DICED FINE
1	TBL. RED ONION, DICED FINE
1	TSP. CILANTRO
$\frac{1}{2}$	TSP. SERRANO CHILI PEPPER, CHOPPED
$\frac{1}{4}$	TSP. SALT
$\frac{1}{8}$	TSP. GRANULATED GARLIC
$\frac{1}{8}$	TSP. WHITE PEPPER
$\frac{1}{8}$	TSP. OREGANO
2	HALVES ADVOCADO
	SALSA, OPTIONAL

SCOOP OUT 2 ADVOCADO HALVES. MASH
ADVOCADO PULP IN BOWL. ADD SEASONINGS
AND MIX. ADD SALSA TO MAKE MIXTURE
THINNER IF SO DESIRED.

*May your day be touched
with the same magic the circus brings when it
comes to town.*

Breads & Starches

FRIED CORNBREAD

1	CUP CORNMEAL
2/3	CUP FLOUR
1½	TSPS. BAKING POWDER
½	TSP. SALT
¾	CUP MILK
¼	CUP BUTTER, MELTED
1	EGG, BEATEN
1	CUP (4 OZ.) SHREDDED SHARP CHEDDAR CHEESE

COMBINE DRY INGREDIENTS. COMBINE MILK, BUTTER AND EGG. ADD TO DRY INGREDIENTS, MIXING JUST UNTIL MOISTENED. STIR IN CHEESE. FOR EACH SERVING, SPOON APPROXIMATELY ¼ CUP MIXTURE ONTO HOT LIGHTLY GREASED GRIDDLE OR SKILLET. FLATTEN SLIGHTLY. COOK UNTIL LIGHTLY BROWNED ON BOTH SIDES. SERVE WARM WITH ADDITIONAL BUTTER. IF BATTER BECOMES TOO THICK, ADD SMALL AMOUNT OF MILK. MAKES 10 SERVINGS

VARIATIONS:

OMIT CHEESE. SUBSTITUTE ½ LB. COOKED AND DRAINED BULK PORK SAUSAGE FOR CHEESE. SERVE WITH SYRUP.

PEPPERONI BREAD

1	LOAF FROZEN BREAD DOUGH, THAWED
12	OZ. PEPPERONI, SLIGHTLY CHOPPED
8	OZ. WHITE CHEDDAR CHEESE
1	SMALL CAN CHOPPED RIPE OLIVES
1	SMALL CAN SLICED MUSHROOMS
	MELTED BUTTER
	GARLIC

DIVIDE DOUGH INTO TWO PORTIONS. ROLL EACH OUT ON FLOURED SURFACE. PLACE PEPPERONI, CHEESE, OLIVES AND MUSHROOMS IN CENTER OF FLAT DOUGH. ROLL CLOSED MAKING SURE TO TUCK ENDS AND SEAL. PLACE ON A BAKING SHEET. BRUSH WITH MELTED BUTTER AND GARLIC.

LET RISE UNTIL DOUBLED IN SIZE. BAKE AT 350° FOR ABOUT 30 TO 45 MINUTES OR UNTIL GOLDEN BROWN.

YOU CAN MAKE SEVERAL OF THESE AT A TIME. STORE IN THE FREEZER AND POP IN THE MICROWAVE OR OVEN WHEN YOU NEED A QUICK SNACK.

ROASTED PEPPER-RED ONION BREAD

1	LARGE (ABOUT 14") LOAF ITALIAN, SEMOLINA OR WHEAT BREAD
1	SMALL RED ONION, PEELED AND SLICED VERY THIN (ABOUT $\frac{1}{2}$ CUP)
$\frac{3}{4}$	CUP THINLY SLICED BOTTLED, ROASTED RED PEPPERS
2	+1 TBLS. OLIVE OIL
3	TBLS. GRATED PARMESAN CHEESE
$\frac{1}{2}$	TSP. SALT
$\frac{1}{4}$	TSP. FRESHLY GROUND BLACK PEPPER

HEAT OVEN TO 400°. SLICE BREAD IN HALF LENGTHWISE. TOSS THE REMAINING INGREDIENTS IN BOWL UNTIL THE ONION SLICES ARE SEPARATED AND ALL INGREDIENTS ARE EVENLY DISTRIBUTED. COVER BOTH SIDES OF THE BREAD WITH AN EVEN LAYER OF THE MIX. BAKE THE BREAD DIRECTLY ON THE RACK OF THE OVEN UNTIL CRISPY AND THE TOP IS LIGHTLY BROWNED, ABOUT 8 MINUTES. REMOVE THE BREAD CAREFULLY AND LET STAND A FEW MINUTES BEFORE SLICING CROSSWISE INTO 2" PIECES. SERVE HOT.

Being close has nothing to do with distance,
it has everything to do with the heart.

BACON JACK MINI-MUFFINS

2	CUPS ALL-PURPOSE FLOUR
3	TSPS. SUGAR
3	TSPS. BAKING POWDER
$\frac{1}{4}$	TSP. SALT
$\frac{1}{4}$	TSP. CAYENNE PEPPER
$1\frac{1}{4}$	CUPS MILK
2	TBLS. VEGETABLE OIL
1	EGG, SLIGHTLY BEATEN
3	SLICES BACON, CRISPLY COOKED AND CRUMBLED
$\frac{3}{4}$	CUP SHREDDED MONTERREY JACK CHEESE

PREHEAT OVEN TO 375°. GENEROUSLY GREASE
MINI-MUFFIN TINS OR LINE WITH PAPER
BAKING CUPS. IN LARGE BOWL, COMBINE
FLOUR, SUGAR, BAKING POWDER AND CAYENNE
PEPPER. BLEND WELL. (RECIPE MAY BE PREPARED
AHEAD TO THIS POINT). ADD MILK, OIL AND
EGG. STIR JUST UNTIL DRY INGREDIENTS ARE
MOISTENED. STIR IN BACON AND CHEESE. FILL
MUFFIN TINS $\frac{3}{4}$ FULL. BAKE UNTIL GOLDEN
BROWN, 15 TO 18 MINUTES. COOL FOR ONE OR
TWO MINUTES BEFORE REMOVING FROM PAN.
SERVE WARM.

There are no endings, only new beginnings.

CAJUN HANUKKAH LATKES

1½	CUPS YELLOW CORNMEAL
1	CUP UNSIFTED ALL PURPOSE FLOUR
1	CUP GRATED AMERICAN CHEESE
¼	CUP MINCED ONION
2	TBLS. CHOPPED PIMENTO
2	TBLS. CHOPPED GREEN PEPPER
3	TSPS. SALT
½	TSP. BAKING SODA
1	CUP MILK
1	EGG, BEATEN
	VEGETABLE OIL FOR FRYING

COMBINE CORNMEAL, FLOUR, CHEESE, ONION, PIMENTO, GREEN PEPPER, SALT AND BAKING SODA. STIR IN MILK AND EGG. BEAT UNTIL BLENDED. DROP BY TEASPOONFULS INTO DEEP HOT FAT (375°). FRY UNTIL GOLDEN BROWN ON BOTH SIDES. DRAIN ON PAPER TOWELS.

Every farewell opens a door to a new adventure.

GARLIC GLAZED CHICKEN PIZZA

2	LARGE PIZZA CRUSTS OR BOBOLIS
¼	CUP SESAME SEEDS, TOASTED
1	4.5 OZ. JAR MINCED GARLIC OR ¾ CUP FRESH GARLIC, CHOPPED
2	TSPS. DRIED RED PEPPER FLAKES
½	CUP SOY SAUCE

5	TBLS. HONEY
$1\frac{1}{2}$	CUPS RICE VINEGAR
$\frac{1}{4}$	CUP VEGETABLE OIL, APPROXIMATELY
5	BONELESS, SKINLESS CHICKEN BREAST HALVES, CUT INTO BITE-SIZE PIECES
3	CUPS GRATED MONTERREY JACK (OR GRUYERE) CHEESE
1	CUP GRATED MOZZARELLA CHEESE
$\frac{1}{2}$	CUP CHOPPED GREEN ONIONS

PREHEAT OVEN AS DIRECTED ON PACKAGED PIZZA CRUST. COMBINE GARLIC, PEPPER, SOY SAUCE, HONEY AND VINEGAR IN BOWL. SET ASIDE. HEAT ABOUT $\frac{1}{4}$ CUP VEGETABLE OIL IN SKILLET AND SAUTE CHICKEN PIECES UNTIL COOKED. REMOVE CHICKEN WITH SLOTTED SPOON AND SET ASIDE. IN SAME SKILLET, ADD THE RESERVED GARLIC, PEPPER AND SOY MIXTURE. COVER OVER MEDIUM HEAT, STIRRING FREQUENTLY, UNTIL MIXTURE THICKENS (LIKE SYRUP). AFTER SAUCE HAS REDUCED, ADD THE COOKED CHICKEN PIECES TO THE GLAZE AND CONTINUE COOKING FOR ABOUT 2 MINUTES. STEPS 2 THROUGH 5 CAN BE DONE AHEAD OF TIME IF NECESSARY.
TOP PIZZA CRUST WITH CHEESE, CHICKEN PIECES AND GREEN ONIONS. SPRINKLE WITH TOASTED SESAME SEEDS AND BAKE IN PREHEATED OVEN. BAKE AT TEMPERATURE RECOMMENDED ON PIZZA CRUST PACKAGE, FOR ABOUT 15 MINUTES OR UNTIL PIZZA IS HEATED THROUGH. MAKES 2 LARGE PIZZAS

LACY BATTY CAKES

¾	CUP WHITE CORNMEAL
½	TSP. BAKING POWDER
½	TSP. BAKING SODA
½	TSP. SALT
1	CUP BUTTERMILK
1	EGG, SLIGHTLY BEATEN
¼	CUP (½ STICK) BUTTER

COMBINE CORNMEAL, BAKING POWDER, BAKING SODA AND SALT. COMBINE BUTTERMILK AND EGG. STIR IN CORNMEAL MIXTURE UNTIL CORNMEAL ABSORBS LIQUID. PREHEAT GRIDDLE TO 400°. LIGHTLY BUTTER GRIDDLE. USE 1 TBL. BATTER FOR EACH CAKE. BAKE 4 AT A TIME. BAKE 2 TO 3 MINUTES, UNTIL CAKES BEGIN TO BUBBLE AND BOTTOMS ARE GOLDEN. TURN AND BAKE 2 TO 3 MINUTES LONGER.

MEXICAN CRAWFISH CORNBREAD

½	LB. GROUND MEAT, SEASONED
½	LB. CRAWFISH TAILS
1	LARGE ONION, CHOPPED

1	CUP YELLOW CORNMEAL
1	TSP. SALT
$\frac{1}{2}$	TSP. BAKING SODA
1	TSP. BAKING POWDER
1	TSP. GARLIC POWDER
1	CUP SWEET MILK
2	EGGS
1	LB. SHARP CHEDDAR CHEESE
$\frac{1}{2}$	CUP CHOPPED JALAPENO PEPPERS
1	LARGE CAN CREAM STYLE CORN

IN SKILLET, FRY GROUND MEAT, CRAWFISH AND
ONION UNTIL MEAT IS DONE. SET ASIDE.
COMBINE CORNMEAL, SALT, BAKING SODA,
BAKING POWDER, GARLIC POWDER, MILK AND
EGGS. MIX WELL. GREASE A LARGE BAKING PAN.
LAYER HALF THE CORNMEAL MIXTURE ON
BOTTOM. NEXT EVENLY SPREAD COOKED MEAT,
CRAWFISH AND ONION MIXTURE, AND A THIN
LAYER OF CHEESE. ADD A LAYER OF JALAPENO
PEPPERS, THEN A LAYER OF CORN. TOP WITH
REMAINING CORNMEAL MIXTURE. BAKE AT 350°
FOR 45 MINUTES.

Beautiful people
cause beautiful things to happen.

TOMATO-BASIL SCONES

| 2 | CUPS ALL PURPOSE FLOUR |
| 1 | TBL. BAKING POWDER |

1	TBL. SUGAR
½	TSP. SALT
½	TO 1 TSP. CRACKED BLACK PEPPER
2	+1 TBLS. MINCED FRESH PARSLEY
2	TBLS. CHOPPED FRESH BASIL OR 2 TSPS. DRIED
⅓	CUP BUTTER
½	CUP OIL-PACKED SUNDRIED TOMATOES, WELL DRAINED AND FINELY CHOPPED
½	CUP MILK
1	EGG, SLIGHTLY BEATEN SEASONED OLIVE OIL OR MELTED BUTTER

PREHEAT OVEN TO 400°. WHISK TOGETHER DRY INGREDIENTS AND HERBS. THEN BLEND IN BUTTER WITH PASTRY CUTTER OR TWO KNIVES UNTIL MIXTURE RESEMBLES COARSE CORNMEAL. STIR IN CHOPPED TOMATOES. MIX MLK TOGETHER WITH BEATEN EGG AND ADD, STIRRING JUST UNTIL MOISTENED. GENTLY KNEAD DOUGH FOR EIGHT TO TEN TURNS. THEN PLACE ON A GREASED COOKIE SHEET AND PAT INTO A 6" CIRCLE. CUT INTO EIGHT WEDGES AND SEPARATE SLIGHTLY. BAKE UNTIL GOLDEN BROWN, 15 TO 20 MINUTES. BRUSH WITH SEASONED OLIVE OIL OR MELTED BUTTER. THEN CUT INTO WEDGES. SERVE WARM

BROCCOLI CORNBREAD

4	EGGS, BEATEN
½	CUP SKIM MILK
1	12 OZ. CONTAINER SMALL CURD COTTAGE CHEESE
1	STICK BUTTER, MELTED
1	10 OZ. BOX CHOPPED BROCCOLI, THAWED AND DRAINED
1	SMALL ONION, FINELY CHOPPED
2	8½ OZ. BOXES CORNBREAD MIX
1	CUP GRATED REDUCED-FAT CHEDDAR CHEESE

PREHEAT OVEN TO 350°. IN LARGE BOWL, COMBINE EVERYTHING EXCEPT CHEDDAR CHEESE. BLEND WELL, INCORPORATING INGREDIENTS. POUR ½ MIXTURE INTO 9"x13" BAKING DISH. TOP WITH CHEESE. POUR REMAINING MIXTURE OVER CHEESE. SPREAD EVENLY. BAKE AT 350° FOR 30 TO 45 MINUTES.

TEXAS CORNBREAD

1	LB. PORK SAUSAGE OR GROUND BEEF
1	TBL. + $\frac{1}{2}$ CUP BUTTER
1	YELLOW ONION, FINELY CHOPPED
1	BELL PEPPER, SEEDED, FINELY CHOPPED
2	EGGS, WELL BEATEN
1	CUP SOUR CREAM
1	CUP COOKED CORN KERNELS, FINELY CHOPPED
$1\frac{1}{4}$	CUPS STONEGROUND CORN MEAL
$\frac{1}{2}$	CUP FLOUR
1	TSP. BAKING SODA
1	TSP. SUGAR
1	TSP. BAKING POWDER
$\frac{3}{4}$	CUP MILK
	FRESH SALSA
8	OZ. LONGHORN CHEESE, FINELY CHOPPED

HEAT OVEN TO 350°. SAUTE SAUSAGE IN A SKILLET UNTIL JUICES NO LONGER RUN PINK. REMOVE SAUSAGE. DISCARD ALL BUT 2 TBLS. OF FAT FROM SKILLET.

ADD 1 TBL. OF THE BUTTER TO THE SAUSAGE DRIPPINGS AND SAUTE THE ONION AND GREEN PEPPER UNTIL ONIONS ARE TRANSLUCENT. SET ASIDE AND RESERVE. BEAT REMAINING $\frac{1}{2}$ CUP BUTTER IN A MIXING BOWL UNTIL VERY SOFT. ADD EGGS, SOUR CREAM AND FINELY CHOPPED COOKED CORN. MIX WELL.

STIR CORNMEAL, FLOUR, BAKING SODA, SUGAR
AND BAKING POWDER TOGETHER IN A SMALL
BOWL. WITH BEATERS RUNNING, ADD TO EGG
MIXTURE AND MIX WELL. THEN STIR IN THE
MILK BY HAND, TAKING CARE NOT TO OVERMIX.
MILK SHOULD BE JUST COMBINED WITH
MIXTURE.

BUTTER A 11"x13" DISH (OR 2 8" PANS). POUR 2/3
OF THE BATTER INTO BUTTERED BAKING PANS.
TOP THE BATTER WITH THE SAUSAGE, THEN
COVER SAUSAGE WITH SAUTEED VEGETABLE
MIXTURE AND ¾ CUP OF THE FRESH SALSA.
SPRINGLE CHEDDAR OVER SALSA, THEN TOP
WITH REMAINING ⅓ BATTER.

BAKE AT 350° 40 TO 45 MINUTES, UNTIL JUST
SET. THE CORNBREAD SHOULD HAVE A QUICH-
LIKE CONSISTENCY. LET REST 10 MINUTES
BEFORE CUTTING INTO LARGE SQUARES FOR
ENTREE SERVINGS, SMALL SQUARES FOR
APPETIZER SERVINGS.

Don't be afraid to believe in yourself,
for you matter in this world.

CARAWAY CLOVERLEAF ROLLS

2   ¼ OZ. PKGS. ACTIVE DRY YEAST
1   TO 1½ CUPS WARM WATER (110° TO 115°)
1   CUP WHOLE WHEAT FLOUR

$\frac{1}{2}$	CUP SUGAR
$\frac{1}{2}$	CUP VEGETABLE OIL
2	TSPS. CARAWAY SEEDS
1	TO 1$\frac{1}{2}$ TSPS. SALT
3$\frac{1}{2}$	TO 4 CUPS ALL PURPOSE FLOUR

IN A MIXING BOWL, DISSOLVE YEAST IN WATER. ADD WHOLE WHEAT FLOUR, SUGAR, OIL, CARAWAY, SALT AND 2 CUPS ALL PURPOSE FLOUR. BEAT UNTIL SMOOTH. ADD ENOUGH OF THE REMAINING ALL PURPOSE FLOUR TO FORM A SOFT DOUGH. TURN ONTO A FLOURED SURFACE. KNEAD UNTIL SMOOTH AND ELASTIC, ABOUT 6 TO 8 MINUTES. PLACE IN A GREASED BOWL, TURNING ONCE TO GREASE TOP. COVER AND LET RISE IN A WARM PLACE UNTIL DOUBLED, ABOUT 1 HOUR. PUNCH DOUGH DOWN. DIVIDE IN HALF, THEN DIVIDE EACH HALF INTO 36 PIECES. SHAPE INTO BALLS. PLACE 3 BALLS EACH IN GREASED MUFFIN CUPS. COVER AND LET RISE UNTIL DOUBLED, ABOUT 30 MINUTES. BAKE AT 375° FOR 15 TO 18 MINUTES OR UNTIL GOLDEN BROWN. YIELDS 2 DOZEN

Let not your heart be impatient,
for time shall teach you all things.

CHEDDAR COCKTAIL BISCUITS

| 2 | CUPS ALL PURPOSE FLOUR |
| 1 | TBL. BAKING POWDER |

1	TSP. SALT
$\frac{1}{4}$	TSP. CAYENNE PEPPER
1	STICK CHILLED BUTTER, CUT INTO 16 PIECES
$1\frac{1}{4}$	CUPS PLAIN YOGURT
1	CUP SHREDDED SHARP OR EXTRA SHARP CHEDDAR CHEESE
$\frac{1}{4}$	CUP MINCED FRESH OR FORZEN CHIVES

PREHEAT OVEN TO 450°. WHISK TOGETHER DRY INGREDIENTS; THEN BLEND IN BUTTER WITH PASTRY CUTTER OR TWO KNIVES UNTIL MIXTURE RESEMBLES COARSE CORNMEAL. STIR IN YOGURT, CHEESE AND CHIVES JUST UNTIL MOISTENED. DROP BY HEAPING TEASPOONS ONTO WELL-GREASED COOKIE SHEETS AND BAKE UNTIL GOLDEN BROWN, 7 TO 10 MINUTES. SERVE WARM. YIELDS ABOUT FOUR DOZEN MINI-BISCUITS

Love is found in enduring friendship when common understanding ignites the candle of our faith.

MAGNOLIA MOUND ROSEMARY MUFFINS

$\frac{3}{4}$	CUP MILK
1	TBL. FRESH ROSEMARY, FINELY CHOPPED
$1\frac{1}{2}$	CUPS PECANS, FINELY CHOPPED

½	CUP SUGAR
¼	TSP. SALT
½	CUP RAISINS
¼	CUP BUTTER, UNSALTED
1½	CUPS ALL PURPOSE FLOUR
2	TSPS. BAKING POWDER
1	LARGE EGG

PREHEAT OVEN TO 375°. SIMMER MILK, RAISINS AND ROSEMARY IN SMALL SAUCEPAN FOR SEVERAL MINUTES, REMOVE FROM HEAT AND ADD BUTTER. STIR UNTIL MELTED. LET COOL. MIX ALL DRY INGREDIENTS AND PECANS IN A LARGE BOWL. BEAT EGG INTO COOLED MILK MIXTURE AND ADD DRY INGREDIENTS. MIX UNTIL JUST MOISTENED. SPOON INTO GREASED OR LINED MUFFIN TINS. BAKE ABOUT 20 MINUTES.

When we accept the seasons of the heart,
age remains a state of mind.

PARMESAN HERB MINI-MUFFINS

2	CUPS ALL PURPOSE FLOUR
1	TBL. SUGAR
1½	TSPS. BAKING POWDER
½	TSP. BAKING SODA
½	TSP. DRIED SAGE LEAVES, CRUSHED
½	CUP CHOPPED FRESH PARSLEY
¾	CUP GRATED PARMESAN CHEESE

1¼	CUPS BUTTERMILK
¼	CUP BUTTER, MELTED
1	EGG, LIGHTLY BEATEN

PREHEAT OVEN TO 375°. GREASE BOTTOMS ONLY OF MINI-MUFFIN TINS OR LINE WITH PAPER BAKING CUPS. IN LARGE BOWL, COMBINE FLOUR, SUGAR, BAKING POWDER, BAKING SODA, SAGE, PARSLEY AND CHEESE. BLEND WELL. (RECIPE MAY BE PREPARED TO THIS POINT A FEW HOURS AHEAD). ADD BUTTERMILK, BUTTER AND EGG. STIR JUST UNTIL DRY INGREDIENTS ARE MOISTENED. FILL MUFFIN TINS ¾ FULL. BAKE UNTIL GOLDEN BROWN, 15 TO 18 MINUTES. SERVE WARM. YIELDS 3 DOZEN

The greatest celebrations are anniversaries of the heart.

DAISY BISCUITS

MAKE YOUR USUAL PIONEER BISCUITS, BUT USE HALF & HALF FOR LIQUID. ROLL DOUGH TO ¼" THICKNESS. USE A 2" ROUND CUTTER TO MAKE BISCUITS, THEN MAKE 6 ¼" CUTS FROM THE EDGE TO THE CENTER OF EACH BISCUIT. PRESS DOWN CENTER OF BISCUITS WITH A SPOON AND PUT A ½ TSP. OF JAM IN THE CENTER OF EACH BISCUIT. BRUSH TOP OF BISCUITS WITH

MELTED BUTTER. BAKE AT 450° FOR 10
MINUTES.

MONKEY BREAD

4 or 5   7.5 OZ. CANS OF BISCUITS
1   CUP SUGAR MIXED WITH 4 TSPS.
              CINNAMON

BUTTER A BUNDT PAN.

CUT BISCUITS IN QUARTERS AND COAT WITH
SUGAR MIXTURE. GENTLY PLACE QUARTERS IN
BUNDT PAN. SPRINKLE REMAINDER OF SUGAR
AND CINNAMON MIXTURE ON TOP.
MELT 1 STICK BUTTER AND POUR OVER
BISCUITS. BAKE AT 250° FOR 30 TO 40
MINUTES. YOU CAN SPRINKLE PECAN HALVES
IN THE BUNDT PAN AS YOU ARE PUTTING IN
THE BISCUIT QUARTERS.

Salads & Greens

STRAWBERRY GREEN SALAD

1	LB. GREENS (SPINACH, RED LEAF OR BOSTON LETTUCE, ETC.)
½	TO 1 PINT SLICED STRAWBERRIES
¼	CUP ALMONDS TOASTED WITH 1 TBL. BUTTER
½	CUP SUGAR
1	TBL. POPPY SEEDS
2	TBLS. SESAME SEEDS
1½	TSPS. MINCED ONION
¼	TSP. PAPRIKA
¼	CUP CIDER VINEGAR
¼	CUP WHITE WINE VINEGAR
¼	CUP VEGETABLE OIL
¼	CUP OLIVE OIL

PREPARE DRESSING BY COMBINING THE SUGAR, POPPY SEEDS AND SESAME SEEDS, MINCED ONION, PAPRIKA, VINEGARS AND OILS. COMBINE GREENS, STRAWBERRIES AND ALMONDS AND TOSS WITH DRESSING.

In the end, what matters most in our lives,
is who we love and who loves us.

TOSSED GREENS WITH PINEAPPLE, APPLE AND FETA CHEESE

3	TBLS. BALSAMIC VINEGAR
3	TBLS. WATER

2	TBLS. HOT-SWEET MUSTARD
1	CLOVE GARLIC, MINCED
	SALT AND PEPPER TO TASTE
6	CUPS TORN BUTTER LETTUCE LEAVES
$1\frac{1}{2}$	CUPS ($\frac{3}{4}$") PINEAPPLE CUBES,
	PREFERABLY FRESH
2	MEDIUM RED DELICIOUS APPLES, CORED
	AND THINLY SLICED
1	SMALL RED ONION, THINLY SLICED
2	TBLS. CRUMBLED FETA CHEESE

TO MAKE VINAIGRETTE: IN SMALL BOWL, WHISK TOGETHER VINEGAR, WATER, MUSTARD AND GARLIC. SEASON WITH SALT AND PEPPER. SET ASIDE.

IN LARGE BOWL, COMBINE REMAINING INGREDIENTS. DRIZZLE WITH VINAIGRETTE AND TOSS GENTLY. SERVE IMMEDIATELY.

When we take time to find quiet moments, we discover the wonder within ourselves.

BACON AND ORANGE SALAD

3	SLICES BACON, FRIED AND CRUMBLED
2	GREEN ONIONS, CHOPPED
1	11 OZ. CAN MANDARIN ORANGES,
	CHILLED AND DRAINED
	SLIVERED ALMONDS
	RED LEAF LETTUCE

DRESSING:

$\frac{1}{4}$	CUP OIL
2	TBLS. SUGAR
2	TBLS. RICE VINEGAR
$\frac{1}{2}$	TSP. SALT
	DASH TABASCO

COMBINE OIL, SUGAR, VINEGAR, SALT AND
TABASCO TO MAKE DRESSING. IN A SALAD
BOWL, COMBINE LETTUCE, MANDARIN
ORANGES, GREEN ONION, TOASTED ALMONDS
AND COOKED BACON PIECES. POUR DRESSING
OVER SALAD, TOSS AND SERVE. SERVES 4

There is music found in dreaming
if we listen with our hearts.

PEAR WALNUT SALAD WITH BALSAMIC VINAIGRETTE

10	CUPS (APPROXIMATELY 16 OZS.) TORN MIXED SALAD GREENS
2	MEDIUM, FIRM PEARS, CORED AND CUT INTO THIN WEDGES
1/3	CUP CRUMBLED BLUE CHEESE
1/3	CUP COARSELY CHOPPED WALNUTS, TOASTED

VINAIGRETTE:

$\frac{1}{4}$	CUP OLIVE OIL
2	TBLS. BALSAMIC VINEGAR
1	CLOVE GARLIC, CRUSHED
$\frac{1}{4}$	TSP. COARSE-GROUND BLACK PEPPER
$\frac{1}{8}$	TSP. SALT

IN A LARGE SALAD BOWL, COMBINE SALAD GREENS, PEARS, CHEESE AND WALNUTS. COVER AND REFRIGERATE UNTIL SERVING TIME.

IN SMALL BOWL, WHISK TOGETHER VINAIGRETTE INGREDIENTS. TO SERVE, TOSS SALAD WITH DRESSING. MAKES 8 SERVINGS

AMBROSIA

8	LARGE NAVEL ORANGES
2	CUPS ORANGE JUICE
1	TO 2 CUPS FLAKED COCONUT
2	CUPS CONFECTIONER'S SUGAR
1	10 OZ. JAR MARASCHINO CHERRIES, SLICED IN HALF

FILL A LARGE SAUCEPAN ABOUT HALF FULL OF WATER AND BRING TO A BOIL. DROP ORANGES INTO BOILING WATER, ONE OR TWO AT A TIME, DEPENDING ON THE SIZE OF SAUCEPAN. ROLL ORANGES AROUND IN BOILING WATER FOR TWO TO THREE MINUTES. THE AMOUNT OF TIME DEPENDS ON THE THICKNESS OF THE

ORANGE RINDS SINCE THE PURPOSE IS TO
SOFTEN THE RIND.

AFTER REMOVING THE ORANGES FROM THE
BOILING WATER, SLICE EACH IN HALF JUST
LIKE A GRAPEFRUIT WITH THE NAVEL ON ONE
SIDE. FLIP THE ORANGE RINDS INSIDE OUT.
THE BOILING SOFTENS THE RIND AND THE
WHITE MEMBRANE SO THAT THE ORANGE
SECTIONS ARE EASY TO FLIP OUT INTO THE
BOWL.

WHEN ALL ORANGES HAVE BEEN PEELED AND
SEGMENTED, MIX IN ORANGE JUICE, FLAKED
COCONUT, SUGAR AND CHERRIES. REFRIGERATE.

CAULIFLOWER SALAD

1	MEDIUM CAULIFLOWER, ABOUT 2 LBS.
1	RED DELICIOUS, GALA OR CRISPIN APPLE, PEELED, CORED AND CUT IN $\frac{3}{4}$" SLICES
2	WHITE SCALLIONS, CHOPPED, ABOUT $\frac{1}{2}$ CUP
$\frac{1}{4}$	RED ONION, THINLY SLICED
3	TBLS. COARSELY CHOPPED DILL
1	TBL. LEMON JUICE
1	TBL. OLIVE OIL
$\frac{1}{2}$	TSP. SALT
	FRESHLY GROUND PEPPER

BOIL A LARGE POT OF WATER. PREPARE THE
CAULIFLOWER BY BREAKING OFF OR CUTTING
AWAY THE LEAVES (IF ANY) WITH A SHARP

KNIFE. CUT THE FLORETS FROM THE STEM OF
THE CAULIFLOWER AND THEN CUT THE LARGE
FLORETS VERTICALLY INTO BITE-SIZE PIECES.

STEAM THE FLORETS UNTIL THEY ARE TENDER-
CRISP, ABOUT 5 MINUTES. IMMEDIATELY
TRANSFER THEM TO A BOWL OF ICE WATER.
WHEN CHILLED, DRAIN THE FLORETS AND PLACE
IN A LARGE BOWL. TOSS THE CAULIFLOWER
WITH THE APPLE, SCALLIONS, ONION AND DILL.
POUR OVER THE LEMON JUICE, OIL AND SALT
AND MIX UNTIL THE FLORETS ARE COATED
WITH THE DRESSING. SEASON TO TASTE WITH
FRESHLY GROUND PEPPER AND SERVE. THIS
SALAD KEEPS WELL IN THE REFRIGERATOR FOR 1
TO 2 DAYS. SERVES 6

*There is no time to leave important word
unsaid or deeds undone.*

COUSCOUS SALAD

3	MEDIUM RED BELL PEPPERS, ROASTED
10	OZS. INSTANT COUSCOUS ($1\frac{1}{2}$ CUPS)
$\frac{1}{4}$	CUP OLIVE OIL
$\frac{1}{4}$	CUP LEMON JUICE
1	TSP. GROUND CUMIN
1	LB. RIPE TOMATOES, PEELED, SEEDED AND DICED
1	LARGE SEEDLESS CUCUMBER, DICED
$\frac{1}{2}$	CUP KALAMATA OLIVES, PITTED AND DICED

        (RIPE OLIVES MAY BE SUBSTITUTED)
2   GREEN ONIONS, SLICED
1   LARGE CLOVE GARLIC, MINCED
2   TBLS. FINELY CHOPPED FLAT LEAF
        PARSLEY
1   PINCH OF CAYENNE PEPPER
        SALT
        FRESHLY GROUND BLACK PEPPER

BRING 2¼ CUPS OF WATER TO A BOIL. STIR IN
COUSCOUS AND ½ TSP. SALT. COVER, AND LET
STAND UNTIL TENDER (ABOUT 5 MINUTES).

IN A SMALL BOWL, COMBINE OLIVE OIL, LEMON
JUICE, CUMIN AND CAYENNE. SEASON WITH
SALT AND FRESHLY GROUND BLACK PEPPER.

FLUFF COUSCOUS WITH A FORK. ADD THE
ROASTED RED PEPPERS, TOMATOES, CUCUMBER,
OLIVES, GREEN ONIONS AND GARLIC.

POUR THE DRESSING FROM THE BOWL OVER THE
COUSCOUS AND TOSS TO COMBINE. LET STAND
AT ROOM TEMPERATURE FOR AT LEAST 1 HOUR.
STIR IN PARSLEY JUST BEFORE SERVING.

*Our children like flowers in a garden, are born
into this world with the right
to blossom and to bloom.*

EMERALD POTATO SALAD

4	LBS. POTATOES, COOKED AND CUT UP INTO SMALL PIECES
2	CUPS MAYONNAISE
4	TBLS. TARRAGON VINEGAR
$\frac{1}{2}$	CUP ONION, FINELY CHOPPED
$\frac{1}{4}$	CUP GREEN ONIONS, FINELY CHOPPED
1	CUP FRESH PARSLEY, CHOPPED
1	CUP CHOPPED CELERY
1	TSP. SALT
	BLACK PEPPER TO TASTE
	DASH OF RED PEPPER
	TOASTED SESAME SEEDS, OPTIONAL

BOIL POTATOES UNTIL TENDER. WHILE STILL WARM, PEEL AND CUT INTO BITE-SIZE PIECES.

IN SEPARATE BOWL, COMBINE MAYONNAISE, VINEGAR, ONIONS, PARSLEY AND CELERY. ADD DRESSING TO THE WARM POTATOES. SEASON WITH SALT, BLACK PEPPER AND RED PEPPER TO TASTE. TOSS UNTIL WELL BLENDED.

TOASTED SESAME SEEDS, OPTIONAL, MAY BE SPRINKLED OVER THE TOP. SERVES 8 TO 10

*Take time to let your heart
celebrate the treasures it holds.*

LAYERED PORK FAJITA SALAD

1½	LBS. BONELESS PORK LOIN CHOPS (ABOUT 6)
¼	CUP OLIVE OIL
2	TBLS. LIME JUICE
1	TSP. DRIED OREGANO
1	TSP. CHILI POWDER
1	CUP RICE
2¼	CUPS CHICKEN BROTH

GUACAMOLE:

2	RIPE ADVOCADOS, PEELED, SEEDED AND MASHED
1	TBL. LEMON JUICE
1	TBL. ONION, FINELY CHOPPED
2	+1 TBLS. FRESH CILANTRO, MINCED
1	MEDIUM RIPE TOMATO, CHOPPED
1	JALAPENO CHILI, SEEDED AND FINELY CHOPPED
1	HEAD ICEBERG LETTUCE, SHREDDED
1	15 OZ. CAN BLACK BEANS, DRAINED
3	+1 OZS. SHARP CHEDDAR CHEESE, GRATED (1 CUP)
1	8 OZ. JAR SALSA, (MILD, MEDIUM OR HOT)
16	OZS. SOUR CREAM
1	2¼ OZ. CAN SLICED BLACK OLIVES, DRAINED
2	GREEN ONIONS, THINLY SLICED

PLACE PORK CHOPS IN A SELF-SEALING PLASTIC
BAG AND ADD THE OLIVE OIL, LIME JUICE AND
SEASONINGS. LET MARINATE OVERNIGHT IN
THE REFRIGERATOR. REMOVE CHOPS FROM
MARINADE. PAT DRY AND GRILL OR BROIL JUST
UNTIL COOKED AND NICELY BROWNED, ABOUT 8
MINUTES TOTAL. SET ASIDE TO COOL. CUT
INTO $\frac{1}{2}$" CUBES.

MEANWHILE, PLACE RICE AND CHICKEN BROTH
IN A SAUCEPAN. BRING TO A BOIL, LOWER HEAT
TO SIMMER AND COOK, COVERED, FOR 12
MINUTES, JUST UNTIL RICE IS COOKED. SET
ASIDE, STILL COVERED, TO COOL.

PREPARE THE GUACAMOLE BY COMBINING THE
ADVOCADOS, LEMON JUICE, ONION, CILANTRO,
CHOPPED TOMATO AND THE CHOPPED JALAPENO.
COVER AND REFRIGERATE.

ASSEMBLE SALAD UP TO AN HOUR BEFORE
SERVING.

IN A 5 QUART STRAIGHT-SIDE GLASS BOWL OR
CASSEROLE DISH, LAYER SHREDDED LETTUCE,
BLACK BEANS, CHEDDAR CHEESE, PORK PIECES
AND GUACAMOLE. SPREAD 1 CUP OF THE SALSA
OVER THE TOP. MIX THE SOUR CREAM AND RICE
TOGETHER AND SPREAD OVER THE TOP OF THE
SALAD, COVERING COMPLETELY. PUT THE

REMAINING SALSA IN THE MIDDLE OF THE
SOUR CREAM LAYER. GARNISH THE SALAD
WITH THE OLIVES AND GREEN ONIONS. SERVE
TORTILLA CHIPS ON THE SIDE.

*Music is a feeling, not a sound and the music
within us is born of the heart.*

MARINATED TOMATOES

6	LARGE, RIPE TOMATOES, PEELED AND CUT INTO EIGHTHS
3	TBLS. WHITE BALSAMIC VINEGAR
5	TBLS. OLIVE OIL
1/3	CUP CHOPPED, PITTED KALAMATA OLIVES
2	TBLS. DRAINED CAPERS
	FRESH BASIL LEAVES OR 1 TBL. DRIED BASIL
1/3	CUP (ABOUT 2 OZS.) CRUMBLED FETA CHEESE

PEEL AND CUT TOMATOES. PUT IN COLANDER
AND LET DRAIN IN REFRIGERATOR ABOUT ONE
HOUR.

ABOUT ONE HOUR BEFORE SERVING, TOSS
TOMATOES WITH REMAINING INGREDIENTS
EXCEPT FETA CHEESE. WHEN READY TO SERVE,
TOP TOMATOES WITH FETA AND TOSS LIGHTLY.
SERVES 6-8

THAI CABBAGE SALAD

3	CUPS COARSELY SHREDDED CABBAGE
1	CUP SHREDDED CARROTS
1	CUP FRESH BEAN SPROUTS
1	6 OZ. PKG. FROZEN COOKED TINY SHRIMP, THAWED
2/3	CUP DRY ROASTED UNSALTED PEANUTS
$\frac{1}{4}$	CUP CHOPPED FRESH CORIANDER LEAVES

DRESSING:

1/3	CUP FRESH LIME JUICE
2	TBLS. NAM PLA (FISH SAUCE) OR SOY SAUCE
1	TBL. MINCED FRESH GINGER ROOT
2	TSPS. SUGAR
1	CLOVE GARLIC, PEELED, CRUSHED

MIX CABBAGE, CARROTS, BEAN SPROUTS, SHRIMP, PEANUTS AND CORIANDER LEAVES IN LARGE SERVING BOWL. MIX DRESSING INGREDIENTS IN SMALL BOWL UNTIL SUGAR DISSOLVES.

POUR DRESSING OVER SALAD. TOSS TO COAT. REFRIGERATE, COVERED, AT LEAST 2 HOURS. SERVE COLD.

EGGPLANT SALAD WITH BASIL

2	MEDIUM EGGPLANTS, ABOUT 3 LBS. TOTAL, CUT INTO 1½" CUBES (DO NOT PEEL)
2/3	CUP OLIVE OIL
2	TSPS. SALT
2	LARGE GARLIC CLOVES, PEELED AND MINCED
2	MEDIUM ONIONS, PEELED, HALVED AND THINLY SLICED
	FRESHLY GROUND PEPPER TO TASTE
2/3	CUP COARSELY CHOPPED FRESH BASIL
	JUICE OF 1 TO 1½ LEMONS, TO TASTE

LINE A ROASTING PAN WITH FOIL AND ADD EGGPLANT. TOSS WITH HALF THE OLIVE OIL, THE SALT AND THE GARLIC. BAKE AT 400° FOR 35 MINUTES OR UNTIL EGGPLANT IS SOFT BUT NOT MUSHY. COOL SLIGHTLY AND TRANSFER TO A LARGE BOWL.

HEAT REMAINING OLIVE OIL IN A LARGE SKILLET. ADD SLICED ONIONS AND COOK, COVERED, OVER LOW HEAT UNTIL TENDER, ABOUT 15 MINUTES. ADD ONIONS TO THE EGGPLANT. SEASON GENEROUSLY WITH BLACK PEPPER. ADD FRESH BASIL AND LEMON JUICE.

TOSS TOGTHER AND ADJUST SEASONINGS. LET
COOL TO ROOM TEMPERATURE AND SERVE.

MARINATED SNAP BEANS

2	14½ OZ. CANS GREEN BEANS, FANCY CUT OR WHOLE
1	ONION, VERY THINLY SLICED
¾	CUP CIDER VINEGAR
4	TBLS. SALAD OIL
¼	CUP WATER
1	CUP SUGAR

LAYER SNAP BEANS AND ONIONS IN A COVERED
CONTAINER. IN A SMALL BOWL, COMBINE
VINEGAR, SALAD OIL, WATER AND SUGAR. STIR
UNIL SUGAR IS DISSOLVED. POUR DRESSING
MIXTURE OVER BEANS AND ONIONS LAYERED
IN BOWL. COVER AND PLACE IN REFRIGERATOR
OVERNIGHT.

MARINATED VEGETABLE SALAD

1	6 OZ. CAN PITTED RIPE OLIVES
2	6 OZ. JARS ARTICHOKE HEARTS IN OIL

2	14½ OZ. CANS GREEN BEANS
1	10 OZ. CAN MUSHROOMS
4	MEDIUM TOMATOES, CUT IN WEDGES
1	8 OZ. BOTTLE ITALIAN DRESSING

COMBINE ALL INGREDIENTS. MARINATE FOR
SEVERAL HOURS, TURNING OCCASIONALLY.

Embrace hellos, and sometimes goodbyes,
for they are each a part of the journey.

SPINACH AND ORANGE SALAD

1	8 OZ. PKG. BABY SPINACH LEAVES
1	CUP FRESH ORANGE OR TANGERINE SECTIONS
1	SMALL RED ONION, THINLY SLICED
1	TBL. BALSAMIC VINEGAR
2	TBLS. OLIVE OIL
	SALT AND FRESHLY GROUND PEPPER

TOSS ALL INGREDIENTS TOGETHER JUST
BEFORE SERVING. SERVES 3

Once we have been graced
by the richness of another's heart, we come to
learn the divine capacity of the human spirit.

SUMMER SALAD

2½	CUPS (6 OZS.) BOW TIE OR ROTINI PASTA, COOKED AND DRAINED
1	MEDIUM EACH ZUCCHINI AND CARROT, THINLY SLICED
1	SMALL EACH GREEN AND RED BELL PEPPER CHOPPED
1	2¼ OZ. CAN SLICED PITTED RIPE OLIVES, DRAINED
½	CUP (2 OZ.) CRUMBLED FETA CHEESE
½	TSP. CRUSHED RED PEPPER
1	CUP PREPARED GOOD SEASONS ROASTED GARLIC OR ITALIAN SALAD DRESSING

MIX ALL INGREDIENTS EXCEPT DRESSING IN LARGE BOWL.

TOSS TO COAT WITH DRESSING. COVER. REFRIGERATE 1 HOUR OR UNTIL READY TO SERVE. MAKES 4 TO 6 SERVINGS

To believe is to find the strength and courage that live within us when it is time to pick up the pieces and begin again.

TORTELLINI ANTIPASTO SALAD

2	9 OZ. PKGS. REFRIGERATED THREE CHEESE TORTELLINI
1	7 OZ. JAR ROASTED RED PEPPERS, DRAINED, RINSED AND CUT INTO SHORT, THIN STRIPS
1	14 OZ. CAN ARTICHOKE QUARTERS, DRAINED
2/3	CUP CREAMY ITALIAN SALAD DRESSING
1	CUP HALVED BLACK OLIVES
$\frac{1}{4}$	CUP CHOPPED FRESH BASIL
	ROMAINE OR RED LEAF LETTUCE FOR GARNISH
	FRESHLY GROUND BLACK PEPPER TO TASTE

COOK TORTELLINI ACCORDING TO PACKAGE DIRECTIONS. DRAIN AND RINSE WITH COLD WATER. COMBINE TORTELLINI, RED PEPPER STRIPS, ARTICHOKE HEARTS AND DRESSING IN LARGE BOWL. TOSS TO COAT. ADD OLIVES. TOSS TO COAT.

AT THIS POINT, SALAD CAN BE COVERED AND REFRIGERATED UP TO 24 HOURS BEFORE SERVING.

STIR IN BASIL. SERVE ON LETTUCE-LINED PLATTER. SPRINKLE WITH PEPPER.

FRUIT SALAD

1	LARGE CAN FRUIT COCKTAIL
1	SMALL CAN PINEAPPLE TIDBITS
1	SMALL CAN MANDARIN ORANGES
	MARASCHINO CHERRIES
	COCONUT
	PECANS
	SOUR CREAM

MIX ALL INGREDIENTS TOGETHER AND
REFRIGERATE BEFORE SERVING.

BASIL PESTO PASTA SALAD

8	OZS. ROTINI, COOKED AS PACKAGE DIRECTS
2/3	CUP PESTO SAUCE
1	CUP CHOPPED, ROASTED BELL PEPPERS
1	CUP SLICED RIPE OLIVES
1	CUP SHREDDED PARMESAN CHEESE
1/3	CUP CHOPPED WALNUTS, TOASTED

IN A LARGE BOWL, GENTLY TOSS PASTA AND
PESTO CAUCE. STIR IN REMAINING
INGREDIENTS, EXCEPT WALNUTS. MIX WELL.
COVER AND REFRIGERATE 1 HOUR.

BEFORE SERVING, SPRINKLE WITH WALNUTS
AND ADDITIONAL PARMESAN CHEESE.

Sandwiches

BASEBALL CLUB SANDWICH

BASIL AIOLI:

2	TBLS. MAYONNAISE
1	TBL. FRESH BASIL, MINCED
½	TSP. FRESH LEMON JUICE

FILLING:

3	SLICES WHITE BREAD
¼	CUP GREENS (ICEBERG LETTUCE, ARUGULA AND MESCLUN MIX)
2	OZS. THINLY SLICED TURKEY BREAST
2	OZS. THINLY SLICED HAM
2	OZS. THIN SLICES RED ONION
2	SLICES APPLE WOOD SMOKED BACON, FRIED CRISP AND DRAINED
2	THIN SLICES SWISS CHEESE

TO MAKE BASIL AIOLI: MIX INGREDIENTS TOGETHER IN SMALL BOWL. LET SIT FOR 1 HOUR TO BLEND FLAVORS. MAKES 2 TBLS.

FOR SANDWICH, TOAST BREAD, SPREAD AIOLI ON ONE SIDE OF EACH SLICE OF BREAD. PLACE ½ GREENS ON BOTTOM SLICE OF TOAST. TOP WITH TURKEY, HAM THEN SECOND SLICE OF TOAST. PLACE REMAINING GREENS ON TOP, ADD ONIONS, TOMATOES, BACON, CHEESE AND THIRD SLICE OF TOAST. TOOTHPICK WITH LARGE FRILL PICK. CUT IN HALF. MAKES 1 SANDWICH

ROAST BEEF HOAGIES

2 12 OZ. CANS ROAST BEEF, PARBOILED
   AND STEAMED WITH GRAVY
8 HOAGIE BUNS
8 SLICES SWISS CHEESE
8 LETTUCE LEAVES
2 TOMATOES, SLICED
   MAYONAISE FOR BUNS

HEAT BEEF IN COVERED MICROWAVE DISH
UNTIL WARM. LIGHTLY TOAST BUNS AND
SPREAD LIGHTLY WITH MAYONAISE. SPREAD
BEEF ON BOTTOM HALF OF BUNS, TOP WITH
CHEESE. PUT ALL BUNS ON BAKING SHEET,
BOTTOMS AND TOPS SEPARATE. PLACE IN 350°
OVEN FOR ABOUT 5 MINUTES OR UNTIL CHEESE
MELTS.

REMOVE FROM OVEN, ADD LETTUCE AND
TOMATOES. PUT TOP BUNS ON AND SERVE.
GARNISH WITH DILL CHIPS

CHEESE STEAK SANDWICH

4	OZS. TOP SIRLOIN STEAK, CHOPPED COARSELY
$\frac{1}{4}$	CUP PROVOLONE CHEESE, CRUMBLED
2	SLICES CRUSTY ITALIAN BREAD
2	SLICES SWEET RED TOMATOES
$\frac{1}{4}$	CUP COLESLAW, DRAINED
2	OZS. FRENCH FRIED POTATOES

OPTIONAL CONDIMENTS:

TRAPPEY'S RED DEVIL HOT SAUCE
RAW ONIONS
MAYONNAISE
YELLOW MUSTARD
KETCHUP

GRILL CHOPPED STEAK MEDIUM RARE. SPRINKLE CHEESE OVER MEAT. AS SOON AS CHEESE HAS MELTED, PLACE ON BREAD. TOP WITH TOMATOES, COLESLAW AND FRENCH FRIES. MAKES ONE SANDWICH

Life speaks through nature. Listen to its song, learn from it and keep the strains of the melody close to heart.

GRILLED PASTRAMI SANDWICH

2½	TSPS. UNSALTED BUTTER, AT ROOM TEMPERATURE
2	SLICES RYE BREAD
1½	TSPS. YELLOW OR DIJON MUSTARD
3	+1 SLICES (ABOUT 2 OZS.) PASTRAMI
2	THIN SLICES WHITE ONION
2	SLICES RIPE TOMATO
2	OZS. SWISS CHEESE

WORKING ON A SHEET OF WAXED PAPER, SPREAD ¾ TSP. BUTTER ON ONE SIDE OF EACH SLICE OF BREAD. TURN SLICES OVER. SPREAD THOUSAND ISLAND ON THE OTHER SIDE. LAY PASTRAMI ON TOP. COVER WITH ONION, TOMATO, AND SWISS CHEESE. TOP WITH REMAINING SLICE OF BREAD, BUTTERED SIDE UP. USING WAXED PAPER, PRESS DOWN ON SANDWICH TO FLATTEN SLIGHTLY.

HEAT REMAINING 1 TSP. BUTTER IN A NONSTICK SKILLET OVER MEDIUM HEAT. ADD SANDWICH, COOK, PRESSING DOWN ON IT WITH A SPATULA, FOR 3 MINUTES UNTIL GOLDEN BROWN. TURN SANDWICH OVER, COOK 2 MINUTES LONGER.

Within us are the keys
to open the doors to any dream.

STEAL HOME TUNA SANDWICH

1	6½ OZ. CAN ALBACORE TUNA IN WATER, DRAINED
2	TBLS. RED ONION, MINCED
1	TBL. FRESH LEMON JUICE
1	TBL. CAPERS (OPTIONAL)
1	TBL. BLACK OLIVES, PITTED AND CHOPPED (OPTIONAL)
¼	CUP CELERY HEARTS, DICED
2	TBLS. MAYONNAISE, PLUS MORE FOR SPREADING
1	TBL. DIJON OR YELLOW MUSTARD
3	+1 SLICES WHEAT BREAD
½	CUP ARUGULA, RINSED AND PATTED DRY
1	TOMATO, THINLY SLICED

PLACE TUNA IN BOWL. ADD ONION, LEMON JUICE, CAPERS, BLACK OLIVES, CELERY HEARTS, MAYONNAISE, DIJON MUSTARD, SALT AND PEPPER. MIX WELL.

SPREAD MAYONNAISE LIGHTLY ON 2 SLICES OF BREAD. PLACE ARUGULA, TOMATOES AND TUNA MIXTURE ON BREAD. TOP WITH SECOND SLICES OF BREAD, CUT IN HALF.

Give yourself time for simple joys.

TRIPLE PLAY BARBECUED CHICKEN SANDWICH

2	SLICES SOURDOUGH BREAD
1	TBL. MELTED BUTTER OR OLIVE OIL
$\frac{1}{4}$	LB. THINLY SLICED TURKEY
2	TBLS. BARBECUE SAUCE
1	THINLY SLICED RED ONION
2	SLICES BACON, FRIED CRISP
3	THIN SLICES SMOKED GOUDA CHEESE

BRUSH 2 SLICES OF BREAD WITH MELTED BUTTER OR OLIVE OIL. PLACE TURKEY ON UNBUTTERED SIDE OF BREAD. BRUSH WITH BARBECUE SAUCE, TOP WITH ONION, BACON AND CHEESE. PLACE SECOND SLICE OF BREAD ON SANDWICH, BUTTERED SIDE OUT. GRILL ON BARBECUE OR IN HEATED SKILLET UNTIL BREAD IS GOLDEN BROWN AND CHEESE MELTED.

To believe in life is to believe there will always be someone to water the geraniums.

MARINATED CHICKEN IN A SANDWICH

8	CHICKEN BREAST HALVES, SKINNED AND BONED
1	CUP SOY SAUCE

$\frac{1}{2}$	CUP PINEAPPLE JUICE
$\frac{1}{4}$	CUP SHERRY
$\frac{1}{4}$	CUP FIRMLY PACKED BROWN SUGAR
$\frac{3}{4}$	TSP. MINCED FRESH GARLIC
8	SLICES MONTERREY JACK CHEESE
8	KAISER ROLLS, SLICED IN HALF
	MUSTARD SAUCE (RECIPE FOLLOWS)
	LEAF LETTUCE

PLACE CHICKEN IN A LARGE, SHALLOW DISH. COMBINE SOY SAUCE, PINEAPPLE JUICE, SHERRY, BROWN SUGAR AND GARLIC, MIXING WELL. POUR OVER CHICKEN AND LET MARINATE FOR ABOUT 30 MINUTES. REMOVE FROM MARINADE. GRILL CHICKEN BREASTS OVER HOT COALS, 25 MINUTES OR UNTIL DONE, TURNING AND BASTING WITH MARINADE APPROXIMATELY EVERY FIVE MINUTES.

PLACE SLICE OF CHEESE ON EACH CHICKEN BREAST AND GRILL FOR THREE MORE MINUTES OR UNTIL CHESE MELTS. REMOVE CHICKEN FROM GRILL.

SPREAD EACH SIDE OF ROLL WITH MUSTARD SAUCE. PLACE CHICKEN BREAST ON BOTTOM HALF OF EACH ROLL. TOP WITH LETTUCE. COVER WITH ROLL TOP AND SERVE SANDWICH IMMEDIATELY.

MUSTARD SAUCE:

$\frac{1}{2}$ CUP DRY MUSTARD
2/3   CUP WHITE VINEGAR
2/3   CUP SUGAR
1   EGG

COMBINE MUSTARD, VINEGAR, SUGAR AND EGG
IN AN ELECTRIC BLENDER. BLEND UNTIL
SMOOTH. POUR MIXTURE INTO TOP OF A
DOUBLE BOILER. BRING WATER IN BOTTOM TO
BOIL. REDUCE HEAT TO LOW. COOK, STIRRING
CONSTANTLY, ABOUT 7 MINUTES OR UNTIL
SMOOTH AND THICKENED. STORE IN AN
AIRTIGHT CONTAINER IN REFRIGERATOR.

Beverages

SPICED TEA

8	CUPS WATER
2	STICKS CINNAMON
½	TSP. WHOLE CLOVES
3	SMALL TEA BAGS
2	CUPS EACH ORANGE & PINEAPPLE JUICE
⅓	CUP LEMON JUICE
¾	CUP SUGAR

BOIL WATER AND SPICES FOR 10 MINUTES. TURN OFF HEAT. ADD 2 TO 3 SMALL TEA BAGS OR 1 LARGE TEA BAG AND STEEP FOR 10 MINUTES. REMOVE SPICES AND TEA BAGS. ADD JUICES AND SUGAR AND STIR UNTIL SUGAR DISSOLVES.

MAY BE REFRIGERATED AND HEATED AS NEEDED.

Every moment gives birth to new beginnings.

ICED THAI COFFEE

3	CUPS COLD STRONG COFFEE
½	CUP SIMPLE SYRUP (RECIPE FOLLOWS)
½	CUP HALF AND HALF

PUT COFFEE, SYRUP AND HALF AND HALF INTO BLENDER OR FOOD PROCESSOR. PROCESS UNTIL MIXED. ADD ICE CUBES. PROCESS UNTI ICE IS

COARSELY CHOPPED. SERVE IMMEDIATELY IN
TALL FROSTED GLASSES. MAKES 4 SERVINGS

SIMPLE SYRUP

PUT 1 CUP WATER AND 1 CUP SUGAR INTO SMALL
HEAVY SAUCEPAN. HEAT TO BOIL, STIRRING
UNTIL SUGAR DISSOLVES. SIMMER COVERED,
WITHOUT STIRRING, 3 MINUTES. REMOVE
FROM HEAT. REFRIGERATE, COVERED, UP TO 1
MONTH. MAKES ABOUT $1\frac{1}{4}$ CUPS

APPLE BLOSSOM ICE CREAM SODA

2   CUPS APPLE JUICE
1   PINT PEACH ICE CREAM
        DRY GINGER ALE

POUR $\frac{1}{2}$ CUP APPLE JUICE IN EACH OF 4 TALL
GLASSES. DIVIDE ICE CREAM EQUALLY AMONG
GLASSES. FILL GLASSES WITH ICE-COLD
GINGERALE. STIR GENTLY TO MIX

GARNISH WITH APPLE SLICES AND SERVE
IMMEDIATELY. SERVES 4

COFFEE ICE CREAM PUNCH

2	CUPS WATER
2	OZ. COMMUNITY INSTANT COFFEE
2	CUPS SUGAR
1	TBL. VANILLA
1	GAL. MILK
$\frac{1}{2}$	GAL. VANILLA ICE CREAM
$\frac{1}{2}$	GAL. FUDGE RIPPLE ICE CREAM
	(MAY SUBSTITUTE CHOCOLATE)

BRING WATER TO BOIL. ADD COFFEE AND SUGAR AND STIR OVER LOWEST HEAT UNTIL SUGAR IS DISSOLVED. REMOVE FROM HEAT AND COOL. ADD VANILLA. THIS IS THE BASE AND CAN BE MADE AHEAD OF TIME AND KEPT REFRIGERATED.

POUR ABOVE INTO 5 GALLON CONTAINER. ADD MILK AND SOFTENED ICE CREAM. SERVES 50

GOLDEN PUNCH

1	12 OZ. CAN FROZEN ORANGE JUICE
2	12 OZ. CAN FROZEN LEMONADE
$\frac{1}{2}$	46 OZ. CAN PINEAPPLE JUICE
$\frac{1}{2}$	CUP SUGAR
8	TO 10 CUPS WATER
1	OR 1$\frac{1}{2}$ BOTTLES GINGER ALE

DISSOLVE SUGAR IN A LITTLE WATER. MIX
JUICES AND WATER (RINSE FROZEN JUICE
CANS WITH PART OF WATER). PUNCH MAY BE
FROZEN AT THIS POINT. WHEN READY TO USE,
THAW TO A SLUSHLY STAGE. POUR INTO PUNCH
BOWL WITH ICE RING. ADD COLD GINGER ALE.
MAKES 40 TO 50 PUNCH CUPS

Dips & Sauces

BLACK BEAN DIP

1	CAN BLACK BEANS, DRAINED
1	CAN SHOEPEG CORN
½	CUP CHOPPED PURPLE ONION
1	LARGE OR 3 PLUM TOMATOES, CHOPPED
1	JALAPENO PEPPER, CHOPPED
½	TSP. CUMIN
	JUICE OF 1 LIME
1	TBL. OLIVE OIL
	CREOLE SEASONING

COMBINE ALL INGREDIENTS. REFRIGERATE
UNTIL READY TO SERVE. BEST IF MADE
SEVERAL HOURS BEFORE SERVING SO FLAVORS
CAN BLEND. SERVE WITH DORITOS OR
TOSTITOS.

Friendship holds love in its hands.
Some people come into our lives and quickly go.
Some stay for a while, leave footprints on our
hearts and we are never, ever the same.

FRESH SALSA

5	RIPE TOMATOES, HALVED
2	FRESH JALAPENO CHILES, STEMS REMOVED, FINELY MINCED (IF YOU WISH TO CUT DOWN ON THE "HEAT", DISCARD STEMS AND VEINS)

1	SMALL YELLOW ONION, FINELY MINCED, THEN RINSED IN A COLANDAR UNDER COLD, RUNNING WATER.
3	SPRIGS FRESH CORIANDER (CILANTRO) OR PARSLEY, FINELY MINCED
½	TSP. SALT
½	CUP CANNED TOMATO SAUCE (OPTIONAL)

PUT TOMATOES ON COOKIE SHEET, CUT SIDE DOWN AND SET UNDER BROILER ABOUT 6" FROM HEAT SOURCE. BROIL, TURNING UNTIL CHARRED ON BOTH SIDES. SET ASIDE TO COOL.

MEANWHILE, MIX MINCED CHILES, ONION, CORIANDER AND SALT IN A MEDIUM BOWL. THEN PEEL SKIN FROM COOLED TOMATOES, CHOP FINELY AND ADD TO BOWL. IF THE SAUCE LACKS A GOOD COLOR, STIR IN ENOUGH TOMATO SAUCE TO MAKE IT A BRILLIANT RED. MAKES 3 CUPS

Love is why we are here. Love is everything.

FRUIT DIP

12	COCONUT MACAROONS
1	PT. NON-FAT SOUR CREAM
2	TBLS. BROWN SUGAR
1	TBL. VANILLA
3	OZS. NONFAT CREAM CHEESE

COMBINE ALL IN FOOD PROCESSOR OR BLENDER.
SERVE WITH FRESH FRUIT.

Our tomorrows, full of surprises,
stay hidden and wait for us somewhere behind
the moon.

HOMEMADE TOMATO SAUCE

COMBINE 24 PEELED HOME GROWN ORGANIC
TOMATOES WITH 6 VERY COARSELY CHOPPED
ONIONS AND 3 VERY COARSELY CHOPPED RED,
GREEN OR YELLOW BELL PEPPERS AND AN
ENTIRE HEAD OF GARLIC, PEELED AND MINCED.
COOK OVER A MEDIUM HEAT WITH $\frac{1}{2}$ CUP SUGAR,
$\frac{1}{4}$ TSP. SALT AND $\frac{1}{4}$ CUP OF FRESHLY GROUND
BLACK PEPPER. COOK FOR 3 HOURS, STIRRING
FREQUENTLY. A HALF HOUR BEFORE REMOVING
FROM STOVE TOP, ADD 1 CUP OF COARSELY
CHOPPED FRESH BASIL AND $\frac{1}{4}$ CUP EACH OF
FRESH THYME AND FRESH OREGANO, BOTH
COARSELY CHOPPED. MAKES 40 TO 48 OUNCES.
CAN BE EATEN ON CRACKERS, THINNED WITH
WINE FOR SPAGHETTI SAUCE OR USED AS IS IN
CHILI OR ON PIZZAS.

Hearts will always seek hearts
and love will come to those who give it.

HOT COCKTAIL SAUCE

1	14 OZ. BOTTLE KETCHUP
½	CUP HORSERADISH
2½	TBLS. TABASCO
	JUICE OF 2½ LEMONS

MIX THESE INGREDIENTS WELL.

*Life's gifts are wondrous and come to us
when it is time.*

HOT CRAB DIP

½	CUP BUTTER (1 STICK)
½	BUNCH CHOPPED GREEN ONIONS
½	BUNCH CHOPPED PARSLEY
2	TBLS. FLOUR
1	CUP GRATED SWISS CHEESE (4 OZ.)
1	LB. CRABMEAT (LUMP OR WHITE)
1	TBL. WHITE WINE OR SHERRY
½	TSP. LEMON JUICE
1	TSP. SALT
¾	TSP. RED PEPPER
	TABASCO

MELT BUTTER. ADD CHOPPED ONION AND
PARSLEY. BLEND IN FLOUR. LET COOK UNTIL
THICKENED.

ADD CREAM AND CHEESE. ADD CRABMEAT AND WINE AND THE REST OF THE SEASONINGS.

THIS CAN BE MADE AHEAD OF TIME AND FROZEN. SERVE WITH MELBA ROUNDS.

Follow your heart wherever it takes you.

OLIVE TAPENADE

¾	CUP CHOPPED RIPE OLIVES
1	TBL. CHOPPED FRESH PARSLEY
2	TBLS. FINELY GRATED FRESH CARROTS
2	TBLS. CHOPPED FROZEN GREEN PEAS
1	TBL. FINELY CHOPPED ONION
1	TBL. FINELY CHOPPED RED PEPPER
2	DROPS RED PEPPER SAUCE
½	TSP. MINCED FRESH GARLIC
1	TBL. LEMON JUICE
½	TSP. ITALIAN SEASONING
1	TSP. FRESH CILANTRO, FINELY CHOPPED
1	FINELY CHOPPED PLUM TOMATO
1	TSP. SPICY MUSTARD

COMBINE ALL INGREDIENTS IN A BOWL. MIX WELL. FOR A SMOOTH TEXTURE, PLACE ALL INGREDIENTS UNCHOPPED IN A FOOD PROCESSOR OR BLENDER AND PROCESS UNTIL SMOOTH. GARNISH WITH A PARSLEY SPRIGS AND OLIVES. MAKES ABOUT 1 CUP

SERVE AS A RELISH, SANDWICH SPREAD, OR A
DIP WITH BREAD, VEGETABLES OR CHIPS.

*FOR SPICIER TASTE, ADD MORE RED PEPPER
SAUCE. *FOR A MIDDLE EASTERN FLAVOR, ADD
CURRY POWDER.

*Embrace the moment and know you are
a part of it all.*

PEANUT-COCONUT SAUCE

$2\frac{1}{2}$	CUPS CREAMY PEANUT BUTTER
$1\frac{1}{4}$	CUPS CHICKEN BROTH
$1\frac{1}{4}$	CUPS CREAM OF COCONUT
2/3	CUP SOY SAUCE
2/3	CUP CIDER VINEGAR
2	TSPS. RED PEPPER, GROUND
$1\frac{1}{2}$	TSPS. GINGER, GROUND

COMBINE ALL INGREDIENTS IN A BOWL.

THIS IS AN EXCELLENT SAUCE FOR DIPPING
CHICKEN WINGS, DRUMMETTES AND
TENDERLOIN STRIPS.

MOROCCAN SPICE BEAN DIP

1	TSP. PAPRIKA
$\frac{1}{4}$	TSP. FENNEL SEEDS, CRUSHED
$\frac{1}{4}$	TSP. GROUND GINGER
$\frac{1}{4}$	TSP. GROUND CUMIN
$\frac{1}{4}$	TSP. GROUND CAYENNE
	PINCH GROUND CINNAMON
1	15 TO 19 OZ. CAN GARBANZO BEANS, RINSED AND DRAINED
2	TBLS. OLIVE OIL
1	TBL. FRESH LEMON JUICE
$\frac{1}{2}$	TSP. SALT
$\frac{1}{4}$	TSP. GROUND BLACK PEPPER
$\frac{1}{4}$	CUP WATER

IN A 1 QT. SAUCEPAN, HEAT FIRST 6 INGREDIENTS OVER MEDIUM-LOW HEAT, STIRRING 1 TO 2 MINUTES, UNTIL VERY FRAGRANT. REMOVE FROM HEAT.

IN FOOD PROCESSOR WITH KNIFE BLADE ATTACHED, COMBINE GARBANZO BEANS, OLIVE OIL, LEMON JUICE, SALT, BLACK PEPPER, TOASTED SPICES AND WATER AND BLEND UNTIL SMOOTH. TRANSFER TO SMALL SERVING BOWL.

SILKY ALMOND DIP

1	8 OZ. PKG. FAT FREE CREAM CHEESE, SOFTENED
$\frac{1}{2}$	CUP NONFAT SOUR CREAM
$\frac{1}{2}$	CUP SUGAR
3	TBLS. SKIM MILK
$\frac{1}{4}$	TSP. ALMOND EXTRACT

MIX CREAM CHEESE WITH ELECTRIC MIXER ON MEDIUM SPEED UNTIL SMOOTH. ADD SOUR CREAM, MIXING UNTIL BLENDED. MIX IN SUGAR, MILK AND EXTRACT. REFRIGERATE. SERVE WITH ASSORTED FRESH FRUIT. MAKES 1 2/3 CUPS

SUN-DRIED TOMATO VINAIGRETTE

4	OZS. WHOLE SUN-DRIED TOMATOES
2	OZS. TOASTED PINE NUTS OR PUMPKIN SEEDS
1	CLOVE GARLIC OR TWO SMALL CLOVES
$\frac{1}{2}$	CUP BALSAMIC VINEGAR
$1\frac{1}{2}$	CUPS EXTRA VIRGIN OLIVE OIL
	SALT AND PEPPER TO TASTE

ADD SUN-DRIED TOMATOES, GARLIC AND PINE
NUTS TO FOOD PROCESSOR AND PUREE. ADD
VINEGAR AND BLEND UNTIL WELL MIXED.
IN A STEADY STREAM, SLOWLY ADD OLIVE OIL.
STOP FOOD PROCESSOR AFTER ALL OIL IS USED.
TASTE AND ADD A PINCH OF SALT AND PEPPER.
MIX ONE MORE TIME TO BLEND. SERVE AS A
VINAGRETTE FOR SALAD GREENS.

Life is only loaned to us, take of its joy.

TEX-MEX BLACK BEAN DIP

1	15 OZ. CAN BLACK BEANS, DRAINED
1	TSP. VEGETABLE OIL
$\frac{1}{2}$	CUP CHOPPED ONION
2	GARLIC CLOVES, MINCED
$\frac{1}{2}$	CUP DICED TOMATO
1/3	CUP MILD PICANTE SAUCE
$\frac{1}{2}$	TSP. GROUND CUMIN
$\frac{1}{2}$	TSP. CHILI POWDER
$\frac{1}{4}$	CUP (1 OZ.) SHREDDED MONTERREY JACK CHEESE
$\frac{1}{4}$	CUP CHOPPED FRESH CILANTRO
1	TBL. FRESH LIME JUICE

PLACE BEANS IN A BOWL. PARTIALLY MASH
UNTIL CHUNKY. SET ASIDE. HEAT OIL IN A
MEDIUM NONSTICK SKILLET OVER MEDIUM
HEAT. ADD ONION AND GARLIC, AND SAUTE 4
MINUTES OR UNTIL TENDER. ADD BEANS,

TOMATO, PICANTE SAUCE, CUMIN, AND CHILI
POWDER. COOK 5 MINUTES OR UNTIL THICK,
STIRRING CONSTANTLY. REMOVE FROM HEAT.
ADD CHEESE, CILANTRO, AND LIME JUICE,
STIRRING WELL. SERVE WARM OR AT ROOM
TEMPERATURE WITH CORN OR FLOUR TORTILLA
CHIPS. YIELDS 1 2/3 CUPS

*Just to be alive and part of the world
is miracle enough.*

BARBEQUE SAUCE

½	LARGE RED BELL PEPPER, CUT IN LARGE PIECES
½	LARGE ONION, CUT IN LARGE PIECES
4	CUPS BOTTLED BARBEQUE SAUCE
3	TBLS. DIJON MUSTARD
3	TBLS. WORCESTERSHIRE SAUCE
½	CUP DARK MOLASSES
2	TBLS. CHOPPED FRESH THYME
2	TBLS. CHOPPED FRESH BASIL
2	TBLS. CHOPPED FRESH PARSLEY

PROCESS BELL PEPPER AND ONION IN FOOD
PROCESSOR UNTIL FINELY CHOPPED.
COMBINE BARBEQUE SAUCE, MUSTARD,
WORCESTERSHIRE SAUCE, MOLASSES, THYME,
BASIL AND PARSLEY IN LARGE BOWL AND ADD
BELL PEPPER-ONION MIXTURE. STIR UNTIL
WELL BLENDED. MAKES 5 CUPS

EXCELLENT SHRIMP DIP

1	8 OZ. PKG. NEUFCHATEL CHEESE
1	8 OZ. PKG. FAT FREE CREAM CHEESE
2	+1 CLOVES GARLIC, MINCED
3	TSPS. WORCESTERSHIRE SAUCE
2	+1 TSPS. TABASCO SAUCE
	MILK
1	LB. COLD BOILED SHRIMP, PREFERABLY SMALL SHRIMP
8	OZ. REDUCED FAT MOZZARELLA CHEESE, GRATED
1	15 OZ. BOTTLE COCKTAIL SAUCE
6	GREEN ONIONS, CHOPPED
1	SMALL GREEN PEPPER, CHOPPED
2	TOMATOES, CHOPPED
1	OZ. GRATED FAT FREE PARMESAN CHEESE

MIX NEUFCHATEL CHEESE, CREAM CHEESE, GARLIC, WORCESTERSHIRE AND TABASCO TOGETHER. ADD A SMALL AMOUNT OF MILK TO THIN THE MIXTURE.

SPREAD ON A ROUND TRAY. SPRINKLE SHRIMP AND REDUCED FAT MOZZARELLA CHEESE ON TOP. SPREAD COCKTAIL SAUCE. SPRINKLE ONIONS, GREEN PEPPERS AND TOMATOES. TOP WITH PARMESAN CHEESE.

FIESTA SALSA

1	8¾ OZ. CAN WHOLE KERNEL CORN, DRAINED
1	4 OZ. CAN DICED GREEN CHILIES
½	CUP SLICED, PITTED RIPE OLIVES
½	CUP DRAINED SONOMA MARINATED SUN DRIED TOMATOES, CUT INTO STRIPS
½	CUP FINELY DICED RED AND/OR GREEN BELL PEPPER
¼	CUP EACH CHOPPED RED ONION AND CILANTRO
2	TSPS. MINCED FRESH OR CANNED JALAPENO PEPPER
1	TBL. LIME JUICE
½	TO 1 TSP. SUGAR
	SALT

IN BOWL, MIX ALL INGREDIENTS EXCEPT CHILI POWDER, SUGAR AND SALT. SEASON TO TASTE WITH CHILI POWDER, SUGAR AND SALT. SERVE WITH GRILLED PORK SAUSAGES. MAKES ABOUT 3 CUPS

HERB WINE BUTTER

1	CUP BUTTER, SOFTENED
2	TBLS. DRY WHITE WINE OR SHERRY
1	TBL. FINELY CHOPPED SHALLOTS
$\frac{1}{2}$	TSP. FINELY CHOPPED FRESH GARLIC
2	TSPS. CHOPPED FRESH PARSLEY
	OR $\frac{1}{2}$ TSP. DRIED
$\frac{3}{4}$	TSP. CHOPPED FRESH THYME
	OR $\frac{1}{4}$ TSP. DRIED

IN SMALL MIXER BOWL, BEAT BUTTER AT
MEDIUM SPEED UNTIL CREAMY (1 TO 2
MINUTES). REDUCE SPEED TO LOW. ADD ALL
REMAINING INGREDIENTS. CONTINUE
BEATING UNTIL WELL MIXED (2 TO 3 MINUTES).
COVER. REFRIGERATE AT LEAST 1 HOUR TO
ENHANCE FLAVORS. MAKES 1 CUP

*Life is change. With every moment in time, a
new you is being born.*

MAPLE TOASTED ONION BUTTER

1	CUP BUTTER, SOFTENED
2	TBLS. FINELY CHOPPED ONIONS
2	TBLS. MAPLE SYRUP
$\frac{1}{2}$	TSP. MAPLE FLAVOR EXTRACT

IN 8" SKILLET, MELT 1 TBL. BUTTER. STIR IN
ONIONS. COOK OVER MEDIUM HEAT, STIRRING
CONSTANTLY, UNTIL ONIONS ARE GOLDEN (1
TO 2 MINUTES). REMOVE FROM HEAT. COOL 5
MINUTES.

MEANWHILE, IN SMALL MIXER BOWL, BEAT
REMAINING BUTTER AT MEDIUM SPEED UNTIL
CREAMY (1 TO 2 MINUTES). REDUCE SPEED TO
LOW. ADD ONIONS, MAPLE SYRUP AND MAPLE
FLAVOR EXTRACT. CONTINUE BEATING UNTIL
WELL MIXED (1 TO 2 MINUTES).

COVER, REFRIGERATE AT LEAST 1 HOUR TO
ENHANCE FLAVOR. MAKES 1 CUP

Time is the soul of the world. Nurture it.

RED PEPPER AND BLACK BEAN SALSA

1½	LBS. RED BELL PEPPER (4 MEDIUM); SEEDS AND RIBS REMOVED AND FINELY DICED
1	CUP FINELY CHOPPED RED ONIONS
1	TBL. MINCED GARLIC
2	TBLS. OLIVE OIL
⅓	CUP CHARDONNAY
½	TSP. DRIED OREGANO
1	15 OZ. CAN BLACK BEANS, DRAINED AND RINSED
1	TSP. TABASCO (OR TO TASTE)

1	TBL. FRESH LIME OR LEMON JUICE
2	+1 TBLS. CHOPPED FRESH CILANTRO
	SALT AND FRESHLY GROUND PEPPER
	GARNISH: CHOPPED FRESH ADVOCADO
	AND CILANTRO SPRIGS, IF DESIRED

SAUTE THE PEPPERS, ONIONS AND GARLIC WITH
THE OLIVE OIL IN A LARGE SAUTE PAN OVER
MODERATE HEAT UNTIL THE VEGETABLES JUST
BEGIN TO SOFTEN, 3 TO 4 MINUTES. ADD THE
WINE AND OREGANO AND CONTINUE TO COOK
FOR 3 TO 4 MINUTES LONGER OR UNTIL
VEGETABLES ARE AL DENTE. TURN OFF HEAT,
COOL AND STIR IN THE BEANS, TABASCO, LIME
JUICE AND CILANTRO. SEASON TO TASTE.

GARNISH, IF DESIRED, WITH CHOPPED
ADVOCADO AND CILANTRO SPRIGS. SERVES 10

*The biggest chance we ever take in life is not
taking a chance.*

SAVORY MUSHROOM SAUCE

2	TBLS. OLIVE OIL
$\frac{1}{2}$	LB. MUSHROOMS, FINELY CHOPPED
$\frac{1}{4}$	CUP CHOPPED ONION
$\frac{1}{2}$	TSP. DRIED THYME LEAVES
$\frac{1}{8}$	TSP. PEPPER
1	12 OZ. JAR BEEF GRAVY
1/3	CUP DRY RED WINE

IN SKILLET, HEAT OIL OVER HIGH HEAT UNTIL
HOT. ADD MUSHROOMS. COOK 3 TO 5 MINUTES
UNTIL MUSHROOMS ARE COOKED AND LIQUID
HAS EVAPORATED, STIRRING OCCASIONALLY.
ADD ONION, THYME AND PEPPER. COOK UNTIL
ONION IS TENDER, ABOUT 3 MINUTES. STIR IN
GRAVY AND RED WINE. BRING TO A BOIL.
REDUCE HEAT TO MEDIUM-LOW AND SIMMER 2
MINUTES. MAKES 2 CUPS

Time has no meaning in matters of the heart.

SUN-DRIED TOMATO AND SHALLOT BUTTER

1	CUP BUTTER, SOFTENED
1	TBL. FINELY CHOPPED SHALLOTS
1	TSP. FINELY CHOPPED FRESH GARLIC
2	TBLS. FINELY CHOPPED SUN DRIED TOMATOES, SOAKED, DRAINED

IN 8" SKILLET, MELT 1 TBL. BUTTER. STIR IN
SHALLOTS AND GARLIC. COOK OVER MEDIUM
HEAT, STIRRING CONSTANTLY, UNTIL
SHALLOTS ARE GOLDEN (1 TO 2 MINUTES).
REMOVE FROM HEAT. COOL 5 MINUTES.

MEANWHILE, IN SMALL MIXER BOWL, BEAT
REMAINING BUTTER AT MEDIUM SPEED UNTIL
CREAMY (1 TO 2 MINUTES). REDUCE SPEED TO
LOW. ADD SHALLOTS, GARLIC AND SUN DRIED

TOMATOES. CONTINUE BEATING UNTIL WELL
MIXED (1 TO 2 MINUTES). COVER, REFRIGERATE
AT LEAST 1 HOUR. MAKES 1 CUP

Believing is everything.

PROVENCAL SPREAD

1	LARGE EGGPLANT
2	CLOVES GARLIC, CHOPPED
2	TBLS. DIJON MUSTARD
1	TBL. LEMON JUICE
2	TBLS. KALAMATA OLIVES, PITTED AND CHOPPED
3	TBLS. CHOPPED SUN DRIED TOMATOES
$\frac{1}{4}$	CUP CHOPPED FRESH PARSLEY
$\frac{1}{4}$	TSP. SALT
$\frac{1}{4}$	TSP. BLACK PEPPER
	CRACKERS

PLACE WHOLE EGGPLANT ON GRILL OVER
MEDIUM HEAT. COOK UNTIL ALL SIDES ARE
EVENLY CHARRED, TURNING OFTEN. COOK
EGGPLANT. PEEL EGGPLANT AND COARSELY CHOP
PULP.

IN FOOD PROCESSOR, PLACE EGGPLANT, GARLIC,
MUSTARD AND LEMON JUICE. PROCESS JUST
UNTIL SMOOTH. FOLD IN OLIVES, SUN DRIED
TOMATOES AND PARSLEY. SEASON WITH SALT
AND PEPPER. SPOON INTO SERVING BOWL.
COVER. CHILL AT LEAST 30 MINUTES. SERVE AS

A SPREAD WITH CRACKERS. MAKES ABOUT 2 CUPS

SALSA

12   CUPS DICED TOMATOES
1   CUP GREEN PEPPER, DICED
1   CUP JALAPENO, DICED
2   CUPS ONION, DICED
4   TSPS. SALT
6   CLOVES GARLIC, MINCED
2   CUPS WHITE VINEGAR
3   TBLS. SUGAR

PUT ALL INGREDIENTS TOGETHER AND SIMMER AT LEAST 20 MINUTES, CAN BE LONGER TO THICKEN (45 MINUTES), PUT IN MEDIUM SIZE ZIPLOC FREEZER BAGS.

SESAME GRILL SAUCE

2/3   CUP VEGETABLE OIL
⅓   CUP SESAME SEEDS
⅓   CUP SOY SAUCE
½   TSP. WORCESTERSHIRE SAUCE

6	TBLS. SUGAR
3	TSPS. MINCED SCALLIONS
3	TBLS. FRESH GINGER, MINCED
1	TSP. DRY MUSTARD
⅓	TSP. SALT

PROCESS ALL INGREDIENTS IN FOOD PROCESSOR USING A STEEL BLADE. THIS MAKES A GREAT DIPPING SAUCE OR MARINADE FOR CHICKEN, PORK OR SHRIMP. IT ALSO MAKES AN EXCELLENT SALAD DRESSING IF YOU ADD A LITTLE MORE VINEGAR.

SPINACH DIP

CREAM TOGETHER:

1	CUP SOUR CREAM
1	CUP MAYONNAISE
	(CREAM CHEESE MAY BE SUBSTITUTED)

ADD:

1	PKG. FROZEN, CHOPPED SPINACH, DRAINED
1	PKG. KNORR VEGETABLE SOUP MIX
1	CAN DICED WATER CHESTNUTS, DRAINED
½	DICED ONION

THREE PEPPER KETCHUP

2	TBLS. OLIVE OIL
$\frac{1}{2}$	CUP MINCED ONION
$\frac{1}{2}$	CUP SLICED GREEN ONION
$\frac{1}{2}$	CUP MINCED RED BELL PEPPER
3	CANNED PICKLED JALAPENO PEPPERS, MINCED
2	GARLIC CLOVES, MINCED
$\frac{1}{4}$	TSP. THYME
$1\frac{1}{2}$	CUPS KETCHUP
$\frac{3}{4}$	CUP CANNED CRUSHED TOMATOES
$\frac{1}{2}$	TSP. PEPPER

HEAT OIL IN MEDIUM SAUCEPAN OVER LOW HEAT. ADD ONIONS, BELL PEPPER, JALAPENO PEPPERS, GARLIC AND THYME. COVER AND COOK UNTIL ALL VEGETABLES ARE TENDER (ABOUT 10 MINUTES). MIX IN KETCHUP, TOMATOES AND PEPPER. COVER PARTIALLY AND SIMMER UNTIL THICKENED, ABOUT FIVE MINUTES, STIRRING OCCASIONALLY. COVER AND CHILL.

MAKES $2\frac{3}{4}$ CUPS. KEEPS TWO WEEKS IN REFRIGERATOR. MAKE AT LEAST 24 HOURS AHEAD OF TIME.

RASBERRY MINT MARINADE

½   CUP OLIVE OIL
⅓   CUP RED WINE OR SHERRY VINEGAR
½   CUP FRESH MINT
1   LARGE CLOVE GARLIC
1   TBL. DIJON MUSTARD
½   TSP. BLACK PEPPER
¼   CUP RASPBERRIES (FRESH OR FROZEN)

THIS MARINARDE IS GREAT FOR POULTRY AND
LAMB. IT IS ALSO GOOD WHEN USED AS A
SALAD DRESSING OR PUT IN A FRUIT SALAD.

Soups & Stews

BAKED GARLIC AND ONION SOUP

6	LARGE ONIONS, CUT INTO $\frac{1}{2}$" SLICES
2	HEADS GARLIC, CLOVES SEPARATED AND PEELED
5	CUPS CANNED CHICKEN BROTH
$1\frac{1}{2}$	TSPS. DRIED THYME LEAVES
1	TSP. COARSELY GROUND BLACK PEPPER
1	TSP. SALT
4	TBLS. ($\frac{1}{2}$ STICK) BUTTER
2	CUPS HEAVY OR WHIPPING CREAM
2	TBLS. CHOPPED FRESH PARSLEY, FOR GARNISH

PREHEAT OVEN TO 350°. PLACE ONIONS AND GARLIC IN A SHALLOW ROASTING PAN AND ADD 3 CUPS OF THE CHICKEN BROTH. SPRINKLE WITH THYME, PEPPER AND SALT. DOT WITH BUTTER.

COVER PAN WITH ALUMINUM FOIL AND BAKE FOR $1\frac{1}{2}$ HOURS. STIR ONCE OR TWICE WHILE BAKING. REMOVE PAN FROM OVEN AND PUREE THE ONIONS AND GARLIC WITH THE LIQUID, IN BATCHES IN A BLENDER OR FOOD PROCESSOR UNTIL SMOOTH. WITH THE MOTOR RUNNING, GRADUALLY ADD THE REMAINING 2 CUPS BROTH AND THE CREAM. POUR THE SOUP INTO A LARGE SAUCEPAN.

ADJUST THE SEASONING AND SLOWLY HEAT
THROUGH. DO NOT ALLOW THE SOUP TO BOIL.
SPRINKLE WITH PARSLEY AND SERVE. SERVES 6

*The mountains are not as high, the seas not as
deep, and the skies not as bright,
as a dream. Every year brings its own pleasures
and sings its own songs.*

CHUNKY CHEESE SOUP

2	CUPS WATER
2	CUPS DICED, PEELED POTATOES
$\frac{1}{2}$	CUP DICED CARROTS
$\frac{1}{2}$	CUP CHOPPED CELERY
$\frac{1}{4}$	CUP CHOPPED ONION
1	TO $1\frac{1}{2}$ TSPS. SALT
$\frac{1}{4}$	TSP. PEPPER
1	CUP CUBED FULLY COOKED HAM
$\frac{1}{4}$	CUP BUTTER
$\frac{1}{4}$	CUP ALL PURPOSE FLOUR
2	CUPS MILK
2	CUPS (8 OZ.) SHREDDED CHEDDAR CHEESE

IN A LARGE SAUCEPAN, COMBINE THE FIRST 7
INGREDIENTS. BRING TO A BOIL. REDUCE
HEAT. COVER AND SIMMER UNTIL THE
VEGETABLES ARE TENDER. ADD HAM. IN
ANOTHER SAUCEPAN, MELT THE BUTTER, STIR
IN FLOUR UNTIL SMOOTH. GRADUALLY ADD

MILK. BRING TO A BOIL. COOK AND STIR FOR 2
MINUTES OR UNTIL THICKENED. STIR IN
CHEESE UNTIL MELTED. ADD TO THE SOUP.
YIELDS 6-8 SERVINGS

IN PLACE OF THE HAM, YOU CAN SUBSTITUTE
ONE OF THE FOLLOWING:

6	OZ. TUNA OR SALMON
1	CUP COOKED GROUND BEEF OR BULK PORK SAUSAGE
1	LB. BACON, COOKED AND CRUMBLED

*Never be afraid to reach for the stars, for the
sky is filled with ageless wonders.*

GUMBO YA-YA

$\frac{1}{4}$	CUP OIL
$\frac{1}{4}$	CUP FLOUR
1	MEDIUM CHOPPED ONION
3	CUPS STOCK OR WATER
1	HEAPING TBL. TOMATO PASTE
1	8 OZ. CAN STEWED TOMATOES
	DASH OF WORCESTERSHIRE
2	PODS GARLIC, CHOPPED FINE
	KITCHEN BOUQUET, TO COLOR
3	SKINLESS CHICKEN THIGHS
1	LARGE LENGTHY CAJUN ANDOUILLE
2	OR 3 BAY LEAVES
	SALT AND PEPPER TO TASTE
$\frac{1}{2}$	CUP CUT OKRA

1	RIB CELERY, SLICED
½	RED BELL PEPPER, CUBED
½	CUP GREEN ONIONS, CHOPPED
	FILE' TO TASTE

MAKE A ROUX OF OIL AND FLOUR. ADD ONION AND COOK UNTIL WILTED. ADD OTHER INGREDIENTS EXCEPT FOR CELERY AND BELL PEPPER AND COOK UNTIL CHICKEN IS TENDER. REMOVE FROM HEAT AND ADD CELERY AND BELL PEPPER. LET SIT FOR 30 MINUTES.

SERVE IN BOWL WITH RICE AND TOPPED WITH GREEN ONIONS AND FILE'.

SHORT RIBS OF BEEF WITH CORNMEAL DUMPLINGS

4	LBS. BEEF RIBS CUT INTO SERVING SIZE PIECES
	SALT AND PEPPER
1	MEDIUM ONION, CUT INTO THIN SLICES
1	CLOVE GARLIC, MINCED
2	28 OZ. CANS TOMATOES
1	12 OZ. CAN BEER
1	FRESH OR DRIED RED CHILI PEPPER, SEEDED AND CHOPPED
2	TBLS. SOY SAUCE
1	TBL. SUGAR

COMBINE ALL INGREDIENTS IN DUTCH OVEN
AND SIMMER SLOWLY FOR ABOUT AN HOUR.
ADD DUMPLINGS.

*May you share love and laughter
with those you love.*

CORNMEAL DUMPLINGS FOR
SHORT RIBS OF BEEF

1	CUP WATER
$\frac{1}{2}$	CUP YELLOW CORNMEAL
$\frac{1}{2}$	TSP. SALT
1	BEATEN EGG
$\frac{1}{2}$	CUP ALL PURPOSE FLOUR
1	TSP. BAKING POWDER
	DASH OF PEPPER
1	7 OZ. CAN WHOLE KERNEL CORN, DRAINED

IN A SAUCEPAN, COMBINE 1 CUP WATER, $\frac{1}{2}$ CUP
YELLOW CORNMEAL AND $\frac{1}{2}$ TSP. SALT. BRING TO
A BOIL, STIRRING CONSTANTLY. COOK AND
STIR UNTIL THE MIXTURE IS THAT OF MEDIUM
CREAM SAUCE. REMOVE FROM HEAT. BEAT THE
EGG IN A SMALL BOWL. STIR A MODERATE
AMOUNT OF THE HOT MIXTURE INTO THE EGG.
RETURN TO THE HOT MIXTURE. MIX TOGETHER
THE FLOUR, BAKING POWDER AND PEPPER. ADD
TO THE CORNMEAL MIXTURE. BEAT WELL. STIR
IN DRAINED CORN. DROP BATTER BY ROUNDED

TABLESPOONS ONTO THE SIMMERING STEW
MIXTURE. COVER AND SIMMER UNTIL DONE
(ABOUT 10 TO 12 MINUTES). SERVES 4 TO 6

*Your journey is just the beginning and all the
world awaits your touch.*

AUSTIN CHILI

½	LB. HICKORY SMOKED BACON
3	LBS. BEEF, LEAN OR COARSE GROUND
2	LARGE ONIONS, CHOPPED FINE
3	CLOVES GARLIC, CHOPPED FINE
1	15 OZ. CAN TOMATO SAUCE
1	6 OZ. CAN TOMATO PASTE
2	+1 TBLS. CUMIN, GROUND
1	TBL. OREGANO, GROUND
1	TBL. SALT
1	TBL. PEPPER
12	OZS. DARK MEXICAN BEER
6	TO 9 DRIED RED CHILIES
2	CUPS WATER

IN A LARGE CAST IRON POT, FRY BACON CRISP.
DISCARD THE BACON AND SAVE THE GREASE.
BROWN THE MEAT. SAUTE THE ONIONS AND
GARLIC. ADD THE GROUND BEEF. ADD
REMAINING INGREDIENTS AND SIMMER UNTIL
DONE. ABOUT 1 HOUR.

CHEESE SOUP

3	TBLS. BUTTER
1	CUP CARROTS, DICED FINE
$\frac{1}{2}$	CUP ONION, DICED FINE
1	CUP CELERY, DICED FINE
2	+1 TBLS. FLOUR
1	QT. HOT CHICKEN BROTH
1	TSP. SEASONED SALT
2	CUPS MILK
3	+1 OZS. AMERICAN CHEESE
4	OZS. CHEDDAR CHEESE
8	OZS. VELVEETA
1	SMALL JAR CHEEZ WHIZ
1	$10\frac{3}{4}$ OZ. CAN CAMPBELL'S CHEESE SOUP
	TONY CHACHERE'S CREOLE SEASONING
	TO TASTE

SAUTE VEGETABLES IN BUTTER UNTIL SOFT. BEING CAREFUL NOT TO SCORCH, BLEND IN FLOUR UNTIL FOAMY. SLOWLY STIR IN LIQUIDS, THEN CHEESES AND CAN OF SOUP AND SEASON TO TASTE. STIR CONSTANTLY UNTIL CHEESES ARE MELTED. DO NOT BOIL.

WINNING WHITE CHILI

½	LB. BONELESS PORK LOIN, (OR 2 BONELESS PORK CHOPS) CUT INTO ½" CUBES
1	TSP. OIL
1½	TSPS. GROUND CUMIN
¼	TSP. GARLIC POWDER
1	CUP COOKED WILD RICE
1	16 OZ. CAN NAVY BEANS, DRAINED
1	16 OZ. CAN CHICKPEAS, DRAINED
1	4 OZ. CAN DICED GREEN CHILIES, DRAINED
1	16 OZ. CAN WHITE WHOLE-KERNEL CORN, DRAINED
⅛	TSP. HOT PEPPER SAUCE
1	14½ OZ. CAN CHICKEN BROTH CHOPPED PARSLEY

IN A 4 QT. SAUCEPAN, SAUTE ONIONS AND PORK IN OIL OVER MEDIUM HIGH HEAT UNTIL ONIONS ARE SOFT AND PORK LIGHTLY BROWNED, ABOUT 5 MINUTES. STIR IN ALL REMAINING INGREDIENTS EXCEPT PARSLEY. COVER AND SIMMER FOR 20 MINUTES. SERVE EACH PORTION GARNISHED WITH CHOPPED PARSLEY.

ZUCCHINI AND SAUSAGE SOUP

1	LB. BULK ITALIAN SAUSAGE
1	MEDIUM ONION, CHOPPED
2	+1 CUPS WATER
$1\frac{1}{2}$	TSPS. FRESH BASIL, CHOPPED (OR $\frac{1}{2}$ TSP. DRIED)
$1\frac{1}{2}$	TSPS. FRESH OREGANO, CHOPPED (OR $\frac{1}{2}$ TSP. DRIED)
3	MEDIUM ZUCCHINIS, COARSELY CHOPPED
2	MEDIUM CARROTS, COARSELY CHOPPED
2	CANS CONDENSED TOMATO SOUP (OR 1 CAN TOMATO PUREE)
8	OZS. UNCOOKED, DRIED (OR FROZEN) MEAT OR CHEESE FILLED TORTELLINI
2	TBLS. CHOPPED CELERY LEAVES

COOK SAUSAGE AND ONION IN DUTCH OVEN UNTIL SAUSAGE IS BROWN. DRAIN. STIR IN REMAINING INGREDIENTS. BRING TO A BOIL. REDUCE HEAT, COVER AND SIMMER ABOUT 20 MINUTES OR UNTIL VEGETABLES ARE DONE. SEASON TO TASTE.

CLAM CHOWDER

½	CUP DICED ONIONS
½	CUP DICED CELERY
¼	CUP DICED GREEN PEPPERS
1	STICK BUTTER
½	CUP FLOUR
½	GALLON MILK
1½	CUPS PEELED, DICED POTATOES
	(3 MEDIUM POTATOES)
1	8 OZ. CAN CLAMS
1	TBL. CLAM BASE
	(4 OZ. OF THE CLAM JUICE)
	SALT AND PEPPER TO TASTE

COOK POTATOES, DRAIN AND SET ASIDE.
IN A 2 QT. POT, SAUTE ONIONS, CELERY AND
GREEN PEPPERS IN BUTTER UNTIL TENDER.
USING A WIRE WHIP, STIR FLOUR INTO
SAUTEED VEGETABLES. SIMMER FOR 3
MINUTES. SLOWLY ADD MILK, STIRRING
CONSTANTLY UNTIL IT STARTS TO THICKEN.
STIR IN CLAMS AND CLAM BASE. SIMMER FOR
15 TO 25 MINUTES. ADD POTATOES. SALT AND
PEPPER TO TASTE.

ENOLA'S PRUDHOMME'S CAJUN STYLE CORN SOUP

1	TBL. QUICK-MIXING FLOUR (WONDRA)
$\frac{1}{2}$	CUP WATER
1	TBL. BUTTER
3	CUPS FRESH CORN, CUT OFF THE COB (ABOUT 6 EARS) (CAN SUBSTITUTE 1 14 OZ. PKG. TENDER WHITE CORN)
$\frac{1}{2}$	CUP FINELY CHOPPED ONIONS
2	MEDIUM TOMATOES, PEELED, SEEDED AND CHOPPED (1 CUP)
2	CUPS SKIM MILK
1	CUP EVAPORATED SKIM MILK
$\frac{1}{4}$	TSP. SALT
$\frac{1}{4}$	TSP. GROUND WHITE PEPPER
$\frac{1}{8}$	TSP. GROUND RED PEPPER
3	TBLS. FINELY CHOPPED GREEN ONIONS

IN A SMALL BOWL, DISSOLVE THE FLOUR IN THE WATER, SET ASIDE. IN A MEDIUM SAUCEPAN OVER MEDIUM HEAT, MELT THE BUTTER. ADD THE CORN, ONIONS AND TOMATOES. COOK FOR 15 MINUTES, STIRRING CONSTANTLY. ADD THE SKIM MILK AND SIMMER FOR AN ADDITIONAL 15 MINUTES. ADD THE EVAPORATED SKIM MILK, DISSOLVED

FLOUR, SALT AND THE WHITE AND RED PEPPERS.
REDUCE THE HEAT AND SIMMER FOR 15
MINUTES, STIRRING OFTEN. ADD THE GREEN
ONIONS. SIMMER FOR 5 MINUTES AND SERVE
HOT.

MOFFITT'S CHILI

1	TBL. OLIVE OIL
1	ONION, FINELY DICED
2	CLOVES GARLIC, FINELY DICED
1	LB. GROUND ROUND
	CHILI PEPPER TO TASTE
	SALT AND BLACK PEPPER TO TASTE
2	CUPS HOMEMADE TOMATO SAUCE*

SAUTE ONIONS AND GARLIC IN THE OLIVE OIL
FOR ABOUT 5 MINUTES OR UNTIL
CARAMELIZED. ADD GROUND MEAT AND
BROWN. SEASON MIXTURE TO TASTE WITH
CHILI PEPPER, SALT AND BLACK PEPPER.
ADD HOMEMADE TOMATO SAUCE AND
CONTINUE COOKING FOR ABOUT 15 MINUTES
OR UNTIL CHILI REACHES DESIRED THICKNESS.
SERVES 4 AS CHILI OR 8 TO 10 AS A HOT DOG
TOPPING.

*Our memories, like our dreams,
are ours alone and tell our story.*

HOMEMADE TOMATO SAUCE

COMBINE 24 PEELED HOME GROWN ORGANIC TOMATOES WITH 6 VERY COARSELY CHOPPED ONIONS AND 3 VERY COARSELY CHOPPED RED, GREEN OR YELLOW BELL PEPPERS AND AN ENTIRE HEAD OF GARLIC, PEELED AND MINCED. COOK OVER A MEDIUM HEAT WITH ½ CUP SUGAR, ¼ TSP. SALT AND ¼ CUP OF FRESHLY GROUND BLACK PEPPER. COOK FOR 3 HOURS, STIRRING FREQUENTLY. A HALF HOUR BEFORE REMOVING FROM STOVE TOP, ADD 1 CUP OF COARSELY CHOPPED FRESH BASIL AND ¼ CUP EACH OF FRESH THYME AND FRESH OREGANO, BOTH COARSELY CHOPPED. MAKES 40 TO 48 OUNCES. CAN BE EATEN ON CRACKERS, THINNED WITH WINE FOR SPAGHETTI SAUCE OR USED AS IS IN CHILI OR ON PIZZAS.

Trust in yourself. There is power in your own mind and heart, let them be your teachers.

MOROCCAN VEGETABLE STEW

3	TBLS. OLIVE OIL
1	LARGE ONION, DICED
1	LARGE RED OR YELLOW BELL PEPPER, DICED
1	LARGE SWEET POTATO, PEELED AND CUT INTO ½" CUBES (2 CUPS)

2	LARGE CLOVES GARLIC, MINCED
3	TSPS. GROUND CUMIN
1	TSP. GROUND CINNAMON
$\frac{3}{4}$	TSP. SALT
$\frac{1}{2}$	TSP. GROUND RED PEPPER
$\frac{1}{8}$	TSP. SAFFRON POWDER, OR $\frac{1}{4}$ TSP. SAFFRON THREADS
1	15 OZ. CAN GARBANZO BEANS, UNDRAINED
1	15 OZ. CAN DICED TOMATOES
$\frac{1}{2}$	CUP VEGETABLE STOCK, CHICKEN STOCK OR WATER
2	SMALL ZUCCHINI, HALVED LENGTHWISE AND CUT INTO $\frac{1}{2}$" SLICES (2 CUPS)
1	SMALL EGGPLANT, CUT IN $\frac{1}{2}$" CUBES (2 CUPS)
$\frac{1}{2}$	CUP RAISINS (OPTIONAL)
$\frac{1}{4}$	CUP CHOPPED FRESH CILANTRO OR PARSLEY
1	7 OZ. BOX WILD PECAN AROMATIC RICE, COOKED ACCORDING TO PACKAGE DIRECTIONS

HEAT OIL IN A 4 QT. SAUCEPAN OVER MEDIUM HIGH HEAT. ADD ONION AND BELL PEPPER AND COOK UNTIL SOFT, ABOUT 5 MINUTES. STIR IN SWEET POTATO, GARLIC, CUMIN, CINNAMON, SALT, RED PEPPER AND SAFFRON. COOK AND STIR 2 TO 3 MINUTES. ADD BEANS, TOMATOES AND STOCK AND BRING TO A BOIL; COVER, REDUCE HEAT, AND SIMMER 15 MINUTES OR UNTIL SWEET POTATOES ARE ALMOST

TENDER, STIRRING OCCASIONALLY. STIR IN
ZUCCHINI AND EGGPLANT. COOK 10 MINUTES
LONGER OR UNTIL VEGETABLES ARE TENDER,
ADDING A LITTLE MORE WATER OR STOCK IF
NEEDED. STIR IN RAISINS, IF DESIRED, AND
CILANTRO. SERVE OVER HOT COOKED WILD
PECAN RICE. MAKES 4 TO 6 SERVINGS

WILD RICE AND SMOKED
CHICKEN SOUP

2	TBLS. BUTTER
1	CUP CARROTS, CUT IN $\frac{1}{4}$" PIECES
1	CUP CELERY, CUT IN $\frac{1}{4}$" PIECES
1	MEDIUM ONION, CUT IN $\frac{1}{4}$" PIECES
$\frac{1}{4}$	TSP. GARLIC, MINCED
$4\frac{1}{2}$	CUPS CHICKEN STOCK, HOMEMADE OR CANNED
1	8 OZ. CAN WHOLE TOMATOES, CHOPPED, JUICE INCLUDED
2	CUPS COOKED WILD RICE
$1\frac{1}{2}$	TBLS. FRESH TARRAGON, CHOPPED WHITE PEPPER TO TASTE JULIENNED SMOKED CHICKEN OR TURKEY BREAST AS DESIRED

IN A LARGE STOCK POT, MELT BUTTER. ADD THE
CARROTS, CELERY, ONION AND GARLIC; COVER.

COOK OVER LOW HEAT UNTIL CARROTS ARE
TENDER. ADD CHICKEN STOCK AND TOMATOES.
SIMMER UNCOVERED FOR 20 MINUTES.
ADD WILD RICE, TARRAGON AND PEPPER TO
TASTE. BRING TO A SIMMER. TO SERVE, PLACE
A PORTION OF JULIENNED SMOKED CHICKEN
BREAST IN THE BOTTOM OF BOWL AND LADLE
IN THE HOT SOUP. MAKES 8 TO 10 SERVINGS

Angels are all around us and every heart that yearns to, can reach out and touch a wing.

BLACK BEAN SOUP

¼	CUP OLIVE OIL
½	CUP ONION, DICED
¼	CUP RED BELL PEPPER, DICED
1	TBL. GARLIC, CHOPPED
¼	TSP. CUMIN
1	16 OZ. CAN REFRIED BLACK BEANS
1	14½ OZ. CAN CHICKEN BROTH
1	10 OZ. CAN TOMATOES
	AND GREEN CHILIES

GARNISH:

SOUR CREAM
FRESH, CHOPPED CILANTRO

IN A 2 QT. SAUCEPAN, HEAT OLIVE OIL. SAUTE
ONIONS AND PEPPERS UNTIL ONIONS BECOME

TRANSLUCENT, ADD GARLIC AND CUMIN. ADD
REFRIED BEANS, CHICKEN BROTH AND
TOMATOES AND GREEN CHILIES. SIMMER 15
MINUTES.

SERVE IN A SOUP CUP OR BOWL. GARNISH WITH
FRESH CHOPPED CILANTRO AND 1 TSP. OF SOUR
CREAM.

NOTE: FOR A THICKER, HEARTIER SOUP, ADD A
SECOND CAN OF REFRIED BLACK BEANS.

CHEDDAR CHOWDER

2	CUPS BOILING WATER
2	CUPS CAULIFLOWER FLORETS
1	CUP DICED POTATOES
$\frac{1}{2}$	CUP SLICED CARROTS
$\frac{1}{2}$	CUP SLICED CELERY
$\frac{1}{4}$	CUP CHOPPED ONION
$1\frac{1}{2}$	TSPS. SALT
$\frac{1}{4}$	TSP. PEPPER
$\frac{1}{4}$	CUP BUTTER
$\frac{1}{4}$	CUP FLOUR
2	CUPS MILK
2	CUPS (8 OZ.) SHREDDED MILD OR SHARP CHEDDAR CHEESE
1	CUP CUBED COOKED HAM, OPTIONAL

IN SAUCEPAN, COMBINE WATER, VEGETABLES,
SALT AND PEPPER. COVER AND SIMMER 10
MINUTES. DO NOT DRAIN. IN LARGE

SAUCEPAN, MELT BUTTER. STIR IN FLOUR, THEN
MILK AND HEAT TO BOILING. CONTINUE
SIMMERING, STIRRING CONSTANTLY, UNTIL
THICKENED. ADD CHEDDAR CHEESE, STIR UNTIL
MELTED. ADD UNDRAINED VEGETABLES AND
HAM, IF USED. HEAT THROUGH, BUT DO NOT
BOIL. MAKES 8 SERVINGS

DARN GOOD CRAB BISQUE

1	STICK BUTTER
1	LARGE ONION, CHOPPED
1	SMALL RED BELL PEPPER, CHOPPED
2	STALKS CELERY, CHOPPED
1	CLOVE GARLIC, MINCED
6	GREEN ONIONS, CHOPPED
$\frac{1}{4}$	CUP FLOUR
2	BAY LEAVES
$1\frac{1}{2}$	QTS. CHICKEN STOCK
$\frac{1}{2}$	TSP. POWDERED THYME
1	TSP. SALT
$\frac{1}{2}$	TSP. BLACK PEPPER
$\frac{1}{2}$	TSP. LIQUID CRAB BOIL
$1\frac{1}{2}$	LBS. CRABMEAT
1	PT. HALF AND HALF CREAM

MELT BUTTER ON LOW HEAT, SAUTE ONION,
BELL PEPPER, CELERY, GARLIC AND GREEN ONION
UNTIL SOFT. ADD FLOUR, INCREASE HEAT TO
MEDIUM AND COOK ABOUT 5 MINUTES,
STIRRING CONSTANTLY. ADD REST OF
INGREDIENTS EXCEPT HALF AND HALF, AND

BRING TO A BOIL. TURN HEAT DOWN AND
SIMMER FOR 20 MINUTES. ADD HALF AND HALF
AND SIMMER FOR 10 MINUTES OR UNTIL
SMOOTH. SERVES 4 TO 6

GINGER-CHICKEN NOODLE SOUP

2   CUPS (3 OZS.) MEDIUM EGG NOODLES
2   14$\frac{1}{2}$ OZS CANS REDUCED-SODIUM
       CHICKEN BROTH
1   5 OZ. CAN CHUNK WHITE CHICKEN IN
       WATER, DRAINED
1   CAN (4 OZS. DRAINED WEIGHT) SLICED
       MUSHROOMS, DRAINED
2   TSPS. GRATED FRESH GINGER
2   TSPS. REDUCED-SODIUM SOY SAUCE
$\frac{1}{4}$ CUP SLICED GREEN ONIONS
3   TBLS. CHOPPED CILANTRO

COOK NOODLES AS PACKAGE DIRECTS. DRAIN
AND SET ASIDE. MEANWHILE, IN 2 QT.
SAUCEPAN OVER HIGH HEAT, BRING BROTH TO
BOIL. REDUCE HEAT TO MEDIUM-LOW. MIX IN
CHICKEN, MUSHROOMS, GINGER AND SOY
SAUCE. SIMMER 3 MINUTES. MIX IN NOODLES,
ONIONS AND CILANTRO. RETURN TO
SIMMERING UNTIL NOODLES ARE AL DENTE.

SOUTHWESTERN VEGETABLE SOUP

1	LB. LEAN GROUND BEEF
5	CUPS WATER
2	15½ OZ. CANS MEXICAN STYLE STEWED TOMATOES, UNDRAINED
1	16 OZ. CAN BLACK BEANS, RINSED AND DRAINED
1	16 OZ. CAN DARK RED KIDNEY BEANS, RINSED AND DRAINED
1	15 OZ. CAN PINTO BEANS, RINSED AND DRAINED
1	15¼ OZ. CAN WHOLE KERNEL CORN, DRAINED
1	15 OZ. CAN TOMATO SAUCE
1	8 OZ. CAN CUT GREEN BEANS, DRAINED
1	1.3 OZ. PKG. CASA FIESTA CHILI SEASONING MIX
1	LARGE ONION, DICED
1	GREEN BELL PEPPER, DICED
1	CUP GRATED MONTERREY JACK CHEESE

BROWN GROUND BEEF IN A LARGE DUTCH OVEN, STIRRING UNTIL IT CRUMBLES, DRAIN. STIR IN 5 CUPS WATER AND NEXT 10 INGREDIENTS. BRING TO A BOIL. REDUCE HEAT, AND SIMMER, STIRRING OCCASIONALLY, FOR 2 HOURS.

SERVE WITH A SPRINKLE OF MONTERREY
CHEESE ON EACH SERVING.

SPICY ITALIAN SKI TEAM SOUP

½	CUP EACH CHOPPED ONION AND CHOPPED GREEN PEPPER
1	TSP. MINCED GARLIC
½	TSP. CRUSHED RED PEPPER
2	TSPS. OLIVE OIL
1	13¾ OZ CAN REDUCED SODIUM BEEF BROTH
1½	CUPS WATER
1	16 OZ. CAN KIDNEY BEANS, DRAINED AND RINSED
1	14½ OZ. CAN ITALIAN STYLE STEWED TOMATOES, UNDRAINED
½	16 OZ. PKG. FROZEN ITALIAN VEGETABLES
1	TSP. DRIED BASIL LEAVES
¾	CUP (3 OZS.) SMALL PASTA SHELLS
1	CUP LOOSELY PACKED, UNCOOKED, BITE SIZE SPINACH LEAVES
	SALT AND PEPPER TO TASTE

SAUTE ONION, PEPPER, GARLIC, AND RED PEPPER
IN OIL IN LARGE SAUCEPAN UNTIL TENDER, 3
TO 4 MINUTES. STIR IN BEEF BROTH, WATER,
BEANS, TOMATOES, ITALIAN VEGETABLES, AND
BASIL. HEAT TO BOILING. ADD PASTA AND
SIMMER, UNCOVERED, UNTIL VEGETABLES AND
PASTA ARE TENDER, ABOUT 10 MINUTES.

STIR SPINACH INTO SOUP. SIMMER 1 TO 2
MINUTES. SEASON TO TASTE WITH SALT AND
PEPPER.

TIP: A TEASPOON OF PREPARED PESTO SAUCE
CAN BE STIRRED INTO EACH BOWL OF SOUP.

*Believe in yourself, for you are important
and you matter in this world.*

THE ULTIMATE MINESTRONE

$\frac{1}{4}$	CUP OLIVE OIL
2	MEDIUM CARROTS, SLICED
2	LARGE STALKS CELERY, CHOPPED
1	MEDIUM ONION, CHOPPED
1	SMALL HEAD SAVOY OR GREEN CABBAGE, COARSELY SHREDDED
6	LEAVES SWISS CHARD, COARSELY SHREDDED
6	LEAVES KALE, COARSELY SHREDDED
7	+1 OZ. GREEN BEANS, TRIMMED AND CUT INTO 2" PIECES
8	OZ. POTATOES, PEELED AND CUBED (OPTIONAL)
9	CUPS CHICKEN BROTH
2	14$\frac{1}{2}$ OZ. CANS TOMATOES, CUT UP, OR 3 CUPS CHOPPED FRESH TOMATOES
$\frac{1}{2}$	TSP. PEPPER
2	15 OZ. CANS WHITE KIDNEY (CANNELLINI) BEANS, DRAINED,

OR 1½ CUPS DRY GREAT NORTHERN
BEANS, COOKED

1   MEDIUM ZUCCHINI OR YELLOW SUMMER
         SQUASH, QUARTERED LENGTHWISE AND
         SLICED

¾   CUP SNIPPED FRESH BASIL

IN A 6 TO 8 QT. POT, HEAT OLIVE OIL OVER
MEDIUM HIGH HEAT. ADD CARROTS, CELERY,
AND ONION. COOK AND STIR FOR 2 MINUTES.
ADD CABBAGE, SWISS CHARD, AND KALE. COOK
AND STIR VEGETABLES ABOUT 6 MINUTES MORE
OR UNTIL GREENS ARE WILTED. ADD GREEN
BEANS AND POTATOES, IF DESIRED. COOK AND
STIR FOR 2 MORE MINUTES. ADD CHICKEN
BROTH, TOMATOES, AND PEPPER. BRING TO A
BOIL. REDUCE HEAT. COVER AND SIMMER FOR
20 MINUTES. STIR IN WHITE KIDNEY OR GREAT
NORTHERN BEANS AND ZUCCHINI OR SQUASH.
RETURN TO BOILING. REDUCE HEAT. COVER
AND SIMMER FOR 20 MINUTES. STIR IN BASIL.

VEGETABLE MEDLEY CHICKEN NOODLE SOUP

2   WHOLE BONELESS, SKINLESS CHICKEN
         BREASTS (ABOUT ½ LB. EACH) CUT INTO
         1" PIECES (ABOUT 2 CUPS)

1   TBL. VEGETABLE OIL, DIVIDED

1   CUP CHOPPED ONION

2/3   CUP CHOPPED RED BELL PEPPER

1   MEDIUM CLOVE GARLIC, MINCED

(ABOUT 1 TSP.)

2   QTS. WATER
1   TBL. CHICKEN BOUILLON GRANULES
$\frac{3}{4}$ TSP. FRESHLY GROUND BLACK PEPPER
$\frac{1}{2}$ TSP. SALT
2   DRIED BAY LEAVES
3   OZ. NOODLES
1   CUP EACH: FROZEN CUT GREEN BEANS
        AND FROZEN SLICED CARROTS
$\frac{1}{4}$ CUP CHOPPED FRESH PARSLEY

SAUTE CHICKEN IN 2 TSPS. OIL IN DUTCH OVEN OVER MEDIUM HEAT FOR 5 MINUTES OR UNTIL CHICKEN IS COOKED THROUGH. REMOVE FROM PAN. SAUTE ONION, RED PEPPER AND GARLIC IN REMAINING 1 TSP. OIL, IF NEEDED, ABOUT 3 MINUTES OR UNTIL VEGETABLES ARE CRISP TENDER. ADD WATER, BOUILLON, BLACK PEPPER, SALT AND BAY LEAVES. BRING TO A BOIL. STIR IN NOODLES, BEANS AND CARROTS. COOK 10 MINUTES, ADD CHICKEN AND PARSLEY. CONTINUE COOKING UNTIL HEATED THROUGH AND NOODLES ARE TENDER, ABOUT 2 MINUTES. REMOVE BAY LEAVES BEFORE SERVING. MAKES 6 SERVINGS

WISCONSIN BROCCOLI-CHEDDAR CHEESE SOUP

2	TBLS. BUTTER
3	TBLS. ALL PURPOSE FLOUR
4	CUPS LOW FAT MILK
$\frac{3}{4}$	TSP. SALT
$\frac{1}{2}$	TSP. DRY MUSTARD
$\frac{1}{4}$	TSP. CAYENNE PEPPER
1	10 OZ. PKG. FROZEN CHOPPED BROCCOLI, THAWED AND DRAINED
$\frac{1}{2}$	CUP FINELY CHOPPED RED BELL PEPPER
6	OZS. SHARP OR EXTRA SHARP CHEDDAR CHEESE, SHREDDED
2	TBLS. CHOPPED CHIVES OR GREEN ONION TOPS

MELT BUTTER IN A LARGE SAUCEPAN OVER MEDIUM HEAT. ADD FLOUR, COOK AND STIR 30 SECONDS OR UNTIL BUBBLY. ADD MILK, SALT, MUSTARD AND CAYENNE PEPPER. BRING TO A SIMMER OVER HIGH HEAT, STIRRING FREQUENTLY. ADD BROCCOLI AND RED BELL PEPPER. RETURN TO A BOIL. REDUCE HEAT TO LOW. SIMMER UNCOVERED 5 MINUTES, STIRRING OCCASIONALLY. ADD CHEESE, STIR

OVER LOW HEAT JUST UNTIL CHEESE MELTS
(DO NOT BOIL). LADLE INTO FOUR SOUP BOWLS.
TOP WITH CHIVES. MAKES 4 SERVINGS

Rain cleanses and brings a peaceful kind of music to the soul.

Casseroles

PINEAPPLE CASSEROLE

2	20 OZ. CANS CHUNK PINEAPPLE, DRAINED
¾	CUP SUGAR
5	TBLS. FLOUR
¾	CUP GRATED CHEDDAR CHEESE
¾	CUP CRUSHED RITZ CRACKERS
1	STICK BUTTER

MIX FIRST 4 INGREDIENTS. PUT CRACKERS ON TOP (MAKE SURE THEY ARE FINELY CRUSHED). MELT BUTTER AND DRIZZLE ON TOP. BAKE COVERED AT 350° FOR 30 MINUTES.

Love is the sharing of songs and silences, and the holding of memories only the heart can see.

POTATO CASSEROLE

2	LB. BAG FROZEN HASH BROWNS
½	CUP BUTTER
1	TSP. SALT (OR TO TASTE)
½	TSP. PEPPER (OR TO TASTE)
1	BAG FROZEN SEASONING MIX (ONION, BELL PEPPER, ETC.)
1	CAN CREAM OF CHICKEN SOUP
1	12 OZ. CONTAINER SOUR CREAM

MIX ALL OF THE ABOVE AND BAKE IN A 9"x12" COVERED DISH AT 350° FOR 30 TO 45 MINUTES. SPRINKLE CHEDDAR CHEESE ON TOP FOR LAST FEW MINUTES (UNCOVERED).

VEGETABLE MEDLEY

1	16 OZ. BAG FROZEN BROCCOLI, CARROTS AND CAULIFLOWER COMBINATION, THAWED AND DRAINED
1	CAN CREAM OF MUSHROOM SOUP
1	CUP SHREDDED SWISS CHEESE
1/3	CUP SOUR CREAM
	BLACK PEPPER
1	4 OZ. JAR CHOPPED PIMIENTO, DRAINED
1	CAN DURKEE FRENCH FRIED ONIONS

COMBINE VEGETABLES, SOUP, ½ CUP CHEESE, PEPPER, PIMIENTO AND ½ OF THE FRIED ONIONS. POUR INTO A 1 QT. CASSEROLE. BAKE COVERED AT 350° FOR 30 MINUTES. TOP WITH REMAINING CHEESE AND FRIED ONIONS AND BAKE UNCOVERED 5 MINUTES LONGER.

EGGPLANT AND TOMATO CASSEROLE

¼	CUP OIL
¾	LB. MUSHROOMS, SLICED
1	MEDIUM EGGPLANT, SEEDED AND CUT IN 1" CUBES
1	TBL. CHOPPED PARSLEY
2	EGGS, BEATEN

1	MEDIUM ONION, CHOPPED
½	MEDIUM GREEN BELL PEPPER, CHOPPED
1	1 LB. CAN PEAR SHAPED TOMATOES
1	CUP EACH, GRATED PARMESAN AND MOZZARELLA CHEESE

USING LARGE FRYING PAN, HEAT OIL AND ADD ONIONS, MUSHROOMS AND GREEN BELL PEPPER. SAUTE OVER MEDIUM HEAT UNTIL VEGETABLES ARE LIMP, TWO MINUTES. STIR IN EGGPLANT, TOMATOES, SALT AND PARSLEY. COVER AND SIMMER SLOWLY UNTIL EGGPLANT IS TENDER (25 MINUTES), STIRRING OFTEN. UNCOVER AND INCREASE HEAT, IF NEEDED, TO REDUCE LIQUID. MEANWHILE, COMBINE PARMESAN AND MOZZARELLA WITH EGGS, SPOON HALF EGGPLANT MIXTURE IN 1½ QT. CASSEROLE AND TOP WITH HALF THE EGG/CHEESE MIXTURE. REPEAT LAYERS, ENDING WITH THE EGG/CHEESE MIXTURE.

BAKE UNCOVERED IN 375° OVEN FOR 25 MINUTES. IF PREPARED AHEAD AND KEPT COLD IN THE REFRIGERATOR, BAKE FOR 45 MINUTES. SERVES 6

It's always morning somewhere in the world.

EGGS DUPLANTIER

4	LOAVES FRENCH BREAD (6"-8" LONG" CUT INTO ½" CROUTONS)
1	LB. BACON, CUT INTO 1" STRIPS
1	MEDIUM ONION, DICED
1½	CUPS GRATED SWISS CHEESE
1	TBL. GARLIC, CHOPPED
6	EGGS, SLIGHTLY WHIPPED
1½	CUPS MILK
1½	CUPS HEAVY CREAM
⅛	TSP. NUTMEG
½	TSP. SALT
¼	TSP. PEPPER
¼	CUP DICED BELL PEPPER
½	CUP DICED TOMATOES
½	CUP SLICED MUSHROOMS

COVER THE BOTTOM OF A 9"x13" NONSTICK
BAKING PAN WITH FRENCH BREAD CROUTONS.
IN A HEAVY SKILLET, COOK BACON UNTIL CRISP.
ADD ONIONS, GARLIC AND MUSHROOMS.
SAUTE 3 TO 5 MINUTES. MIX EGGS, CHEESE,
CREAM, MILK, NUTMEG, SALT, PEPPER, BELL
PEPPER AND TOMATOES TOGETHER. COMBINE
WITH THE BACON MIXTURE AND POUR OVER
CROUTONS.

BAKE AT 350° UNTIL CUSTARD IS WELL SET (20
TO 30 MINUTES).

GREEN CHILI AND POTATO TART

5	NEW RED POTATOES (UNPEELED)
2	TBLS. OLIVE OIL
1	LARGE ONION, CHOPPED
4	GARLIC CLOVES, MINCED
1	4 OZ. CAN CHOPPED GREEN CHILIES, DRAINED
1	7.25 OZ. JAR ROASTED RED BELL PEPPERS, DRAINED
4	EGGS
1	CUP SHREDDED MONTERREY JACK CHEESE
1	CUP SHREDDED MEDIUM CHEDDAR CHEESE
	PINCH CRUSHED RED PEPPER
$\frac{1}{2}$	TSP. SALT
	DASH PEPPER

PREHEAT OVEN TO 375°. WASH AND BOIL
POTATOES UNTIL NEARLY COOKED (POTATOES
SHOULD REMAIN FIRM). SET ASIDE. WHEN
COOL, CUT INTO $\frac{1}{2}$" SLICES. IN MEDIUM
SKILLET, SAUTE ONION AND GARLIC IN OLIVE
OIL UNTIL SOFT. REMOVE FROM HEAT. ADD
GREEN CHILIES AND ROASTED RED PEPPERS TO
ONION MIXTURE. IN LARGE BOWL, BEAT EGGS.
STIR IN VEGETABLES, CHEESES, AND

SEASONINGS. LAYER HALF OF THE POTATOES
IN GREASED 10" DEEP DISH PIE PLATE. SPOON
HALF OF THE EGG MIXTURE OVER POTATOES.
REPEAT WITH SECOND LAYER OF POTATOES
AND REMAINING EGG MIXTURE. BAKE 30 TO 35
MINUTES OR UNTIL GOLDEN AND SET. SERVES 6

*Each of us is given a measure of time that gives
even as it takes.*

GRINGO CHILI RELLENO
CASSEROLE

1	LB. CHEDDAR CHEESE, GRATED (4 CUPS)
4	4 OZ. CANS CHOPPED GREEN CHILIES, DRAINED
1	LB. MONTERREY JACK CHEESE, GRATED (4 CUPS)
2	+1 CUPS HALF AND HALF
4	EGGS, BEATEN
$\frac{1}{4}$	CUP CORNMEAL
1	TSP. SALT
1	TSP. WORCESTERSHIRE SAUCE
1	CUP PURCHASED SALSA (MILD, MEDIUM OR HOT)

PREHEAT OVEN TO 350°. GREASE A 13"x9"
BAKING PAN. SPRINKLE GRATED CHEDDAR OVER
BOTTOM OF PAN, TOP EVENLY WITH GREEN
CHILIES AND THEN WITH MONTERREY JACK.

IN A LARGE BOWL, BEAT TOGETHER THE HALF
AND HALF, EGGS, CORNMEAL, SALT AND
WORCESTERHIRE SAUCE. POUR OVER CHEESE
AND CHILIES. TOP EVENLY WITH SALSA. BAKE
FOR 40 MINUTES. LET COOL SLIGHTLY. CUT
INTO ½" SQUARES TO SERVE.

It is never easy reaching for dreams,
but those who reach, walk in stardust.

SPINACH & ARTICHOKE
CASSEROLE

½	CUP SOUR CREAM
1	LB. FROZEN SPINACH
8	OZS. CREAM CHEESE
½	STICK BUTTER
2	TSPS. WORCESTERSHIRE SAUCE
½	TSP. GRANULATED GARLIC
4	OZS. ARTICHOKE HEARTS
⅛	CUP PARMESAN CHEESE
⅛	CUP BREAD CRUMBS

STRAIN, CUT AND PLACE ARTICHOKE HEARTS IN
A 9"x8" CASSEROLE DISH, SET ASIDE. IN A
MEDIUM TO LARGE SKILLET, MELT BUTTER AND
CREAM CHEESE. REMOVE FROM HEAT, ADD SOUR
CREAM AND MIX WELL. IN A LARGE MIXING
BOWL, COMBINE SPINACH, GARLIC,
WORCESTERSHIRE SAUCE AND THE CREAM

CHEESE MIXTURE. MIX WELL. POUR MIXTURE
OVER THE ARTICHOKE HEARTS, SPREAD EVENLY.
SPRINKLE PARMESAN CHEESE AND BREAD
CRUMBS ON TOP. BAKE FOR 30 MINUTES IN A
350° PREHEATED OVEN. SERVES 10

LASAGNA

1	LB. GROUND BEEF
½	LB. SAUSAGE
1	MEDIUM ONION, FINELY CHOPPED
½	LB. FRESH MUSHROOMS, SLICED
2	15 OZ. CANS TOMATO SAUCE
2	6 OZ. CANS TOMATO PASTE
½	CUP GRATED PARMESAN CHEESE
3	TSPS. GARLIC POWDER
1	TSP. DRIED BASIL, CRUSHED
1	TSP. DRIED OREGANO, CRUSHED
1	TSP. DRIED THYME, CRUSHED
1	TSP. DRIED ROSEMARY, CRUSHED
2	BAY LEAVES
10	FENNEL SEEDS
1	PT. RICOTTA OR COTTAGE CHEESE
1	EGG, BEATEN
1	LB. MOZZARELLA CHEESE, SHREDDED (4 CUPS)
½	LB. CHEDDAR CHEESE, SHREDDED (2 CUPS)
1	LB. LASAGNA NOODLES, COOKED

IN A LARGE SKILLET OR DUTCH OVEN, BROWN
MEAT AND ONION, ABOUT 5 MINUTES. DRAIN
OFF DRIPPINGS AND STIR IN MUSHROOMS,

TOMATO SAUCE AND PASTE, PARMESAN CHEESE AND SEASONINGS. COVER AND SIMMER 2 TO 3 HOURS, STIRRING OCCASIONALLY.

COMBINE RICOTTA OR COTTAGE CHEESE AND EGG. MIX WELL. COMBINE MOZZARELLA AND CHEDDAR CHEESE. IN A 13"x9" BAKING PAN, LAYER INGREDIENTS IN THE FOLLOWING ORDER:

⅓ OF THE SAUCE
⅓ OF THE LASAGNA NOODLES
ALL OF THE RICOTTA MIXTURE
⅓ OF THE NOODLES
⅓ OF THE SAUCE
½ OF THE CHEESE
⅓ OF THE NOODLES
⅓ OF THE SAUCE
⅓ OF THE CHEESE

BAKE UNCOVERED IN A 325° OVEN FOR 30 MINUTES. MAKES 12 SERVINGS

Become a searcher, for only those who seek are the finders of treasures.

ZESTY BEEF AND CHEESE CASSEROLE

1¼   LBS. GROUND BEEF
1   16 OZ. BAG OF UNCOOKED LARGE SHELL NOODLES (NOT JUMBO)

SAUCE:

1	16 OZ. JAR MEDIUM PICANTE SAUCE
1	4.5 OZ. CAN CHOPPED CHILIES
	(OMIT FOR LESS ZEST)
1	CAN CREAM OF CELERY SOUP
1/3	CUP SKIM MILK
4	CUPS SHREDDED MILD CHEDDAR CHEESE

PREHEAT OVEN TO 375°. BRING 2 QTS. OF WATER TO A BOIL AND COOK NOODLES IN A LIGHT BOIL FOR 7 MINUTES, DRAIN. MEANWHILE, BROWN AND DRAIN BEEF. GREASE A 9"x13" BAKING DISH. MIX TOGETHER THE REMAINING INGREDIENTS, RESERVING 1 CUP OF CHEESE AND 1 TBL. OF CHILIES. MIX BEEF AND NOODLES INTO THE SAUCE. COVER DISH AND COOK FOR 25 MINUTES. UNCOVER, STIR, THEN SPRINKLE THE REMAINING CHEESE OVER THE ENTIRE DISH. CONTINUE COOKING FOR 10 MINUTES.

Those who truly love, stay close to heaven.

BROCCOLI CASSEROLE

1	BAG FROZEN BROCCOLI
1	CAN DURKEE'S FRENCH FRIED ONIONS
1/3	CUP SOUR CREAM
1	$10\frac{3}{4}$ OZ. CAN CREAM OF MUSHROOM SOUP
1 1/3	CUPS GRATED CHEESE

$\frac{1}{8}$ TSP. BLACK PEPPER

THAW BROCCOLI. MIX TOGETHER BROCCOLI,
SOUR CREAM, SOUP AND PEPPER. ADD HALF OF
THE ONIONS AND HALF OF THE CHEESE. BAKE
COVERED AT 350° FOR 30 MINUTES. UNCOVER.
ADD REMAINING CHEESE AND ONIONS TO THE
TOP. BAKE 5 MORE MINUTES. SERVES 4 TO 6

Time's true measure of value is discovered not in its duration, but in the sharing of its moments.

HERB CHEESE CAKE

CRUST:

1	CUP ALL PURPOSE FLOUR
$\frac{1}{2}$	CUP UNSALTED BUTTER
$\frac{1}{2}$	TSP. SALT
1	EGG YOLK
2	TSPS. GRATED LEMON ZEST

FILLING:

2	CLOVES GARLIC
1	LARGE ONION, CHOPPED
2/3	CUP CHOPPED FRESH PARSLEY
$\frac{3}{4}$	CUP FRESHLY GRATED PARMESAN CHEESE
24	OZS. CREAM CHEESE AT ROOM TEMPERATURE
3	TBLS. ALL PURPOSE FLOUR

4	EGGS
2	TSPS. SALT
$\frac{3}{4}$	TSP. TABASCO SAUCE
3	TBLS. FRESH LEMON JUICE
$\frac{1}{8}$	TSP. CAYENNE
1	TSP. DRIED OREGANO
1	TSP. DRIED TARRAGON
1	TSP. DRIED BASIL
$\frac{1}{2}$	TSP. DRIED ROSEMARY
$\frac{1}{2}$	CUP CHOPPED PEPPERONI

FOR CRUST, BLEND 1 CUP FLOUR, BUTTER, $\frac{1}{2}$ TSP.
SALT, EGG YOLK AND LEMON ZEST IN FOOD
PROCESSOR. REMOVE DOUGH FROM BOWL AND
KNEAD LIGHTLY. SHAPE INTO A BALL AND WRAP
IN WAXED PAPER. REFRIGERATE UNTIL
SLIGHTLY CHILLED.

PRESS A THIRD OF THE DOUGH EVENLY INTO
THE BOTTOM OF AN 8" SPRINGFORM PAN. PRESS
REMAINING DOUGH AROUND SIDES OF PAN.
PUT PAN WITH DOUGH IN FREEZER WHILE
PREPARING FILLING.

TO PREPARE FILLING IN A FOOD PROCESSOR
CHOP GARLIC. ADD ONION, PARSLEY AND
PARMESAN CHEESE. ADD CREAM CHEESE, 8 OZS.
AT A TIME AND PROCESS.

ADD 3 TBLS. FLOUR AND 1 EGG. PROCESS UNTIL
SMOOTH. ADD REMAINING EGGS, ONE AT A
TIME, BLENDING AFTER EACH ADDITION. ADD

REMAINING FILLING INGREDIENTS, EXCEPT
PEPPERONI, AND PROCESS UNTIL JUST BLENDED.
STIR IN PEPPERONI. POUR MIXTURE INTO
DOUGH-LINED PAN. BAKE AT 400° FOR 10
MINUTES. REDUCE TEMPERATURE TO 325° AND
BAKE 50 MINUTES LONGER. LET STAND 1 HOUR
BEFORE SERVING WITH YOUR FAVORITE
CRACKERS.

How sad for those who never sing their songs,
and keep all of their music inside them.

SPINACH ARTICHOKE CASSEROLE

1	STICK BUTTER
½	CUP FINELY CHOPPED ONION
2	PACKS FROZEN, CHOPPED SPINACH
1	LARGE CAN ARTICHOKES, DRAINED
16	OZS. SOUR CREAM
	DASH TABASCO SAUCE
	SALT AND PEPPER TO TASTE
½	CUP GRATED PARMESAN CHEESE
½	TO 1 CUP GRATED MOZZARELLA CHEESE

MELT BUTTER IN SAUCE PAN. SAUTE ONIONS
UNTIL SOFT. COOK SPINACH ACCORDING TO
DIRECTIONS. DRAIN WELL. ADD SPINACH,
ARTICHOKES, SOUR CREAM, ¼ CUP PARMESAN
CHEESE AND APPROXIMATELY ½ CUP
MOZZARELLA CHEESE. HEAT THOROUGHLY.
SEASON WITH DASH OF TABASCO SAUCE AND
SALT AND PEPPER TO TASTE. PLACE IN 8"x8"

CASSEROLE DISH. TOP WITH REMAINING
PARMESAN CHEESE AND MOZZARELLA CHEESE.
BAKE UNCOVERED AT 350° FOR 20 TO 30
MINUTES, UNTIL BUBBLY. GREAT AS DIP WITH
TORTILLA CHIPS.

CORNBREAD, PECAN & OYSTER DRESSING

1	"PONE" OF CORN BREAD (JIFFY WILL DO)
½	LB. BULK PORK SAUSAGE
1	CUP (4 OZ.) PECANS, COARSELY CHOPPED
¾	CUP UNSALTED BUTTER
1	CUP COARSELY CHOPPED ONION
1	CUP CHOPPED CELERY
½	CUP CHOPPED PARSLEY
1	PT. SHUCKED OYSTERS, WITH LIQUOR
1	TSP. POULTRY SEASONING
	SALT AND FRESHLY GROUND PEPPER

PREPARE CORNBREAD ACCORDING TO PACKAGE
INSTRUCTIONS. IN A DUTCH OVEN, MELT
BUTTER AND SAUTE VEGETABLES (EXCEPT FOR
PARSLEY) UNTIL TRANSLUCENT. ADD PORK
SAUSAGE AND COOK UNTIL SAUSAGE IS
THOROUGHLY COOKED. BREAK UP CORNBREAD
INTO SMALL PIECES AND ADD TO DUTCH OVEN,
FOLD IN PECANS, POULTRY SEASONING, SALT,
PEPPER AND OYSTERS, UNTIL DRESSING IS
NICELY COMBINED. IF DRESSING IS TOO
THICK, ADD OYSTER LIQUOR.

Vegetables

152

DO-AHEAD COLORFUL POTATOES

1	22 OZ. PKG. FROZEN MASHED POTATOES
2	CUPS MILK
1	CUP SOUR CREAM
2	TBLS. PREPARED HORSERADISH
$\frac{1}{8}$	TSP. PEPPER
3	TBLS. BUTTER
$\frac{1}{2}$	CUP FINELY CHOPPED RED BELL PEPPER
$\frac{1}{2}$	CUP CHOPPED GREEN ONIONS
$\frac{1}{4}$	TSP. SALT
	CHOPPED GREEN ONION FOR GARNISH

HEAT OVEN TO 425°. PREPARE POTATOES ACCORDING TO PACKAGE DIRECTIONS USING 2 CUPS MILK. STIR IN SOUR CREAM, HORSERADISH AND PEPPER.

MEANWHILE IN SMALL SKILLET, HEAT BUTTER OVER MEDIUM-HIGH HEAT. ADD RED BELL PEPPER AND COOK 2 TO 3 MINUTES UNTIL TENDER. STIR IN $\frac{1}{2}$ CUP GREEN ONIONS. ADD VEGETABLE MIXTURE AND SALT TO POTATOES. MIX LIGHTLY.

POUR MIXTURE INTO GREASED $1\frac{1}{2}$ QT. ROUND CASSEROLE. (CAN BE PREPARED A DAY AHEAD, IF DESIRED. COVER AND REFRIGERATE.) BAKE IN 425° OVEN 35 TO 40 MINUTES (45 TO 50 MINUTES, IF REFRIGERATED) OR UNTIL HOT IN CENTER. GARNISH WITH ADDITIONAL GREEN ONION. MAKES 8 SERVINGS

GINGER-GLAZED CARROTS

2	LBS. PEELED BABY CARROTS
$\frac{1}{2}$	CUP WATER
$\frac{1}{4}$	CUP BUTTER
2	TBLS. PACKED BROWN SUGAR
$1\frac{1}{2}$	TSPS. GROUND GINGER
$\frac{1}{8}$	TO $\frac{1}{4}$ TSP. GROUND RED PEPPER
$\frac{1}{4}$	TSP. SALT

IN LARGE SAUCEPAN, BRING CARROTS AND
WATER TO A BOIL. COVER PAN. REDUCE HEAT
TO MEDIUM-LOW AND COOK 15 TO 20 MINUTES
OR UNTIL TENDER. DRAIN.

ADD REMAINING INGREDIENTS. INCREASE
HEAT TO HIGH. COOK AND STIR UNTIL
CARROTS ARE GLAZED, ABOUT 1 MINUTE.
MAKES 8 SERVINGS

GREEK STUFFED BELL PEPPERS

4	RED OR YELLOW BELL PEPPERS
3	CUPS PART-SKIM RICOTTA
2	CLOVES GARLIC, MINCED
½	CUP FETA CHEESE, CRUMBLED
1	EGG, SLIGHTLY BEATEN
2	TSPS. OREGANO
½	CUP WALNUTS, CHOPPED AND TOASTED
¾	CUP FRESH BREAD CRUMBS
2	TSPS. OLIVE OIL

PLACE PEPPERS IN A LARGE MICROWAVE SAFE PIE PLATE, COVER WITH PLASTIC WRAP AND MICROWAVE 4 TO 6 MINUTES ON HIGH, ROTATING AFTER TWO MINUTES. PEPPERS SHOULD SOFTEN BUT NOT COLLAPSE. CUT OFF THE TOPS AND REMOVE THE SEEDS. LEAVE THE PEPPERS IN THE PIE PLATE WITH THE LIDS ON THE SIDE FOR GARNISH. PREHEAT THE BROILER.

IN A SMALL BOWL, COMBINE THE RICOTTA, GARLIC, FETA, EGG, OREGANO AND WALNUTS. FILL PEPPERS WITH THIS MIXTURE. MIX BREAD CRUMBS WITH OLIVE OIL AND SPRINKLE OVER CHEESE FILLING. COVER THE STUFFED PEPPERS LOOSELY WITH THE PLASTIC WRAP AND MICROWAVE FOR 8-12 MINUTES, ROTATING AFTER 4 MINUTES. FILLING SHOULD BE HOT IN THE CENTER. REMOVE THE PLASTIC WRAP AND

BROIL THE PEPPERS FOR A MINUTE OR TWO TO
BROWN THE CRUMBS. SERVE IMMEDIATELY.
SERVES 4

BARBEQUE-HERBED POTATO WEDGES

2	TBLS. BUTTER
$\frac{1}{4}$	CUP OLIVE OIL
$\frac{1}{4}$	CUP CHOPPED ONION
3	TBLS. FRESH CHOPPED PARSLEY
1	TSP. CHILI POWDER
$\frac{1}{4}$	TSP. GARLIC POWDER
$\frac{1}{4}$	TSP. BASIL
$\frac{1}{4}$	TSP. SALT
	DASH PEPPER
6	MEDIUM POTATOES

MELT BUTTER AND COMBINE WITH OLIVE OIL.
SET ASIDE. BUTTER A LARGE PIECE OF HEAVY
ALUMINUM FOIL. COMBINE CHOPPED ONION,
HERBS AND SEASONINGS. SCRUB POTATOES
AND CUT IN $\frac{1}{2}$" THICK WEDGES, CUTTING THE
POTATOES LENGTHWISE. PLACE POTATOES ON
FOIL. BRUSH WITH BUTTER AND OIL MIXTURE.
SPRINKLE WITH HERBS. SEAL THE EDGES OF
FOIL WELL. PLACE ON GRILL 4" FROM COALS
AND COOK UNTIL TENDER FOR 30 TO 45
MINUTES. SERVES 6

CAULIFLOWER CASSEROLE

3	CUPS COOKED RICE
1	HEAD CAULIFLOWER, CUT INTO FLORETS, SLICE STEMS
1	$10\frac{3}{4}$ OZ. CAN CREAM OF MUSHROOM SOUP
$\frac{1}{2}$	LB. MUSHROOMS, SLICED
2	CUPS GRATED CHEESE, MONTERREY JACK OR CHEDDAR
$\frac{1}{2}$	CUP WATER
1	MEDIUM ONION, DICED

SPRAY SLOW COOKER WITH NONSTICK COOKING SPRAY. COMBINE ALL INGREDIENTS. MIXTURE WILL BE CHUNKY, BUT STIR WELL. COOK ON LOW FOR 4 TO 6 HOURS. MAKES 10 SERVINGS

LIGHT SPINACH MADELAINE

1	SMALL ONION, CHOPPED FINE
4	CLOVES GARLIC, MINCED
1	HOT GREEN SERRANO OR JALAPENO PEPPER, MINCED

2	TBLS. VEGETABLE OIL
3	TBLS. FLOUR
1	12 OZ. CAN SKIMMED EVAPORATED MILK
2	10 OZ. PKGS. FROZEN CHOPPED SPINACH, THAWED
3	TSPS. CREOLE SEASONING

SAUTE FINELY CHOPPED ONION, GARLIC AND HOT PEPPER IN THE OIL, UNTIL SOFT. STIR IN FLOUR AND COOK FOR A FEW MINUTES. ADD EVAPORATD MILK AND STIR UNTIL SAUCE IS SMOOTH. ADD THAWED, BUT NOT DRAINED, SPINACH AND SEASON TO TASTE. COOK COVERED ON LOW HEAT UNTIL SPINACH IS COOKED. SERVES 6

Joy may be found in the tiniest of moments.

MUSTARD GREEN BEANS AND CHERRY TOMATOES

$1\frac{1}{2}$	LBS. GREEN BEANS, TRIMMED AND CUT INTO 1" PIECES
3	TBLS. BALSAMIC VINEGAR
2	TSPS. SUGAR
2	TSPS. DIJON STYLE MUSTARD
1	TSP. SALT
$\frac{1}{4}$	CUP OLIVE OIL
$\frac{1}{4}$	CUP FINELY CHOPPED RED ONION
1	PT. CHERRY TOMATOES, HALVED FRESHLY GROUND BLACK PEPPER

IN A LARGE POT OF BOILING WATER, COOK THE
BEANS UNTIL JUST CRISP-TENDER, ABOUT 3
MINUTES (OR LONGER IF DESIRED), DRAIN AND
PLACE IN SERVING BOWL. IN MEDIUM BOWL,
WHISK TOGETHER VINEGAR, SUGAR, MUSTARD,
SALT AND OIL. STIR IN RED ONIONS. SHAKE
OR STIR WELL. DRIZZLE DRESSING OVER WARM
BEANS, TOP WITH TOMATOES AND SPRINKLE
WITH BLACK PEPPER. SERVE WARM, ROOM
TEMPERATURE OR COLD. SERVES 8

*When life seems to fall apart one piece at a
time, it will always fit back together again.*

ROASTED CORN WITH
CUMIN AND LIME

6	EARS FRESH CORN, IN THE HUSK
1	TBL. FRESH LIME
1	TSP. GROUND CUMIN
1	TSP. SALT
2	TSPS. OLIVE OIL
	FRESHLY GROUND PEPPER
3	LIMES, CUT LENGTHWISE INTO WEDGES

HEAT THE GRILL, OR PREHEAT THE OVEN TO
500°. MEANWHILE, IN A SMALL BOWL, WHISK
TOGETHER THE LIME JUICE, CUMIN, SALT AND
OLIVE OIL. SEASON TO TASTE WITH PEPPER.

TO CLEAN THE CORN, PULL OFF AND DISCARD
THE 2 TO 3 DARK, TOUGH OUTER LEAVES.
CAREFULLY PULL BACK THE REMAINING LEAVES,
ONE AT A TIME, EXPOSING AS MUCH OF THE
EAR OF CORN AS POSSIBLE. IT IS BETTER TO
UNCOVER ONLY HALF THE EAR THAN TO TEAR
THE HUSKS. PULL OFF ALL THE SILK.

BRUSH THE KERNELS WITH THE LIME JUICE-OIL
MIXTURE, USING JUST ENOUGH TO COAT THE
CORN LIGHTLY, ABOUT ½ TSP. ONE BY ONE,
SMOOTH THE FOLDED LEAVES BACK INTO PLACE,
UNTIL THE EAR IS ENVELOPED IN ITS HUSK.
CLEAN AND SEASON EACH REMAINING EAR OF
CORN.

ARRANGE THE CORN ON THE GRILL OR PLACE IT
IN THE OVEN. ROAST THE CORN FOR 15
MINUTES. IF USING THE GRILL, TURN THE EARS
2 TO 3 TIMES. THIS IS NOT NECESSARY IF
ROASTING THE CORN IN THE OVEN. SERVE THE
ROASTED CORN IMMEDIATELY, ACCOMPANIED
BY THE WEDGES OF LIME. SQUEEZE THE LIME
OVER THE CORN AS YOU EAT IT.

BEANS-N-BACON

3	TO 4 CANS WHOLE SNAP BEANS
1	LB. SLICED BACON
1	CUP BROWN SUGAR

DRAIN SNAP BEANS. CUT BACON SLICES IN
HALF. GATHER BEANS IN SMALL BUNDLES AND
WRAP WITH BACON PIECES. PLACE BEAN ROLLS
CLOSELY IN PAN. COVER WITH BROWN SUGAR.
COVER AND BAKE 25 TO 35 MINUTES AT 350°.
SERVES 12

Our lives are directed by the choices we make.

CHEESE MARINATED ONIONS

3   OZS. BLUE CHEESE, CRUMBLED, ABOUT $\frac{3}{4}$
            CUP
$\frac{1}{2}$ CUP SALAD OIL
2   TBLS. LEMON JUICE
1   TSP. SALT
$\frac{1}{2}$ TSP. SUGAR
            DASH PEPPER
            DASH PAPRIKA
4   MEDIUM ONIONS, THINLY SLICED AND
            SEPARATED IN RINGS, ABOUT 4 CUPS.

MIX ALL INGREDIENTS, EXCEPT ONIONS. POUR
MIXTURE OVER ONION RINGS AND
REFRIGERATE AT LEAST 3 TO 4 HOURS.

TRADITIONAL POTATO LATKES

6	LARGE POTATOES
2	EGGS
2	TBLS. FLOUR
1	TSP. SALT
	PEPPER TO TASTE
1	SMALL ONION, GRATED
¼	TSP. BAKING POWDER
	VEGETABLE OIL FOR FRYING

GRATE POTATOES AND DRAIN WELL. ADD
REMAINING INGREDIENTS, EXCEPT VEGETABLE
OIL AND MIX WELL. DROP BY TABLESPOONFULS
INTO HOT OIL AT LEAST ¼" DEEP. FRY UNTIL
BROWN ON BOTH SIDES, TURNING ONLY ONCE
SO THAT PANCAKES DO NOT GET SOGGY.

POTATO-ONION NESTS

POTATO-ONION NESTS:

	VEGETABLE OIL
1	CUP GRATED BAKING POTATO
2	TBLS. GRATED RED ONION
¼	TSP. SALT

CREAMED SPINACH:

2	TBLS. BUTTER
3	TBLS. UNBLEACHED WHITE FLOUR
1	TO 1¼ CUPS MILK (WHOLE OR 2%)
⅓	CUP GRATED ASIAGO CHEESE
½	TSP. DRY MUSTARD
	GENEROUS PINCH OF FRESHLY GROUND NUTMEG
1	LB. FRESH SPINACH, STEAMED, CHOPPED AND SQUEEZED DRY
2	EGGS

PREHEAT THE OVEN TO 450°. OIL TWO 1-CUP
RAMEKINS OR CUSTARD CUPS. MIX THE
POTATO, ONION AND SALT TOGETHER AND
DIVIDE BETWEEN THE RAMEKINS. PRESS IT
INTO THE SIDES AND BOTTOMS, FORMING CUPS
ABOUT ¼" THICK. BRUSH THE NESTS LIGHTLY
WITH OIL. BAKE FOR 30 TO 40 MINUTES, UNTIL
LIGHTLY BROWNED AND CRISP. SET ASIDE ON
COOLING RACK.

WHILE THE POTATO CUPS ARE BAKING, MELT
BUTTER IN HEAVY SAUCEPAN OVER MEDIUM
HEAT. STIR IN FLOUR; WHEN IT BEGINS TO
BUBBLE, REDUCE HEAT TO LOW AND COOK,
WHISKING CONSTANTLY, FOR ABOUT 3
MINUTES. GRADUALLY POUR IN MILK, STILL
WHISKING, AND SIMMER UNTIL THICKENED,
ABOUT 5 MINUTES. ADD CHEESE, AND STIR

UNTIL MELTED. STIR IN MUSTARD, NUTMEG,
SALT AND PEPPER TO TASTE, ADD SPINACH.

REMOVE PAN FROM HEAT. PREHEAT BROILER.
POACH OR LIGHTLY SCRAMBLE EGGS IN A LITTLE
BUTTER, LEAVING THEM SLIGHTLY UNDERDONE.
DIVIDE EGGS BETWEEN POTATO NESTS, AND
COVER WITH WARM CREAMED SPINACH. PUT
RAMEKINS UNDER BROILER FOR A MINUTE OR
TWO, UNTIL LIGHTLY BROWNED. SERVE
IMMEDIATELY.

How lovely the time when shared with a friend.

RATATOUILLE

1	SMALL EGGPLANT, CUT INTO ½" CUBES
	SALT TO TASTE
2	TBLS. OLIVE OIL
3	LARGE RED PEPPERS, CUT INTO ¾" PIECES
4	SMALL ZUCCHINI, SLICED
1	SMALL ONION, COARSELY CHOPPED
4	CLOVES GARLIC, MINCED
1	LB. TOMATOES, CHOPPED OR 1 (28 OZ.)
	CAN WHOLE TOMATOES,
	DRAINED AND CHOPPED
⅓	CUP CHOPPED FRESH BASIL

SPRINKLE THE EGGPLANT WITH SALT AND PLACE
IT IN A COLANDER TO DRAIN FOR 30 MINUTES.
PAT DRY WITH PAPER TOWELS. HEAT A TBL. OF
THE OIL IN A NONSTICK SKILLET. ADD THE

EGGPLANT, STIR AND COOK 6 TO 7 MINUTES, OR
UNTIL SOFT AND BROWN. (IF MORE COOKING
LIQUID IS NECESSARY, ADD 2 TBLS. CHICKEN
BROTH). PUSH THE COOKED EGGPLANT TO THE
SIDE OF PAN BEFORE ADDING RED PEPPERS,
ZUCCHINI, ONION AND GARLIC TO THE CENTER
OF THE PAN. COOK THE VEGETABLES, STIRRING,
3 TO 5 MINUTES OR UNTIL TENDER. ADD THE
TOMATOES TO THE PAN, MIX IN WITH THE
OTHER VEGETABLES AND COOK ON LOW HEAT
BETWEEN 15 TO 20 MINUTES, OR UNTIL ALL OF
THE VEGETABLES ARE VERY TENDER, STIRRING
OCCASIONALLY. STIR IN THE BASIL AND
SERVE.

ROLLED MELANZANA

1	($\frac{1}{8}$") SLICE OF A LARGE EGGPLANT, SLICED LENGTHWISE
1	THIN SLICE HAM (TO COVER EGGPLANT)
1	THIN SLICE MOZZARELLA CHEESE (TO COVER HAM)
	FLOUR
1	BEATEN EGG
	BREAD CRUMBS

ROLL HAM AND CHEESE INTO A TUBE. ROLL
EGGPLANT AROUND HAM AND CHEESE.
DIP ROLL FLOUR, THEN IN EGG WASH, AND
FINALLY IN BREAD CRUMBS, MAKING SURE ENDS
ARE COMPLETELY BREADED. SECURE WITH A
SKEWER AND FRY SUBMERGED IN OIL WHICH,
HAS BEEN HEATED ON LOW, 3 TO 5 MINUTES.

SLICE INTO ¾" PIECES ACROSS THE TUBE.
SERVE OVER PASTA TOPPED WITH RED SAUCE.

Beef Entrees

BEEF TENDERLOIN
EXTRAORDINAIRE

1	STICK BUTTER
$\frac{1}{4}$	CUP OLIVE OIL
$\frac{1}{2}$	LB. PORTABELLO MUSHROOMS, DICED
$\frac{3}{4}$	CUP CHOPPED ONION
$\frac{1}{2}$	CUP CHOPPED GREEN PEPPER
$\frac{1}{4}$	CUP CHOPPED PARSLEY
$\frac{1}{4}$	CUP CHOPPED ONION TOPS
$\frac{1}{2}$	CUP CHOPPED RED BELL PEPPER
	ITALIAN-STYLE BREAD CRUMBS
	SALT AND BLACK PEPPER TO TASTE
1	BEEF TENDERLOIN, TRIMMED

MARINADE PASTE:

1	SMALL JAR GREY POUPON MUSTARD
2	TBLS. OLIVE OIL
	BLACK PEPPER

SAUCE:

$\frac{1}{2}$	CUP BEEF STOCK OR BROTH
1	SHALLOT, DICED VERY FINE
1	TBL. OLIVE OIL
$\frac{1}{4}$	CUP PORT WINE
1	TBL. BUTTER

SAUTE MUSHROOMS AND CHOPPED VEGETABLES
IN BUTTER AND OLIVE OIL UNTIL TENDER.
SEASON TO TASTE WITH SALT AND BLACK

PEPPER. ADD ITALIAN-STYLE BREAD CRUMBS TO SOAK UP LIQUID. BUTTERFLY TENDERLOIN AND SPREAD VEGETABLE FILLING INSIDE. TIE TENDERLOIN INTO A ROLL.

MAKE MARINADE PASTE WITH MUSTARD AND OLIVE OIL. COAT MEAT AND SEASON WITH MORE BLACK PEPPER. COVER AND REFRIGERATE OVERNIGHT.

GRILL TENDERLOIN 15 TO 20 MINUTES PER SIDE OVER A HOT CHARCOAL FIRE.

MAKE SAUCE BY SAUTEING SHALLOT IN OLIVE OIL UNTIL CLEAR. ADD PORT WINE AND COOK 2 TO 3 MINUTES UNTIL IT THICKENS. ADD STOCK OR BROTH AND HEAT UNTIL IT BUBBLES. TURN OFF HEAT. WHISK IN BUTTER AND SERVE WITH SLICED TENDERLOIN.

Sweet is the quiet time of beginning.

DILLY STEAK KABOBS

$1\frac{1}{2}$	TO 2 LBS. BEEF TOP ROUND STEAK, CUT $1\frac{1}{2}$" THICK
1	$8\frac{1}{4}$ OZ. CAN PINEAPPLE CHUNKS IN HEAVY SYRUP
$\frac{1}{2}$	CUP LEMON JUICE
$\frac{1}{4}$	CUP SALAD OIL
1	TBL. WORCESTERSHIRE SAUCE
$\frac{1}{4}$	CUP FIRMLY PACKED BROWN SUGAR

2	TSPS. SALT
1½	TSPS. DILL WEED
1	LARGE GREEN PEPPER, CUT IN 12 PIECES
6	CHERRY TOMATOES, HALVED

PARTIALLY FREEZE STEAK. CUT INTO STRIPS ¼"
THICK OR LESS AND PLACE IN RECLOSABLE
PLASTIC BAG. DRAIN PINEAPPLE CHUNKS.
RESERVE SYRUP AND COMBINE WITH LEMON
JUICE, OIL, WORCESTERSHIRE SAUCE, BROWN
SUGAR, SALT AND DILL WEED IN SMALL
SAUCEPAN. COOK SLOWLY 5 MINUTES. COOL
AND POUR OVER STEAK STRIPS, TURNING TO
COAT. MARINATE IN REFRIGERATOR 4 TO 6
HOURS OR OVERNIGHT. POUR OFF MARINADE
AND RESERVE.

THREAD STEAK STRIPS ON SIX 15" METAL
SKEWERS (WEAVING BACK AND FORTH)
ALTERNATELY WITH PINEAPPLE CHUNKS, PIECES
OF GREEN PEPPER AND CHERRY TOMATOES
HALVES.

BRUSH WITH MARINADE AND PLACE ON GRILL
SO SURFACE OF MEAT IS 3" TO 4" FROM HEAT.
GRILL OVER MEDIUM HEAT FOR 3 MINUTES.
BRUSH WITH MARINADE, TURN AND GRILL 3 TO
4 MINUTES.

VERY TRADITIONAL, BUT WONDERFUL FLAVOR.
SERVE WITH WILD RICE. ADD OTHER
VEGETABLES WHEN FRESH AND AVAILABLE.

STEAK AND PEPPER FAJITAS

1	LB. BONELESS BEEF SIRLOIN STEAK, $\frac{3}{4}$" THICK
1	CUP BOTTLED PICANTE SAUCE
1	TBL. VEGETABLE OIL
2	MEDIUM GREEN OR RED PEPPERS, CUT INTO STRIPS (ABOUT 3 CUPS)
1	MEDIUM RED ONION, SLICED
1	TBL. CHOPPED FRESH CILANTRO
8	6" FLOUR TORTILLAS
1	CUP (4 OZS.) SHREDDED CHEDDAR CHEESE

PLACE STEAK ON RACK IN BROILER PAN. BROIL 4" FROM HEAT TO DESIRED DONENESS (ALLOW 15 MINUTES FOR MEDIUM), TURNING ONCE AND BRUSHING OFTEN WITH ⅓ CUP OF THE PICANTE SAUCE.

IN MEDIUM SKILLET OVER MEDIUM HEAT, HEAT OIL. ADD PEPPERS AND ONIONS. COOK UNTIL TENDER-CRISP. ADD REMAINING PICANTE SAUCE AND CILANTRO. HEAT THROUGH.

WARM TORTILLAS ACCORDING TO PACKAGE DIRECTIONS. SLICE EACH STEAK INTO THIN STRIPS AND PLACE DOWN CENTER OF EACH

TORTILLA. TOP WITH PEPPER MIXTURE AND
CHEESE. ROLL UP. SERVE WITH ADDITIONAL
PICANTE SAUCE.

*Flower gardens awaken sleeping symphonies
whose listeners will be those who love the spring.*

QUICK BEEF STROGANOFF

1	LB. BEEF TOP ROUND, CUT INTO THIN STRIPS ACROSS THE GRAIN ON A DIAGONAL
2	TBLS. FLOUR
	SALT & PEPPER
3	TBLS. VEGETABLE OIL
1	SMALL ONION, SLICED THIN
$\frac{1}{2}$	LB. FRESH MUSHROOMS, SLICED THIN
1	CUP BEEF BROTH
	DASH OF WORCESTERSHIRE
1	CUP SOUR CREAM

HEAT OIL IN SAUTE PAN. DREDGE THE BEEF IN
SEASONED FLOUR. BROWN QUICKLY IN HOT
OIL. ADD ONION AND CONTINUE COOKING
UNTIL ONION SLICES ARE TENDER AND
TRANSLUCENT, NOT BROWN. ADD THE
MUSHROOMS AND COOK UNTIL LIMP. POUR ON
BEEF BROTH AND ADD A DASH OF
WORCESTERSHIRE SAUCE. STIR IN SOUR
CREAM. COOK, STIRRING FOR A MINUTE OR
TWO AND SERVE OVER NOODLES. SERVES 4

DIJON GLAZED CORNED BEEF

1	3 LB. CORNED BEEF BRISKET
	WATER
	SAVORY CABBAGE WITH RED POTATOES
	(RECIPE FOLLOWS)

FOR THE GLAZE:

2	TBLS. HONEY
1	TBL. FROZEN ORANGE JUICE
	CONCENTRATE, THAWED
2	TSPS. DIJON-STYLE MUSTARD

IN DUTCH OVEN, PLACE CORNED BEEF BRISKET AND ADD WATER TO COVER. BRING TO A BOIL. REDUCE HEAT TO LOW. COVER TIGHTLY AND SIMMER $2\frac{1}{2}$ TO $3\frac{1}{2}$ HOURS OR UNTIL TENDER.

MEANWHILE, PREPARE SAVORY CABBAGE WITH RED POTATOES.

COMBINE GLAZE INGREDIENTS. SET ASIDE.

REMOVE BRISKET FROM COOKING LIQUID. TRIM FAT FROM OUTER SURFACE OF BRISKET, IF NECESSARY. PLACE BRISKET ON RACK IN BROILER PAN SO SURFACE OF MEAT IS 3" TO 4"

FROM HEAT. BRUSH GLAZE OVER BRISKET.
BROIL 2 TO 3 MINUTES OR UNTIL BRISKET IS
GLAZED.

CARVE BRISKET DIAGONALLY ACROSS THE
GRAIN INTO THIN SLICES. SERVE WITH
VEGETABLES.

Today and always know how special you are.

SAVORY CABBAGE WITH RED POTATOES

	WATER
1	SMALL HEAD CABBAGE (ABOUT $1\frac{1}{2}$ LBS.), CUT INTO WEDGES
1	LB. SMALL RED POTATOES, QUARTERED

FOR THE SAUCE:

$\frac{1}{4}$	CUP BUTTER
2	TBLS. SLICED GREEN ONIONS
3	TSPS. PREPARED HORSERADISH
$\frac{1}{8}$	TSP. SALT
$\frac{1}{8}$	TSP. PEPPER

IN DUTCH OVEN, PLACE STEAMER BASKET IN $\frac{1}{2}$"
WATER (WATER SHOULD NOT TOUCH THE
BOTTOM OF THE BASKET). PLACE CABBAGE AND
POTATOES IN BASKET. COVER TIGHTLY AND
BRING TO A BOIL. REDUCE HEAT AND STEAM 20
TO 25 MINUTES OR UNTIL TENDER.

MEANWHILE, IN 1-CUP GLASS MEASURE,
COMBINE SAUCE INGREDIENTS. MICROWAVE
ON HIGH FOR 45 SECONDS TO 1 MINUTE OR
UNTIL BUTTER IS MELTED. DRIZZLE OVER
VEGETABLES. SERVE WITH CORNED BEEF.

May your wishes touch the sky and may all of your dreams come true.

TEXAS BARBECUE BRISKET
"CAJUN STYLE"

10	LB. BEEF BRISKET
	SALT, BLACK AND RED PEPPER, PAPRIKA, WORCESTERSHIRE SAUCE AND LIQUID SMOKE FOR SEASONING MEAT
6	12 OZ. CANS BEER
	TABASCO, WATER, WORCESTERSHIRE SAUCE AND LIQUID SMOKE FOR FILLING WATER PAN IN WATER SMOKER
¼	CUP VEGETABLE OIL
1	MEDIUM ONION, CHOPPED
2	CLOVES CHOPPED GARLIC
½	BELL PEPPER, CHOPPED
¼	CUP BROWN SUGAR
2/3	CUP KETCHUP
2	TBLS. SOY SAUCE
1	TBL. PREPARED MUSTARD
1	CUP WORCESTERSHIRE SAUCE
2	TBLS. LIQUID SMOKE
⅓	CUP LEMON JUICE

$\frac{1}{4}$ TSP. BLACK PEPPER
$1\frac{1}{2}$ TSPS. SALT

TRIM ALL FAT FROM BEEF BRISKET. CUT IN
TWO PIECES TO FIT ON SMOKER. GENEROUSLY
RUB IN SALT, PEPPER, PAPRIKA,
WORCESTERSHIRE SAUCE AND LIQUID SMOKE.
PLACE IN PLASTIC BAG AND REFRIGERATE FOR
AT LEAST 24 HOURS. PREPARE WATER SMOKER
BY SOAKING HICKORY CHIPS IN WATER
OVERNIGHT. PLACE CHIPS ON TOP OF PAN OF
COALS. FILL WATER PAN WITH BEER. ADD TWO
TBLS. TABASCO AND ENOUGH WATER,
WORCESTERSHIRE SAUCE AND LIQUID SMOKE
UNTIL WATER PAN IS FULL. SMOKE BRISKET 6
TO 7 HOURS, ROTATING EVERY 3 HOURS.

*Rain comes. Listen to it, take walks in it, and
taste its sweetness.*

ITALIAN LAYERED MEAT PIE

1   ONION, CHOPPED
1   LB. GROUND BEEF (BROWN AND DRAIN)
1   CUP SPAGHETTI SAUCE
$\frac{1}{2}$ TSP. SALT
$\frac{1}{2}$ TSP. PEPPER
$\frac{1}{2}$ TSP. GARLIC POWDER
1   9" FROZEN PIE CRUST
         (BROWN PER INSTRUCTIONS)
$6\frac{1}{2}$ OZS. MUSHROOMS, SLICED AND DRAINED

8	OZS. MOZZARELLA CHEESE, GRATED
2	OZS. BLACK OLIVES, SLICED, DRAINED
10	OZS. CHOPPED FROZEN BROCCOLI, THAWED
2	EGGS, BEATEN
$\frac{1}{4}$	CUP PARMESAN CHEESE

SAUTE ONIONS IN GROUND BEEF. ADD SPAGHETTI SAUCE, SALT, PEPPER, AND GARLIC POWDER. PLACE $\frac{1}{2}$ OF MEAT MIXTURE IN PREPARED PIE CRUST. LAYER $\frac{1}{2}$ OF MUSHROOMS, MOZZARELLA, AND BLACK OLIVES, IN THAT ORDER. IN MIXING BOWL, MIX BROCCOLI, BEATEN EGGS AND PARMESAN CHEESE. POUR OVER PIE. ADD SECOND HALF OF GROUND MEAT MIXTURE TO PIE, MAKING SURE TO COVER BROCCOLI MIXTURE COMPLETELY, TO SEAL PIE. BAKE AT 350° FOR 20 MINUTES. REMOVE FROM OVEN. LAYER REST OF MUSHROOMS, MOZZARELLA AND BLACK OLIVES, IN THAT ORDER. RETURN TO 350° OVEN FOR 5 MINUTES. SERVES 8

Some people move our souls to sing and make our spirits dance.

MEXICAN CHILI BEANS

| 1 | LB. LEAN GROUND BEEF |
| | SALT, PEPPER AND GARLIC POWDER TO TASTE |

1	CUP CHOPPED ONIONS
1/3	CUP CHOPPED GREEN ONIONS
1/2	CUP CHOPPED BELL PEPPER (1/2 MEDIUM)
1/3	CUP CHOPPED CELERY (3 STALKS)
1	14.5 OZ. CAN DICED TOMATOES
1	10 OZ. CAN DICED TOMATOES AND GREEN CHILIES
2	TBLS. CHILI POWDER
2	15 OZ. CANS RED KIDNEY BEANS
1/4	TSP. BASIL
1	TBL. DRIED PARSLEY
1	CUP WATER

OPTIONAL GARNISH:

CHEDDAR CHEESE, GRATED
CHOPPED ONIONS

BROWN BEEF WITH SALT, PEPPER AND GARLIC POWDER. DRAIN FAT AND ADD ONIONS, GREEN ONIONS, BELL PEPPER AND CELERY. SIMMER UNTIL THEY ARE TENDER. ADD TOMATOES AND TOMATOES WITH GREEN CHILIES. BLEND WELL AND ADD CHILI POWDER, BEANS, BASIL, DRIED PARSLEY AND WATER. SIMMER FOR ABOUT 30 MINUTES.

PUT IN SERVING BOWLS AND GARNISH AS YOU WISH. SERVE WITH CRACKERS. MAKES 8 SERVINGS

OKLAHOMA-STYLE CHILI

6	LBS. BEEF, COARSE GROUND
2	LBS. PORK, COARSE GROUND
3	+1 LARGE ONIONS, CHOPPED
4	CANS DICED TOMATOES
5	+1 GARLIC CLOVES, CHOPPED FINE
2	OZS. PAPRIKA
1	TSP. BLACK PEPPER
2	TSPS. SEASONED SALT
3	OZS. CHILI POWDER
1	TSP. OREGANO
1	OZ. GROUND CUMIN
2	+1 JALAPENO PEPPERS, CHOPPED

BROWN MEAT WITH PAPRIKA. DRAIN FAT AND SAUTE ONIONS AND GARLIC IN A SEPARATE PAN. COMBINE MEAT WITH REMAINING INGREDIENTS. COOK SLOWLY OVER LOW HEAT FOR 3 HOURS. SERVES 8 TO 10

PEPPER STEAK

2	TBLS. SOY SAUCE, DIVIDED
2	TBLS. WHITE WINE, DIVIDED

⅓	CUP PEANUT OIL, DIVIDED
2	TBLS. CORNSTARCH
1	LB. BEEF TOP ROUND (PARTILLY FROZEN), SLICED INTO VERY THIN DIAGONAL STRIPS, ACROSS THE GRAIN
2	SMALL ONIONS, SLICED THIN
1	BELL PEPPER, SEEDED AND SLICED
1	LARGE OR 2 SMALL TOMATOES, CUT INTO WEDGES
1	CUP BEEF BROTH

MIX TOGETHER 1 TBL. EACH OF SOY SAUCE, WINE, OIL AND CORNSTARCH IN A SMALL BOWL. TOSS THE BEEF STRIPS IN THE MIXTURE TO COAT. HEAT 2 TBLS. OF THE OIL IN A WOK OR FRY PAN OVER HIGH HEAT. ADD THE MEAT AND COOK QUICKLY TO BROWN (2 TO 3 MINUTES). SET ASIDE. ADD A BIT MORE OIL TO THE PAN AND SAUTE THE ONION FOR A MINUTE OR TWO, THEN ADD THE BELL PEPPER AND COOK FOR A MINUTE MORE. PUT THE MEAT BACK IN AND ADD THE TOMATOES AND BEEF BROTH. COOK UNTIL THE BROTH BOILS. STIR TOGETHER THE REMAINING SOY SAUCE, WINE AND CORNSTARCH. WHEN THE BROTH BOILS, THICKEN IT WITH THE CORNSTARCH MIXTURE AND THEN SERVE OVER COOKED RICE. SERVES 4

Life holds gifts in its hands and gives them to each of us when it is time.

SALT-ENCRUSTED RIB-EYE ROAST

1 4 TO 6 LB. WELL-TRIMMED BEEF RIB-EYE
   ROAST, SMALL END
1 TBL. VEGETABLE OIL
2 TO 3 TSPS. CRACKED BLACK PEPPER

SALT CRUST:

1 BOX (3 LBS.) COARSE KOSHER SALT
$1\frac{1}{4}$ CUPS WATER

HEAT OVEN TO 425°. LINE SHALLOW ROASTING
PAN WITH HEAVY-DUTY ALUMINUM FOIL.
COMBINE SALT CRUST INGREDIENTS. MIX
WELL. (MIXTURE MAY APPEAR DRY BUT DO NOT
ADD ADDITIONAL WATER.) IN ROASTING PAN,
PAT $1\frac{1}{2}$ CUPS SALT MIXTURE INTO A
RECTANGULAR SHAPE APPROXIMATELY $\frac{1}{2}$" TO 1"
LARGER THAN THE SIZE OF THE BEEF ROAST.
BRUSH ROAST WITH OIL. PRESS PEPPER EVENLY
INTO SURFACE. INSERT OVENPROOF MEAT
THERMOMETER INTO THICKEST PART OF ROAST,
NOT RESTING IN FAT. CENTER ROAST ON SALT
LAYER. STARTING AT BASE OF ROAST, PACK
REMAINING SALT MIXTURE ONTO SIDES AND
TOP OF ROAST TO ENCASE ROAST IN SALT.
(OCCASIONALLY, SOME SALT MIXTURE MAY
FALL OFF EXPOSING SMALL AREAS OF THE
ROAST. THIS WILL NOT EFFECT COOKING.)

DO NOT ADD WATER OR COVER PAN. ROAST IN 425° OVEN APPROXIMATELY 1½ TO 1¾ HOURS FOR MEDIUM RARE. 1¾ TO 2 HOURS FOR MEDIUM DONENESS. REMOVE FROM OVEN WHEN MEAT THERMOMETER REGISTERS 130° FOR MEDIUM RARE, 145° FOR MEDIUM. REMOVE PAN WITH ROAST TO COOLING RACK. LET STAND 10 TO 15 MINUTES. (TEMPERATURE WILL CONTINUE TO RISE APPROXIAMTELY 15° TO REACH DESIRED DONENESS.) REMOVE AND DISCARD SALT CRUST FROM ROAST, BRUSHING OFF ANY REMAINING SALT. CARVE ROAST INTO ½" THICK SLICES.

TOTAL PREPARATION AND COOKING TIME WILL BE 2 TO 2½ HOURS.

COOK'S TIP: SALT CRUST SHOULD BE SLIGHTLY THICKER AT THE BASE OF ROAST THAN AT THE TOP. FOR EASIER PACKING OF SALT ONTO VERTICAL SURFACES, USE ONE HAND TO HOLD THE SALT CRUST IN PLACE WHILE USING THE OTHER HAND TO PACK ON ADDITIONAL SALT TO COVER. SALT CRUST SHOULD BE APPLIED TO ROAST JUST BEFORE ROASTING.

OCCASIONALLY, A SMALL AMOUNT OF LIQUID MAY COLLECT IN THE BOTTOM OF ROASTING PAN DURING PACKING PROCESS. THIS IS NORMAL.

ROAST BEEF AU JUS

EARLY IN THE AFTERNOON, PREHEAT OVEN AT 500° FOR ONE HOUR. *DON'T OPEN OVEN DOOR.* WHILE THE OVEN IS PREHEATING, TAKE A FIVE POUND ROAST (PREFERABLY A SIRLOIN TIP, EYE OF ROUND OR SIMILAR CUT, JUST MAKE SURE IT HAS NO BONE, FAT OR GRIZZLE) AND RUB IN *LOTS* AND *LOTS* OF DRIED TARRAGON, GARLIC POWDER AND CRACKED PEPPERCORNS. PLACE THE ROAST (UNCOVERED) IN A SHALLOW MICROWAVE DISH. ONCE THE OVEN HAS BEEN PREHEATED FOR A FULL HOUR, PLACE THE ROAST IN THE OVEN (UNCOVERED) AND BAKE AT 500° FOR ONE HOUR. *DO NOT OPEN THE OVEN DOOR ONCE THE ROAST HAS BEEN PLACED IN THE OVEN.* TURN OFF THE OVEN AFTER THE ROAST HAS BAKED FOR ONE HOUR. *DO NOT OPEN THE OVEN DOOR.* LEAVE THE ROAST IN THE OVEN TO FINISH COOKING FOR A COUPLE OF HOURS. WHEN CUTTING THE ROAST, CUT IT ACROSS THE GRAIN OF THE MEAT. THE CENTER OF THE ROAST WILL BE MEDIUM RARE AND THE OUTER ENDS WILL BE MEDIUM. PUT A LITTLE WATER IN THE MICROWAVE DISH AND MICROWAVE UNTIL BOILING. BREAK UP THE BROWNED FROND ON THE BOTTOM OF THE DISH. STRAIN THE LIQUID FROM THE DISH. VOILA, AU JUS GRAVY TO GO WITH THE ROAST BEEF. PREPARATION IS SIMPLE AND CAN BE SERVED WITH HORSERADISH, A SALAD, BAKED POTATO

AND A VEGETABLE FOR A VERY NICE DINNER FOR COMPANY THAT ISN'T BURDENSOME FOR THE HOSTESS.

Pork Entrees

BRANDIED CHERRY GLAZED HAM

1	HAM
1	(21 OZ.) CAN CHERRY PIE FILLING
2	TBLS. BRANDY

BAKE HAM ACCORDING TO PACKAGE DIRECTIONS. 30 MINUTES BEFORE HAM IS DONE, SPOON PIE FILLING OVER HAM. CONTINUE BAKING. JUST BEFORE SERVING, HEAT BRANDY. POUR BRANDY OVER HAM AND IGNITE.

Hold close the ever present blessing of this journey we all share.

GRILLED HAM WITH DIJON GLAZE

1/3	CUP PACKED BROWN SUGAR
1/4	CUP DIJON MUSTARD
	DASH GROUND CLOVES
1	HALF HAM, CUT INTO 1/2" STEAKS

COMBINE BROWN SUGAR, MUSTARD AND CLOVES. GRILL HAM STEAKS OVER MEDIUM HOT COALS 5 TO 10 MINUTES, TURNING AND BRUSHING WITH GLAZE FREQUENTLY.

Those who reach, touch the stars.

GRILLED HAM
WITH PINEAPPLE GLAZE

1	HALF HAM
$\frac{3}{4}$	CUP PINEAPPLE JUICE
$\frac{1}{4}$	CUP PACKED BROWN SUGAR
1	TBL. CORNSTARCH
$\frac{1}{2}$	TSP. GROUND GINGER

PREPARE CHARCOAL GRILL FOR INDIRECT HEAT GRILLING. ARRANGE DRIP PAN IN BOTTOM OF GRILL. SURROUND WITH CHARCOAL. LIGHT CHARCOAL. WHEN CHARCOAL IS COVERED WITH ASH, PLACE HAM ON GRILL FACE DOWN (HAM SHOULD BE POSITIONED OVER DRIP PAN). PUT HOOD ON GRILL WITH VENTS OPEN. GRILL HAM 1 HOUR. IN SAUCEPAN, COMBINE REMAINING INGREDIENTS. COOK, STIRRING CONSTANTLY, UNTIL MIXTURE THICKENS AND BOILS. REMOVE FROM HEAT. BRUSH HAM WITH PINEAPPLE GLAZE. CONTINUE GRILLING AND BRUSHING HAM FOR 30 MINUTES. SERVE WITH GLAZE.

Music bridges the silence when our words are empty of hand.

HAM STEAKS WITH PLUM SALSA

4	PLUMS, SEEDED AND DICED

2	TBLS, THAWED, FROZEN ORANGE JUICE CONCENTRATE
1	TSP. LEMON JUICE
1	TBL. MINCED JALAPENO PEPPER
$\frac{1}{4}$	TSP. GROUND GINGER
$\frac{1}{4}$	TSP. GROUND CINNAMON
3	$\frac{1}{2}$" THICK SLICES HAM

COMBINE PLUMS, ORANGE JUICE CONCENTRATE, LEMON JUICE, JALAPENO PEPPER, GINGER AND CINNAMON. COVER AND LET STAND AT ROOM TEMPERATURE FOR 1 HOUR. BROIL HAM STEAKS UNTIL GOLDEN BROWN. SERVE WITH PLUM SALSA.

Time is a friend, a healer, a maker of dreams.

HONEY MUSTARD GLAZED HAM

1	HAM
1	CUP PACKED BROWN SUGAR
$\frac{1}{2}$	CUP HONEY
2	TBLS. PREPARED MUSTARD

BAKE HAM ACCORDING TO DIRECTIONS. COMBINE BROWN SUGAR, HONEY AND MUSTARD. 30 MINUTES BEFORE HAM IS DONE, REMOVE FROM OVEN. SCORE SURFACE AND SPOON ON GLAZE. CONTINUE BASTING WITH GLAZE DURING LAST 30 MINUTES OF BAKING.

MUSTARD AND RAISIN GLAZED HAM

1	HALF HAM
½	CUP PACKED BROWN SUGAR
2	TBLS. CORNSTARCH
1¼	CUPS WATER
½	CUP RAISINS
3	TBLS. LEMON JUICE
1	TSP. DIJON MUSTARD
¼	TSP. CINNAMON

BAKE HAM ACCORDING TO PACKAGE DIRECTIONS. COMBINE BROWN SUGAR AND CORNSTARCH. STIR IN WATER. COOK, STIRRING CONSTANTLY, UNTIL CLEAR AND THICKENED. STIR IN REMAINING INGREDIENTS. 30 MINUTES BEFORE HAM IS DONE, SPOON GLAZE OVER HAM. CONTINUE BAKING. SERVE HAM WITH REMAINING GLAZE.

PINEAPPLE MARMALADE GLAZED HAM

1	HAM
1	8 OZ. CAN CRUSHED PINEAPPLE

¼	CUP ORANGE MARMALADE
2	TSPS. DIJON MUSTARD
	DASH GROUND CLOVES

BAKE HAM ACCORDING TO PACKAGE
DIRECTIONS. COMBINE REMAINING
INGREDIENTS. 30 MINUTES BEFORE HAM IS
DONE, REMOVE FROM OVEN. SCORE SURFACE
AND SPOON ON GLAZE. CONTINUE BASTING
WITH GLAZE DURING LAST 30 MINUTES OF
BAKING.

Let your dreams take flight
for life is meant to be an adventure.

ROAST PORK WITH ROSEMARY

1	3 LB. PORK LOIN ROAST
2	TBLS. CHOPPED FRESH ROSEMARY
	OR 1 TBL. DRIED
4	CLOVES GARLIC
1	TSP. SALT
1	TSP. BLACK PEPPER
¼	CUP OLIVE OIL
2	TBLS. BUTTER
1	SMALL ONION, CHOPPED

FINELY CHOP ROSEMARY AND GARLIC
TOGETHER. MAKE 8 TO 10 DEEP CUTS IN ROAST.
INSERT SMALL AMOUNTS OF GARLIC MIXTURE.

SPRINKLE ROAST WITH SALT AND PEPPER. HEAT
BUTTER IN ROASTING PAN IN OVEN. SCATTER
ONION PIECES IN PAN. PLACE ROAST IN PAN
AND BAST WITH OLIVE OIL. ROAST UNCOVERED
FOR 1¾ TO 2 HOURS.

PORK TENDERLOIN DIANE

1	LB. PORK TENDERLOIN, CUT CROSS-WISE INTO 8 PIECES
3	TSPS. LEMON PEPPER SEASONING
2	TBLS. BUTTER
2	TBLS. LEMON JUICE
1	TBL. WORCESTERSHIRE SAUCE
1	TSP. DIJON STYLE MUSTARD
1	TBL. PARSLEY OR CHIVES, MINCED

PRESS EACH TENDERLOIN SLICE TO A 1"
THICKNESS. SPRINKLE SURFACES OF
MEDALLIONS WITH LEMON PEPPER SEASONING.
HEAT BUTTER IN HEAVY SKILLET, COOK
TENDERLOIN MEDALLIONS 3 TO 4 MINUTES ON
EACH SIDE. REMOVE MEDALLIONS TO SERVING
PLATTER AND KEEP WARM. ADD LEMON JUICE,
WORCESTERSHIRE SAUCE AND MUSTARD TO
THE SKILLET. COOK, STIRRING WITH PAN
JUICES, UNTIL HEATED THROUGH. POUR SAUCE
OVER MEDALLIONS, SPRINKLE WITH PARSLEY
AND SERVE.

CARNITAS

3   LBS. OF PORK (BUTT OR SHOULDER)

MARINADE MIXTURE:

½   TBL. BLACK PEPPER
¼   YELLOW ONION
         JUICE OF 1 ORANGE
         JUICE OF 1 LEMON
4   CLOVES GARLIC
1   TBL. SALT
2   CUPS WATER

CUT PORK INTO ½" CUBES, PLACE CUBED PORK
INTO LARGE MIXING BOWL. MIX ALL OTHER
INGREDIENTS IN BLENDER UNTIL LIQUID.
POUR MIXTURE OVER MEAT AND MIX
THOROUGHLY. COVER MEAT WITH MARINADE.
PLACE MEAT AND MIXTURE IN LARGE SAUCEPAN,
COVER. COOK SLOWLY ON LOW HEAT UNTIL
LIQUID IS REDUCED. UNCOVER, CONTINUE
COOKING MEAT SLOWLY, STIRRING THROUGH
REMAINING OILS AND FATS OF MARINADE.
MEAT WILL BE COMPLETELY STEAMED WHEN
GOLDEN BROWN AND TENDER. IF DESIRED,
SERVE MEAT WITH FRIED BEANS, QUACAMOLE,

SALSA PICANTE, AND CORN OR FLOUR
TORTILLAS. SERVES 6

Poultry

BBQ CHICKEN KABOBS

3	SWEET POTATOES, PEELED AND CUT INTO 1½" CHUNKS (NEW POTATOES MAY BE SUBSTITUTED)
2	SLICES BACON
¼	CUP FINELY CHOPPED ONION
1	CLOVE GARLIC, FINELY CHOPPED
2	TBLS. WATER
1	8 OZ. CAN TOMATO SAUCE
½	CUP KETCHUP
3	TBLS. BROWN SUGAR
3	TBLS. CIDER VINEGAR
2	TBLS. WORCESTERSHIRE SAUCE
⅛	TSP. SALT
2	DASHES HOT PEPPER SAUCE
2	ONIONS, PEELED AND CUT INTO 1½" PIECES
6	BONELESS, SKINLESS CHICKEN BREASTS (1½ LBS.) CUT INTO 1½" CHUNKS

PREPARE GRILL OR HEAT BROILER. SIMMER POTATOES IN WATER IN COVERED SAUCEPAN UNTIL JUST TENDER (ABOUT 12 MINUTES). DRAIN.

TO MAKE SAUCE, COOK BACON, ONION AND GARLIC IN SKILLET FOR SIX MINUTES. ADD 2 TBLS. WATER. COOK 2 MINUTES. STIR IN TOMATO SAUCE, KETCHUP, VINEGAR, BROWN SUGAR, WORCESTERSHIRE SAUCE, SALT AND

HOT PEPPER SAUCE. SIMMER 6 MINUTES TO THICKEN. SKEWER PIECES OF ONION, CHICKEN AND POTATO ON 6 SKEWERS. RESERVE HALF OF SAUCE TO SERVE WITH KABOBS.

GRILL 5" OVER MEDIUM HOT COALS, OR BROIL 5" FROM HEAT, BASTING FREQUENTLY WITH HALF THE SAUCE, FOR 6 TO 7 MINUTES PER SIDE OR UNTIL CHICKEN IS COOKED THROUGH. SERVE KABOBS WITH RESERVED SAUCE. SERVES 6

Somewhere in the sky, a web made of clouds, stars and moonlight, holds our tomorrows.

SESAME ALMOND CHICKEN

$\frac{3}{4}$	CUP CRUSHED SALTINE CRACKERS
$\frac{1}{4}$	CUP TOASTED SESAME SEED
$2\frac{1}{4}$	OZ. PKG. (2/3 CUP) SLIVERED ALMONDS
1	TBL. DRIED GREEN ONION
$\frac{1}{2}$	TSP. DRIED PARSLEY FLAKES
$\frac{1}{2}$	TSP. DRIED THYME LEAVES
1	CRUSHED BAY LEAF
1	TSP. DRY MUSTARD
$\frac{1}{2}$	TSP. SALT
$\frac{1}{2}$	CUP BUTTER
$3\frac{1}{2}$	LB. FRYING CHICKEN, CUT INTO 8 PIECES

HEAT OVEN TO 350°. COMBINE ALL INGREDIENTS EXCEPT BUTTER AND CHICKEN.

DIP CHICKEN IN MELTED BUTTER, THEN COAT
WITH CRUMB MIXTURE. RESERVE REMAINING
BUTTER. PLACE CHICKEN IN UNGREASED 13"x9"
BAKING DISH. SPRINKLE WITH REMAINING
CRUMBS. POUR REMAINING BUTTER OVER
CHICKEN. BAKE FOR 65 TO 70 MINUTES OR
UNTIL CHICKEN IS FORK TENDER. SERVES 4

*Every day is a new beginning.
Believe in your heart that something wonderful is
about to happen.*

CHICKEN CREOLE

1	CUP CHICKEN BROTH
1	6 OZ. CAN TOMATO PASTE
1	LARGE ONION, CHOPPED
2	CUPS CHOPPED CABBAGE
1	LARGE GREEN BELL PEPPER, SEEDED AND DICED
2	LARGE CLOVES GARLIC, MINCED
1	BAY LEAF
1	TBL. LEMON JUICE
1	TBL. WORCESTERSHIRE SAUCE
1	TBL. GRANULATED SUGAR
2	TSPS. DRIED BASIL LEAVES
2	TSPS. DIJON STYLE MUSTARD
$\frac{1}{4}$	TSP. BLACK PEPPER
3	DROPS HOT PEPPER SAUCE
4	LBS. BONE IN CHICKEN BREAST HALVES, SKIN AND FAT REMOVED

1¼   CUPS UNCOOKED LONG GRAIN
          WHITE RICE

IN BOTTOM OF LARGE SLOW COOKER, WHISK TOGETHER CHICKEN BROTH AND TOMATO PASTE UNTIL SMOOTH. ADD ONION, CABBAGE, GREEN PEPPER, GARLIC, BAY LEAF, LEMON JUICE, WORCESTERSHIRE SAUCE, SUGAR, BASIL, MUSTARD, BLACK PEPPER AND HOT PEPPER SAUCE. STIR TO MIX WELL. ADD CHICKEN. COVER AND COOK ON HIGH 1 HOUR. STIR CHICKEN INTO SAUCE. REDUCE HEAT TO LOW AND COOK AN ADDITIONAL 5 TO 6 HOURS. REMOVE AND DISCARD BAY LEAF.

A HALF HOUR BEFORE SERVING, COOK RICE ACCORDING TO PACKAGE DIRECTIONS. REMOVE CHICKEN. WHEN COOL ENOUGH TO HANDLE, CUT INTO SLICES AND DISCARD BONES. SERVE INDIVIDUAL PORTIONS OF CHICKEN AND VEGETABLES OVER RICE. SERVES 4 TO 5

Sunshine gives warmth to the earth like a mother gives warmth to her child.

CHICKEN POTATO LATKES

1½	LBS. BONELESS, SKINLESS CHICKEN BREASTS, SHREDDED
2	CUPS SHREDDED POTATOES
1	GREEN ONION, CHOPPED
1	EGG
1	EGG YOLK
1	TSP. POULTRY SEASONING
2	CLOVES GARLIC, MINCED
	ADDITIONAL SALT AND PEPPER TO TASTE
3	TBLS. BUTTER

PLACE POTATOES IN BOWL AND COVER WITH COLD WATER. LET SIT FOR 5 MINUTES. REMOVE POTATOES FROM BOWL AND PAT DRY. IN A LARGE BOWL, MIX REMAINING INGREDIENTS, EXCEPT BUTTER, UNTIL THOROUGHLY BLENDED, APPROXIMATELY 3 MINUTES. HEAT BUTTER ON MEDIUM HIGH HEAT IN A LARGE, DEEP NON-STICK SKILLET. DROP POTATO BATTER BY TABLESPOONS, FLATTENING SLIGHTLY WITH A SPATULA. COOK ON LOW TO MEDIUM HEAT UNTIL BROWN ON BOTH SIDES.
SERVES 4

CHICKEN TOMATILLO ENCHILADAS

1	8 OZ. PKG. CREAM CHEESE, SOFTENED
1¾	CUPS BOTTLED PICANTE SAUCE
2	CUPS CHOPPED COOKED CHICKEN
2	CUPS MONTERREY JACK CHEESE (8 OZ.)
12	6" CORN TORTILLAS
1	CUP TOMATO PUREE
2	TBLS. CHOPPED FRESH CILANTRO
¼	TBL. GARLIC POWDER
	OR 1 CLOVE GARLIC, MINCED
1	11 OZ. CAN TOMATILLOS, DRAINED AND CHOPPED
	FRESH CILANTRO FOR GARNISH

STIR CREAM CHEESE UNTIL SMOOTH. STIR IN ¾ CUP OF THE PICANTE SAUCE, THE CHICKEN AND 1 CUP OF THE MONTERREY JACK CHEESE. WARM TORTILLAS ACCORDING TO PACKAGE DIRECTIONS. SPOON ABOUT ¼ CUP CHICKEN MIXTURE DOWN CENTER OF EACH TORTILLA. ROLL UP AND PLACE SEAM SIDE DOWN IN 3 QT. SHALLOW BAKING DISH. MIX REMAINING PICANTE SAUCE, TOMATO PUREE, CHOPPED CILANTRO, GARLIC POWDER AND TOMATILLOS. POUR OVER ENCHILADAS. COVER AND BAKE AT 350° FOR 35 MINUTES OR UNTIL HOT.

UNCOVER. TOP WITH REMAINING MONTERREY
JACK CHEESE. BAKE 5 MINUTES MORE OR UNTIL
CHEESE IS MELTED. GARNISH WITH CILANTRO.
MAKES 6 SERVINGS

*Sometimes it's the simplest touch that brings the
heart its greatest passion.*

CHICKEN WITH LIME BUTTER

6	CHICKEN BREASTS, BONED AND SKINNED
½	TSP. SALT
½	TSP. PEPPER
⅓	CUP COOKING OIL
	JUICE OF 1 LIME
8	TBLS. BUTTER
½	TSP. MINCED CHIVES
½	TSP. DILL WEED

SPRINKLE CHICKEN ON BOTH SIDES WITH SALT
AND PEPPER. PLACE OIL IN A LARGE FRYING PAN
AND HEAT TO MEDIUM TEMPERATURE. ADD
CHICKEN AND SAUTE ABOUT 4 MINUTES, OR
UNTIL LIGHTLY BROWNED. TURN CHICKEN,
COVER, AND REDUCE HEAT TO LOW. COOK 10
MINUTES, OR UNTIL FORK CAN BE INSERTED IN
CHICKEN WITH EASE. REMOVE CHICKEN AND
KEEP WARM. DRAIN OFF OIL AND DISCARD. IN
SAME PAN, ADD LIME JUICE AND COOK OVER
LOW HEAT UNTIL JUICES BEGIN TO BUBBLE.
ADD BUTTER, STIRRING UNTIL BUTTER

BECOMES OPAQUE AND FORMS A THICKENED
SAUCE. STIR IN CHIVES AND DILL WEED.
SPOON SAUCE OVER CHICKEN. SERVES 6

*You are what you believe you are
and you can do whatever you believe you can do.*

JERK CHICKEN

PASTE:

1	CUP DICED ONION
3	SCALLIONS, GREEN AND WHITE PARTS, CHOPPED
2	TBLS. FRESH THYME LEAVES, OR 2 TSPS. DRIED
1	TBL. COARSELY CHOPPED GINGER ROOT
2	TO 4 SCOTCH BONNET OR HABANERO CHILI PEPPERS
1	TBL. VEGETABLE OIL
1	TSP. GROUND ALLSPICE
$\frac{1}{2}$	TSP. FRESHLY GROUND BLACK PEPPER
$\frac{1}{2}$	TSP. GROUND CINNAMON
$\frac{1}{4}$	TSP. FRESHLY GROUND NUTMEG
$\frac{1}{2}$	TSP. SALT
2	WHOLE CHICKEN BREASTS, SPLIT AND SKINNED

IN A FOOD PROCESSOR OR BLENDER, COMBINE
THE ONION, SCALLION, THYME, GINGER,
CHILIES, OIL, ALLSPICE, PEPPER, CINNAMON,

NUTMEG AND SALT. PROCESS TO A PULPY PASTE.
THERE WILL BE ABOUT A CUP. SPREAD THE
PASTE LIBERALLY OVER THE CHICKEN BREASTS.
ARRANGE THE CHICKEN ON A PLATE. COVER
WITH PLASTIC WRAP AND MARINATE IN THE
REFRIGERATOR 2 TO 3 HOURS, OR OVERNIGHT.
PREHEAT THE OVEN TO 300°. PLACE THE
CHICKEN IN A BAKING DISH, COVER AND BAKE
30 MINUTES.

MEANWHILE, LIGHT THE GRILL, OR IF COOKING
INDOORS, HEAT A GRILL PAN OR RIDGED
GRIDDLE. WHEN THE CHICKEN COMES OUT OF
THE OVEN, GRILL IT UNTIL IT IS COOKED
THROUGH, TURNING THE PIECES ONCE. THIS
TAKES ABOUT 10 MINUTES, DEPENDING ON THE
SIZE OF THE CHICKEN BREASTS.

Never be ashamed of age or imperfections,
for it is life's touch that creates the richest
beauty of all.

SMOTHERED CHICKEN BRULOT

1	LARGE FRYER, CUT INTO SERVING PIECES
	WATER FOR CHICKEN
½	CUP OIL
⅓	CUP SUGAR
1½	CUPS WATER
1	CUP CHOPPED ONION
½	CUP CHOPPED CELERY

½	CUP CHOPPED BELL PEPPER
¼	CUP DICED GARLIC
2	CUPS CHICKEN STOCK
1	TSP. THYME
2½	TSP. BASIL
½	CUP SLICED GREEN ONIONS
¼	CUP CHOPPED PARSLEY
	SALT AND BLACK PEPPER
	LOUISIANA GOLD PEPPER SAUCE

SEASON CHICKEN USING SALT, PEPPER, THYME AND BASIL. IN A CAST-IRON CHICKEN FRYER, HEAT OIL OVER MEDIUM-HIGH HEAT. ADD CHICKEN, SKIN-SIDE DOWN AND COOK UNTIL GOLDEN BROWN ON ALL SIDES. ALLOW CHICKEN TO STICK TO PAN, ADDING A LITTLE WATER EACH TIME. WHILE CHICKEN IS COOKING, MELT SUGAR IN AN 8" CAST-IRON SKILLET UNTIL ALMOST BROWNED. SLOWLY ADD 1½ CUPS WATER TO SUGAR MIXTURE UNTIL BRULOT IS COMPLETELY DISSOLVED. SET ASIDE.

INTO CHICKEN SKILLET, ADD ONIONS, CELERY, BELL PEPPER AND GARLIC. SAUTE 3 TO 5 MINUTES OR UNTIL VEGETABLES ARE WILTED. POUR IN CHICKEN STOCK, ONE LADLE AT A TIME, UNTIL ALL IS INCORPORATED. POUR SUGAR/WATER MIXTURE OVER CHICKEN, COVER AND ALLOW TO SIMMER FOR APPROXIMATLEY 15 MINUTES. ADD GREEN ONIONS AND PARSLEY. SEASON TO TASTE USING SALT, PEPPER AND LOUISIANA GOLD. SERVES 4

CHICKEN AND PEPPERS WITH PENNE PASTA

12	OZS. BONELESS, SKINLESS CHICKEN BREASTS, CUT INTO $\frac{1}{2}$" BY 2" STRIPS
1	CUP FAT FREE CHICKEN BROTH
8	OZS. DRIED PENNE PASTA
1	MEDIUM GREEN BELL PEPPER
1	MEDIUM RED BELL PEPPER
1	$14\frac{1}{2}$ OZ. CAN ITALIAN SEASONED TOMATOES, CUT INTO BITE SIZE CHUNKS, RESERVING JUICE
1	TBL. BUTTER
1	LARGE GARLIC CLOVE, MINCED
1	TBL. CHOPPED FRESH PARSLEY OR 1 TSP. DRIED FLAKES
$\frac{1}{2}$	TSP. SALT
$\frac{1}{4}$	TSP. FRESHLY GOUND BLACK PEPPER

MARINATE CHICKEN IN BROTH IN REFRIGERATOR FOR AT LEAST 1 HOUR. COOK PASTA ACCORDING TO PACKAGE DIRECTIONS, UNTIL AL DENTE, ABOUT 10 MINUTES. DRAIN AND SET ASIDE. CUT PEPPERS INTO 1" DIAMOND SHAPES OR SQUARES. SET ASIDE. IN SMALL SAUCEPAN, BRING TOMATOES TO A BOIL OVER MEDIUM HIGH HEAT. TURN HEAT TO LOW AND COVER SAUCEPAN, LEAVING TOMATOES ON

BURNER UNTIL READY TO SERVE. MELT BUTTER
IN SKILLET OVER MEDIUM HIGH HEAT. TURN
HEAT TO HIGH AND ADD CHICKEN (DISCARD
MARINADE BROTH). QUICK FRY UNTIL CHICKEN
PIECES ARE LIGHTLY BROWNED, 3 TO 4
MINUTES. REDUCE HEAT TO MEDIUM HIGH AND
ADD RESERVED PEPPERS, GARLIC, PARSLEY, SALT
AND PEPPER. COOK STIRRING FREQUENTLY, FOR
ABOUT 5 MINUTES MORE, OR UNTIL NO TRACE
OF PINK REMAINS WHEN YOU CUT INTO
THICKEST PART OF CHICKEN.

DIVIDE PASTA INTO 4 EQUAL PORTIONS IN
LARGE, SHALLOW BOWLS. SPOON ¼ OF HOT
TOMATOES OVER EACH PASTA SERVING. TOP
WITH ¼ OF CHICKEN AND PEPPER MIXTURE.
SERVE IMMEDIATELY. SERVES 4

*Wildflowers gather together and spill their colors
like fallen rainbows covering a hillside.*

FRIED CHICKEN WITH GARLIC
AND GREEN ONIONS

2	WHOLE CHICKEN BREASTS, BONED, SKINNED, SPLIT
3	CLOVES GARLIC, MINCED, ABOUT 2 TSPS.
2	TBLS. SOY SAUCE
2	TSPS. SESAME OIL
1	TSP. BLACK PEPPER
1	TSP. CRUSHED CORIANDER SEEDS

$\frac{1}{2}$	TSP. SUGAR
$\frac{1}{8}$	TSP. RED PEPPER FLAKES
8	GREEN ONIONS, SLICED
2	TBLS. PEANUT OIL
3	CUPS STEAMED RICE OR COOKED ORIENTAL NOODLES

CUT CHICKEN BREASTS INTO 1" CUBES. MIX REMAINING INGREDIENTS, EXCEPT PEANUT OIL AND RICE IN LARGE BOWL. ADD CHICKEN PIECES. TURN TO COAT. MARINATE IN REFRIGERATER UP TO 2 HOURS. TURN CHICKEN OCCASIONALLY WHILE MARINATING. HEAT 3 TBLS. PEANUT OIL IN WOK OR LARGE SKILLET UNTIL HOT, BUT NOT SMOKING. ADD CHICKEN MIXTURE, STIR-FRY OVER HIGH HEAT 3 TO 5 MINUTES, UNTIL CHICKEN IS OPAQUE. SERVE OVER RICE OR NOODLES. MAKES 4 SERVINGS

Don't lose sight of your journey for the sake of your destination.

OVEN BAKED PARMESAN CHICKEN

10	LB. BAG CHICKEN
1	16 OZ. CONTAINER NON-FAT PLAIN YOGURT
6	TBL. DIJON MUSTARD
1	CONTAINER MINUTE MAID LEMON JUICE CONCENTRATE
	CHOPPED BASIL LEAVES
	BREAD CRUMBS
	PARMESAN CHEESE

COMBINE YOGURT, MUSTARD, LEMON JUICE, AND BASIL IN A LARGE MIXING BOWL. ADD CHICKEN AND COAT WELL WITH MARINADE. COVER FOR A LITTLE AS ONE HOUR OR FOR AS LONG AS A DAY OR SO. TURN CHICKEN PERIODICALLY. PREHEAT OVEN TO 350°. SHAKE OFF EACH PIECE OF CHICKEN AND COAT IN MIXTURE OF EQUAL PORTIONS OF BREAD CRUMBS AND PARMESAN CHEESE. PLACE ON GREASED COOKIE SHEET AND BAKE FOR AN HOUR OR SO.

*Learn the language of your heart
and say the words.*

HONEY-MUSTARD GLAZED CHICKEN WINGS WITH
SCALLION-SESAME CONFETTI

6	LBS. WHOLE CHICKEN WINGS (ABOUT 25 WINGS)
$\frac{1}{2}$	CUP HONEY
$\frac{1}{2}$	CUP ORANGE JUICE
6	TBLS. PREPARED MUSTARD
2	TBLS. SOY SAUCE
$\frac{1}{2}$	TSP. HOT RED PEPPER SAUCE
3	SCALLIONS, TRIMMED AND THINLY SLICED
2	TBLS. SESAME SEEDS

PREHEAT OVEN TO 375°. CUT OFF AND DISCARD
THE WING TIPS. CUT THE REMAINING WINGS
INTO 2 PIECES AT THE JOINT. SPRAY 13"x9"
OBLONG BAKING DISH WITH NON-STICK
COOKING SPRAY. ARRANGE THE WINGS IN 2
LAYERS IN THE DISH. BAKE FOR 30 MINUTES.
REMOVE AS MUCH OIL AS POSSIBLE WITH A
BASTER.

WHILE THE WINGS ARE BAKING, HEAT THE
HONEY, ORANGE JUICE, MUSTARD, SOY SAUCE
AND HOT RED PEPPER SAUCE TO BOILING IN A 2
QT. SAUCEPAN. BOIL 5 MINUTES. POUR THE
HONEY-MUSTARD SAUCE OVER THE BAKED
WINGS. (THE RECIPE CAN BE PREPARED TO THIS
POINT UP TO 2 DAYS IN ADVANCE. COVER THE
DISH WITH PLASTIC LID AND REFRIGERATE).
RETURN TO OVEN. BAKE THE WINGS UNTIL THE
SAUCE IS THICK ENOUGH TO COAT THE WINGS
AND THE WINGS ARE LIGHTLY BROWNED,
ABOUT 40 TO 50 MINUTES. TAKE THE WINGS
OUT OF THE OVEN SEVERAL TIMES DURING
THIS PERIOD, AND USING TONGS, MOVE THEM
AROUND TO PREVENT STICKING. REARRANGE
THEM EVENLY EACH TIME AFTER YOU STIR
THEM.

SPRINKLE THE SCALLIONS AND SESAME SEEDS
OVER THE WINGS AND STIR GENTLY TO COAT.
MAKES ABOUT 50 PIECES

PESTO PASTA WITH GRILLED CHICKEN

½   CUP PREPARED ITALIAN SALAD DRESSING
½   CUP, PLUS 2 TBLS. PESTO SAUCE
1   LB. SKINLESS, BONELESS
      CHICKEN BREASTS
8   OZS. FETTUCCINE,
      COOKED AS PACKAGE DIRECTS

IN RESEALABLE PLASTIC FOOD STORAGE BAG, COMBINE SALAD DRESSING AND 2 TBLS. PESTO SAUCE. ADD CHICKEN, RESEAL BAG. REFRIGERATE AT LEAST 1 HOUR. GRILL OR BROIL CHICKEN UNTIL FULLY COOKED. TOSS HOT FETTUCCINE WITH REMAINING PESTO SAUCE. SLICE CHICKEN BREASTS. SERVE WITH FETTUCCINE. SERVES 4

Seafood Entrees

CRAWFISH IN BLACK BEAN SAUCE

CRAWFISH:

2"	FRESH GINGER ROOT, PEELED AND COARSELY CHOPPED
4	MEDIUM CLOVES GARLIC, PEELED AND COARSELY CHOPPED
3	LBS. FRESH LIVE CRAWFISH

SAUCE:

1	TSP. CANOLA OIL
1	MEDIUM CLOVE GARLIC, PEELED AND MINCED
2	TSPS. FINELY MINCED FRESH GINGER ROOT
$\frac{1}{4}$	CUP DRY SHERRY
$\frac{1}{2}$	CUP CLAM JUICE
1	TBL. ASIAN BLACK BEAN GARLIC SAUCE
1	TSP. SOY SAUCE
1	TSP. RICE VINEGAR
$\frac{1}{4}$	TSP. HOT CHILI OIL
$\frac{1}{2}$	TSP. ARROWROOT OR CORNSTARCH DISSOLVED IN 2 TSPS. WATER
1	TSP. LEMON JUICE
1	GREEN ONION, FINELY CHOPPED
2	CUPS HOT COOKED WHITE RICE

TO PREPARE THE CRAWFISH:

BRING A LARGE STOCKPOT OF WATER TO BOIL,
ADD THE GINGER AND GARLIC. RINSE
CRAWFISH WELL IN SEVERAL CHANGES OF
WATER. WHEN THE POT OF WATER COMES TO A
BOIL, ADD THE CRAWFISH ALL AT ONCE. COVER
AND COOK 7 MINUTES. DRAIN WELL.

WHEN COOL ENOUGH TO HANDLE, PEEL THE
CRAWFISH. (REFRIGERATE IF NOT USING
IMMEDIATELY).

IN A LARGE NON-STICK SKILLET, HEAT THE OIL
OVER MEDIUM HEAT. SAUTE THE GARLIC AND
GINGER 30 SECONDS. ADD SHERRY AND COOK
UNTIL REDUCED TO A COUPLE OF TBLS. THEN
ADD CLAM JUICE, BLACK BEAN SAUCE, VINEGAR
AND CHILI OIL. COOK 2 MINUTES, THEN STIR
IN DISSOLVED ARROWROOT. COOK 1 MINUTE.
STIR IN CRAWFISH, LEMON JUICE AND GREEN
ONION. HEAT ON MEDIUM LOW HEAT. SPOON
OVER THE HOT RICE AND SERVE.

GALVESTON CRAB CAKES

1	LB. FRESH LUMP CRABMEAT
¾	CUP ITALIAN FLAVORED BREADCUMBS
1	LARGE EGG, BEATEN
¼	CUP GOOD QUALITY MAYONNAISE
1	TSP. WORCESTERSHIRE SAUCE
1	TSP. DRY MUSTARD
½	TSP. SALT
¼	TSP. PEPPER
½	TSP. PARSLEY
	(OR 2 TBLS. CHOPPED FRESH)
	OIL FOR FRYING
	LEMON WEDGES

PLACE CRABMEAT IN LARGE BOWL AND, WITHOUT BREAKING UP THE LUMPS, CAREFULLY REMOVE CARTILAGE AND SHELL. ADD BREADCRUMBS AND MIX GENTLY.

IN A SEPARATE BOWL, COMBINE EGG, MAYONNAISE, WORCESTERSHIRE SAUCE, MUSTARD, SALT, PEPPER AND PARSLEY. GENTLY BLEND WITH CRABMEAT MIXTURE. FORM MIXTURE INTO 6 PATTIES.

IN A LARGE SKILLET, FRY THE CAKES IN OIL
UNTIL GOLDEN BROWN. (ABOUT 3 MINUTES ON
EACH SIDE.) SERVE WITH LEMON WEDGES AND
SOUR CREAM-DILL SAUCE.

SOUR CREAM-DILL SAUCE:

BLEND A LITTLE DIJON MUSTARD, DILL WEED
AND A FEW CHOPPED CAPERS INTO SOUR CREAM.

*The human heart, being true to itself, will
always reveal the presence of the love it tries so
hard to hide.*

SHRIMP LOUISIANE

$\frac{1}{4}$	CUP BUTTER
1	CUP FINELY CHOPPED ONIONS
$\frac{1}{2}$	CUP CHOPPED GREEN ONIONS
2	STALKS CELERY, FINELY CHOPPED
2	TO $2\frac{1}{2}$ LBS. RAW SHRIMP, PEELED
3	TBLS. FLOUR
1	TBL. SALT
1	TBL. CHILI POWDER
2	CUPS MILK
4	TBLS. KETCHUP
1	TBL. DRIED PARSLEY

MELT BUTTER IN LARGE, HEAVY SKILLET. SAUTE
ONIONS AND CELERY UNTIL LIMP. ADD SHRIMP

AND SAUTE UNTIL SHRIMP ARE PINK. STIR IN
FLOUR, SALT AND CHILI POWDER. ADD MILK
GRADUALLY AND COOK 5 MINUTES OVER LOW
HEAT. ADD KETCHUP AND PARSLEY. COOK
COVERED 10 TO 15 MINUTES. SERVE OVER RICE
WITH GREEN SALAD AND FRENCH BREAD.
SERVES 4 TO 6

Our lives are woven by the weavers of time,

in a pattern we cannot see.

CRAWFISH AND SHRIMP ENCHILADAS

8	TBLS. UNSALTED BUTTER
2	CUPS CHOPPED ONION (ABOUT 2 LARGE)
1	CUP DICED RED PEPPER (ABOUT 1 LARGE)
1	LB. CREAM CHEESE
1	CUP SOUR CREAM
$2\frac{1}{2}$	TSPS. DRIED OREGANO
$2\frac{1}{2}$	TSPS. GROUND CUMIN
$\frac{1}{4}$	TSP. CAYENNE PEPPER
2	TSPS. SALT
$2\frac{1}{2}$	CUPS HEAVY CREAM
3	LBS. SMALL SHRIMP, PEELED AND DEVEINED OR CRAWFISH TAILS OR HALF SHRIMP AND HALF CRAWFISH
4	TSPS. ALL-PURPOSE SEASONING (RECIPE FOLLOWS)
$\frac{1}{2}$	CUP SLICED SCALLIONS
12	6" FLOUR TORTILLAS

2   CUPS FRESHLY GRATED
        MONTERREY JACK CHEESE
        FRESH PARSLEY, FOR GARNISH

IN A 5 QT. SAUCEPAN OVER MODERATELY HIGH HEAT, MELT 4 TBLS. OF THE BUTTER. ADD ONION AND BELL PEPPER. COOK FOR 5 MINUTES, STIRRING. REDUCE HEAT TO MEDIUM. COOK AN ADDITIONAL 5 MINUTES. ADD CREAM CHEESE, SOUR CREAM, OREGANO, CUMIN, CAYENNE AND SALT. COOK, STIRRING FOR 3 MINUTES. ADD CREAM AND COOK FOR 5 ADDITIONAL MINUTES. KEEP WARM UNTIL READY TO SERVE.

IN A MEDIUM SKILLET OVER MODERATLY HIGH HEAT, SAUTE THE SHRIMP IN THE REMAINING BUTTER FOR 3 MINUTES. ADD THE SEASONING AND SCALLIONS. COOK FOR 2 ADDITIONAL MINUTES. ADD THE SHRIMP AND CRAWFISH TO THE CREAM MIXTURE, AND MIX WELL. SPOON A GENEROUS AMOUNT OF THE SHRIMP MIXTURE IN THE CENTER OF EACH TORTILLA. FOLD EACH TORTILLA IN THIRDS AND PLACE SEAM SIDE DOWN. SPOON MORE OF THE SHRIMP MIXTURE OVER THE TORTILLAS AND TOP WITH CHEESE. GARNISH WITH PARSLEY LEAF.

ALL-PURPOSE SEASONING

4	TBLS. SALT
5	TBLS., PLUS 1 TSP. GRANULATED GARLIC
2	TSPS. GROUND BLACK PEPPER
2	TBLS. GRANULATED ONION
2	TSPS. CAYENNE PEPPER
3	TBLS. PAPRIKA
2	TSP. GROUND WHITE PEPPER
2	TSP. DRIED OREGANO
2	TSP. DRIED THYME LEAVES

IN A SMALL BOWL, COMBINE ALL INGREDIENTS.
MIX WELL. STORE IN AIRTIGHT PLASTIC BAGS
OR JARS.

Within each of us there are wings.

CRAWFISH, ARTICHOKE, ORZO
PASTA SALAD

1	LB. CRAWFISH TAILS, DRAINED
1	LB. ORZO (RICE SHAPED PASTA)
1	LARGE RED BELL PEPPER, CUT IN STRIPS
1	16 OZ. CAN BLACK OLIVES, SLICED
1	16 OZ. CAN ARTICHOKE HEARTS IN WATER, QUARTERED
1	SMALL JAR TINY CAPERS, DRAINED
1	CUP CHOPPED PARSLEY

MARINADE:

1   BUNCH CHOPPED GREEN ONIONS
1   CUP CHOPPED CELERY
         (LEAVES AND STALKS)
5   PODS GARLIC, CHOPPED
2   CUPS PURE OLIVE OIL
2   CUPS WHITE WINE VINEGAR
         JUICE OF 6 LEMONS
3   TSPS. CAVENDER'S GREEK SEASONING
         SALT AND PEPPER TO TASTE

COMBINE MARINADE INGREDIENTS AND LET
SET OVERNIGHT. MAKES AT LEAST 4 CUPS.
COOK PASTA AL DENTE. DO NOT RINSE.
MARINATE CRAWFISH TAILS FOR 30 MINUTES
IN 2 CUPS OF MARINADE. TOSS ALL OF THE
SALAD INGREDIENTS TOGETHER.

Believe in the sharing of friendship, for having
people in our lives who care is
a most precious gift.

OYSTERS SICILY

1   QT. OYSTERS
5   CLOVES GARLIC, PRESSED AND MINCED
1   TSP. ROSEMARY
1   TSP. BASIL
1   TSP. OREGANO
1   TSP. ITALIAN SEASONING

2   BAY LEAVES
1   CUP, PLUS 1 TBL. OLIVE OIL
½   BUNCH GREEN ONIONS, CHOPPED
        ITALIAN BREAD CRUMBS

COMBINE THE MINCED GARLIC, ROSEMARY,
BASIL, OREGANO, ITALIAN SEASONINGS AND
BAY LEAF. ADD TO 1 CUP OF THE OLIVE OIL. SET
ASIDE.

WHEN READY TO PREPARE OYSTERS, PREHEAT
OVEN TO 450°. DRAIN OYSTERS, RESERVE
LIQUOR. CAREFULLY REMOVE ANY SHELL
FRAGMENTS. POUR ABOUT ⅛ CUP OF THE
LIQUOR BACK INTO OYSTERS. SET ASIDE.

INTO A 9" SQUARE BAKING PAN, ADD 1 TBL. OIL
AND THE CHOPPED GREEN ONIONS. PLACE IN
HOT OVEN UNTIL BUBBLY. PULL OUT OVEN TRAY
AND ADD OIL MIXTURE AND OYSTERS TO PAN.
PUT IN OVEN UNTIL SIZZLING AROUND EDGES.
PULL OUT OVEN TRAY AGAIN AND POUR
ITALIAN BREAD CRUMBS IN PAN UNTIL ALL OIL
HAS BEEN SOAKED UP. THE TOP LAYER SHOULD
LOOK DRY. PUT BACK INTO OVEN TO BROWN
TOP OF CRUMBS.

CRAWFISH CHEESECAKE

1	QT. CHOPPED, ROASTED PECANS
6	OZS. MELTED BUTTER
2	CUPS GRATED PARMESAN CHEESE
4	TSPS. FRESH DILL WEED
3	LBS. CREAM CHEESE
4	EGGS
$\frac{1}{4}$	CUP CREOLE MUSTARD
$\frac{1}{2}$	CUP SKIM MILK
1	LB. CRAWFISH TAILS
1	CUP GREEN ONIONS, CHOPPED
1	CUP BELL PEPPERS, DICED
2	TBLS. CREOLE SEASONING
	SALT AND PEPPER TO TASTE

ROAST PECANS UNTIL BROWN. CHOP PECANS IN BLENDER UNTIL THE CONSISTENCY OF BREAD CRUMBS. MIX PECANS, MELTED BUTTER, PARMESAN CHEESE AND DILL WEED IN LARGE MIXING BOWL TO FORM DOUGH. DIVIDE AND PRESS MIXTURE INTO TWO 9" UNGREASED PIE PLATES. BAKE FOR 7 TO 10 MINUTES AT 350°.

IN A LARGE MIXING BOWL, BEAT CREAM CHEESE WITH MIXER UNTIL FLUFFY. ADD EGGS, MUSTARD, MILK, SALT, PEPPER AND CREOLE

SEASONING. MIX WELL. FOLD IN CRAWFISH
TAILS, ONIONS AND BELL PEPPERS. POUR
FILLING OVER PRE-BAKED CRUST AND BAKE AT
400° UNTIL GOLDEN BROWN, APPROXIMATELY 15
MINUTES. LET COOL.

Listen to the dream makers
for they are the guardians of wonder.

CRUSTLESS CRAB QUICHE

2	TSPS. OLIVE OIL
1	ONION, CHOPPED
1	RED BELL PEPPER, SEEDED AND CHOPPED
¾	LB. MUSHROOMS, SLICED
	(ABOUT 4½ CUPS)
2	LARGE EGGS
2	LARGE EGG WHITES
1½	CUPS LOW FAT (1%) COTTAGE CHEESE
½	CUP NON-FAT PLAIN YOGURT
¼	CUP ALL PURPOSE WHITE FLOUR
¼	CUP FRESHLY GRATED PARMESAN CHEESE
¼	TSP. CAYENNE PEPPER
¼	TSP. SALT
¼	TSP. FRESHLY GROUND BLACK PEPPER
½	LB. COOKED LUMP CRABMEAT
	(FRESH OR FROZEN, THAWED),
	DRAINED AND PICKED OVER
	(ABOUT 1 CUP)
½	CUP GRATED SHARP CHEDDAR CHEESE
	(2 OZS.)
¼	CUP CHOPPED SCALLIONS

PREHEAT OVEN TO 350°. LIGHTLY OIL A 10" PIE
PAN OR PORCELAIN QUICHE DISH, OR COAT IT
WITH NON-STICK COOKING SPRAY.

IN LARGE NON-STICK SKILLET, HEAT 1 TSP. OF
THE OIL OVER MEDIUM HIGH HEAT. ADD
ONIONS AND PEPPERS AND COOK, STIRRING,
UNTIL SOFTENED, ABOUT 5 MINUTES.
TRANSFER TO A MIXING BOWL. ADD THE
REMAINING 1 TSP. OIL TO THE SKILLET AND
HEAT OVER HIGH HEAT. ADD MUSHROOMS AND
COOK, STIRRING, UNTIL THEY HAVE SOFTENED
AND MOST OF THE LIQUID HAS EVAPORATED, 5
TO 7 MINUTES. ADD TO THE ONION MIXTURE.
IN A FOOD PROCESSOR OR BLENDER, BLEND
EGGS, EGG WHITES, COTTAGE CHEESE, YOGURT,
FLOUR, PARMESAN, CAYENNE, SALT AND PEPPER
UNTIL SMOOTH. ADD TO THE BOWL WITH THE
VEGETABLES. WITH A RUBBER SPATULA, FOLD
IN CRAB, CHEDDAR AND SCALLIONS. TRANSFER
TO THE PREPARED PIE PAN OR QUICHE DISH.
BAKE FOR 40 TO 50 MINUTES, OR UNTIL A KNIFE
INSERTED INTO THE CENTER COMES OUT
CLEAN. LET STAND FOR 5 MINUTES BEFORE
SERVING. MAKES 6 SERVINGS

FISH FILLETS WITH PECAN CRUST

2	LBS. FISH FILLETS
1/3	CUP FLOUR
1	CUP BREAD CRUMBS
1	CUP FINELY CHOPPED PECANS
2	EGGS
2	TBLS. WATER
3	TBLS. OLIVE OIL
	SALT AND PEPPER

CUT FISH INTO SERVING SIZE PORTIONS. SALT AND PEPPER AND LIGHTLY DUST WITH FLOUR. COMBINE CRUMBS AND PECANS IN A FLAT PAN.

BEAT EGG YOLKS AND WHITES WITH 2 TBLS. WATER IN ANOTHER PAN.

HEAT OIL IN SKILLET.

DREDGE EACH FISH PORTION IN EGG WASH, THEN CRUMB-NUT MIXTURE. SAUTE FISH ON EACH SIDE FOR 2 MINUTES OR UNTIL GOLDEN BROWN. CAREFULLY PLACE FISH ON BAKE AND SERVE PLATTER AND BAKE FOR 5 MINUTES AT 350° TO FINISH. MAKES 5 TO 6 SERVINGS

GREEK STYLE SCAMPI

1	TSP. OLIVE OIL
5	CLOVES GARLIC, MINCED
2	28 OZ. CANS WHOLE TOMATOES, DRAINED AND COARSELY CHOPPED
$\frac{1}{2}$	CUP CHOPPED FRESH PARSLEY, DIVIDED
$1\frac{1}{4}$	LBS. LARGE SHRIMP, PEELED AND DEVEINED
1	CUP (4 OZ.) CRUMBLED FETA CHEESE
2	TBLS. FRESH LEMON JUICE
$\frac{1}{4}$	TSP. FRESH GROUND PEPPER

PREHEAT OVEN TO 400°. HEAT OIL IN A LARGE DUTCH OVEN. ADD GARLIC AND SAUTE 30 SECONDS. ADD TOMATOES. REDUCE HEAT. SIMMER 10 MINUTES. ADD $\frac{1}{4}$ CUP CHOPPED PARSLEY AND SHRIMP. POUR MIXTURE INTO A 13"x9" DISH. TOP WITH CHEESE. BAKE AT 400° FOR 10 MINUTES. ADD $\frac{1}{4}$ CUP PARSLEY, LEMON JUICE AND PEPPER.

Every single moment is bursting
with its own beauty.

LINGUINE WITH SHRIMP AND TOMATOES

4	OZS. LINGUINE
1	TBL. VEGETABLE OIL

1	CLOVE GARLIC, CHOPPED
2	TBLS. FINELY CHOPPED SHALLOTS
3	LARGE TOMATOES, COARSELY CHOPPED
$\frac{1}{4}$	TSP. DRIED BASIL
$\frac{1}{2}$	LB. SMALL OR MEDIUM SHRIMP
	(RAW, PEELED)
2	GREEN ONIONS, CHOPPED
	SALT AND FRESHLY GROUND PEPPER

IN A LARGE POT OF BOILING WATER, COOK LINGUINE UNTIL IT IS AL DENTE. DRAIN AND SET ASIDE, KEEPING WARM IN THE POT WITH A LITTLE WATER. MEANWHILE, IN A HEAVY FRYING PAN, HEAT THE OIL OVER MEDIUM HEAT. ADD THE GARLIC AND SHALLOTS AND COOK, STIRRING, FOR ABOUT 30 SECONDS. ADD THE TOMATOES AND BASIL AND COOK FOR 1 TO 2 MINUTES. STIR IN THE SHRIMP AND COOK UNTIL THEY ARE PINK. SPRINKLE THE SAUCE WITH GREEN ONIONS AND SEASON WITH SALT AND PEPPER. SERVE OVER HOT LINGUINE.

Time is the stuff life is made of.
Don't let it slip through your hands.

SEAFOOD PIZZA

1	12" BOBOLI PIZZA CRUST
$\frac{1}{2}$	CUP PESTO SAUCE (MORE IF DESIRED)
2/3	CUP MARINARA SAUCE, OR AS DESIRED

1	LB. SEAFOOD (SHRIMP, CRAB OR COMBINATION)
$\frac{3}{4}$	CUP SHREDDED MOZZARELLA CHEESE
$\frac{3}{4}$	CUP SHREDDED MONTERREY JACK CHEESE
	GARLIC SALT

BOIL SHRIMP IN SEASONED WATER UNTIL JUST COOKED AND TENDER, DRAIN AND SET ASIDE. SPREAD LAYER OF PESTO SAUCE OVER PIZZA CRUST. TOP WITH MARINARA SAUCE. LAYER WITH SEAFOOD AND CHEESES. SPRINKLE WITH GARLIC SALT PLACE ON UNGREASED COOKIE SHEET AND BAKE IN PREHEATED 450° OVEN UNTIL CHEESE IS MELTED.

Give someone's spirit wings, and their dreams will have a reason to take flight.

SHRIMP A LA FEIN

10	PEELED, RAW SHRIMP
2	GREEN ONIONS
	TONY CHACHERE'S
	GARLIC POWDER
	JUICE OF 1 LEMON
1	TBL. BUTTER
	TABASCO
	WORCESTERSHIRE SAUCE

PUT RAW SHRIMP IN A BOWL AND SEASON WITH SPRINKLE OF TONY CHACHERE'S AND

GARLIC POWDER. ADD DASH OF TABASCO,
WORCESTERSHIRE SAUCE AND LEMON JUICE.
COVER SHRIMP WITH PLASTIC WRAP AND PUT
THEM IN THE REFRIGERATOR FOR AT LEAST 30
MINUTES SO THAT THE SHRIMP ABSORB THE
SEASONINGS.

MELT BUTTER IN SAUCEPAN, ADD SHRIMP AND
GREEN ONIONS AND COOK FOR SEVERAL
MINUTES UNTIL SHRIMP TURN PINK AND ARE
COOKED THROUGH. SERVES 2

*Strength is born of love and nothing is
impossible to the believing heart.*

SHRIMP KABOBS WITH HONEY-MUSTARD GLAZE

¼	CUP HONEY
¼	CUP DIJON MUSTARD
2	TBLS. FRESH LEMON JUICE
	PINCH OF DRIED SAGE
24	LARGE UNCOOKED SHRIMP, PEELED, TAILS INTACT
4	RED BELL PEPPERS, CUT INTO 2" PIECES
4	YELLOW BELL PEPPERS, CUT INTO 2" PIECES
1	RED ONION, CUT INTO 1" PIECES
12	LARGE MUSHROOMS
12	CHERRY TOMATOES

12	BAMBOO SKEWERS, SOAKED 30 MINUTES IN WATER

MIX HONEY, DIJON MUSTARD, LEMON JUICE AND SAGE IN SMALL BOWL. ALTERNATE SHRIMP AND VEGETABLES ON BAMBOO SKEWERS. CAN BE MADE 8 HOURS AHEAD. LET HONEY-MUSTARD MIXTURE STAND AT ROOM TEMPERATURE, BUT COVER KABOBS AND CHILL.

HEAT GRILLING PIT TO MEDIUM-HIGH. BRUSH KABOBS WITH HONEY MUSTARD MIXTURE. GRILL UNTIL SHRIMP ARE COOKED THROUGH, BASTING OCCASIONALLY, ABOUT 3 MINUTES PER SIDE. TRANSFER TO PLATTER AND SERVE. SERVES 6

Life itself is the prize.

BARBECUED RED SNAPPER

1	RED SNAPPER
2	OR 3 PIECES OF SOAKED MESQUITE FOR THE COALS
2	STICKS BUTTER
¼	CUP FINELY CHOPPED PARSLEY
2	TO 3 PODS FINELY CHOPPED GARLIC
	PINCH OF SALT
	DASH OF PEPPER OR TO TASTE
1	TSP. FRESH ROSEMARY, MORE IF DESIRED
½	CUP DRY WHITE WINE

JUICE FROM A WHOLE LEMON, PLUS
EXTRA LEMON JUICE TO SPRINKLE OVER
FISH JUST BEFORE SERVING

CLEAN, SCALE AND REMOVE HEAD FROM FISH.
PLACE A SHEET OF ALUMINUM FOIL COVERING
THE GRILL ON YOUR BARBECUE PIT. HEAT GRILL
WITH A MEDIUM FIRE (ABOUT 375° TO 400°)
FOR APPROXIMATELY 20 MINUTES. PLACE 2 OR 3
PIECES OF SOAKED MESQUITE IN COALS JUST
BEFORE PUTTING FISH ON GRILL TO GIVE A
SLIGHT HINT OF MESQUITE. PLACE SNAPPER
ON HOT GRILL. COOK APPROXIMATELY 10
MINUTES PER SIDE FOR A 5 TO 8 LB. FISH AND
20 MINUTES PER SIDE FOR LARGER FISH.

AFTER COOKING THE FIRST SIDE, CAREFULLY
TURN FISH OVER USING TWO LARGE SPATULAS.
BE CAREFUL NOT TO TEAR THE FOIL. THE SKIN
WILL STICK TO THE FOIL AND LEAVE THE
WHITE MEAT EXPOSED.

IN A SAUCEPAN, COMBINE BUTTER, PARSLEY,
GARLIC, SALT, PEPPER, ROSEMARY, WHITE WINE
AND JUICE FROM ONE LEMON. SIMMER SAUCE,
BUT DO NOT BOIL.

BASTE THE EXPOSED SIDE WITH WARMED
SAUCE. REPEAT ONCE MORE WHILE COOKING.

WHEN SNAPPER IS FLAKY AND STILL MOIST,
REMOVE FROM GRILL USING SPATULAS.

REMAINING SKIN WILL STICK TO FOIL, GIVING
YOU A WHOLE SKINLESS FISH TO SERVE.

PLACE ON SERVING PLATTER AND POUR
REMAINING SAUCE OVER FISH. SPRINKLE
LIGHTLY WITH LEMON JUICE.

BROWNSVILLE SHRIMP

5	LBS. FRESH SHRIMP, PEELED
$\frac{1}{2}$	TSP. CAYENNE PEPPER
3	CLOVES GARLIC, CRUSHED
2	LEMONS, THINLY SLICED
2	CUPS BUTTER
$\frac{1}{2}$	CUP LEMON JUICE
$\frac{1}{4}$	CUP CHIVES, CHOPPED
1	TSP. SALT
2	OZS. TABASCO
	FILE' POWDER
	PAPRIKA

IN A LARGE, OBLONG BAKING DISH, ARRANGE A
LAYER OF SHRIMP. SPRINKLE HALF THE
CAYENNE AND HALF THE GARLIC OVER THE
SHRIMP. DUST WITH PAPRIKA AND FILE'
POWDER, AND ARRANGE HALF THE LEMON
SLICES OVER THE SHRIMP. ADD ANOTHER
LAYER OF SHRIMP AND REPEAT THE SAME
PROCEDURE.

COMBINE REMAINING INGREDIENTS IN A
LARGE SAUCEPAN AND SIMMER SLOWLY UNTIL

BUTTER IS MELTED. POUR BUTTER SAUCE OVER SHRIMP AND BAKE AT 350° FOR 20 MINUTES.

SERVE WITH PLENTY OF HOT FRENCH BREAD TO DIP IN SAUCE.

CATFISH COURTBOUILLON

SAUCE:

1	STALK CELERY, SLICED THIN
10	CLOVES GARLIC, MINCED
1	LARGE WHITE ONION, MINCED
1	GREEN PEPPER, MINCED
$\frac{1}{4}$	CUP BUTTER
4	LARGE WHOLE TOMATOES, DICED
1	CUP DRY WHITE WINE
1	CUP FISH STOCK
	OR $\frac{1}{2}$ CUP BOTTLED CLAM JUICE
$\frac{1}{2}$	TSP. WHITE PEPPER
	DASH OF TABASCO

SAUTE CELERY, GARLIC, ONION AND GREEN PEPPER IN THE BUTTER UNTIL THE VEGETABLES ARE JUST LIMP. ADD THE TOMATOES, WINE AND FISH STOCK. STIR IN THE PEPPER. BRING TO A BOIL, REDUCE HEAT AND SIMMER UNCOVERED FOR 20 TO 30 MINUTES TO BLEND THE SAUCE AND THICKEN THE SAUCE SLIGHTLY.

PREPARE THE CATFISH TO YOUR LIKING, BROIL, FRY, GRILL, WHATEVER YOU CHOOSE.

SPOON A GOOD PORTION OF THE
COURTBOUILLON SAUCE ON EACH OF SIX WARM
PLATES. PUT A SERVING OF RICE ON ONE SIDE
AND A CATFISH FILLET ON THE OTHER AND
SERVE. MAKES ENOUGH SAUCE FOR SIX
FILLETS.

Life's moments are woven into songs and silences
only the heart can hear.

CATFISH, OYSTER AND BLACK BEAN STEW

WHILE THE LIST OF INGREDIENTS IS LONG,
THIS SAVORY STEW IS QUICK AND EASY TO
MAKE. PLUS, IT TASTES BETTER IF MADE ONE
DAY IN ADVANCE. SIMPLY ADD THE SEAFOOD
AFTER YOU REHEAT IT.

2	TBLS. CORN OIL
1	CUP RED BELL PEPPER, CHOPPED
$1\frac{1}{2}$	CUPS SHALLOTS, MINCED
$1\frac{1}{2}$	TBLS. GARLIC, MINCED
3	CUPS CLAM JUICE OR CHICKEN BROTH (FAT SKIMMED)
3	TBLS. WORCESTERSHIRE SAUCE
$\frac{1}{2}$	TSP. DRIED THYME
$\frac{1}{2}$	TSP. DRIED BASIL
$\frac{1}{4}$	TO $\frac{1}{2}$ TSP. HOT RED PEPPER FLAKES
$\frac{1}{2}$	TSP. SALT
$\frac{1}{2}$	CUP FRESH PARSLEY, MINCED

½	CUP TOMATO PASTE
1	CUP COOKED BLACK BEANS (2 15 OZ.) CANS, DRAINED, RINSED
½	10 OZ. PKG. FROZEN OKRA (THAWED, CUT INTO ½" ROUNDS)
1	LB. FARM RAISED CATFISH FILLETS, CUT INTO ¾" CUBES
1	8 OZ. CONTAINER SHUCKED OYSTERS (DRAINED)
½	TSP. WHITE PEPPER
2/3	CUP COOKED RICE

IN A HEAVY 5 QT. POT, HEAT OIL ON MEDIUM HEAT UNTIL HOT. ADD THE PEPPERS, SHALLOTS AND GARLIC. SAUTE UNTIL SOFTENED, ABOUT 10 MINUTES, STIRRING. STIR IN CLAM JUICE OR BROTH, WORCESTERSHIRE SAUCE, THYME, BASIL, RED PEPPER FLAKES, SALT AND PARSLEY. WHISK IN TOMATO PASTE. ADD BEANS AND OKRA AND SIMMER, UNCOVERED ON MEDIUM HEAT FOR 10 MINUTES, STIRRING. ADD CATFISH AND OYSTERS AND SIMMER UNTIL THE CATFISH IS BARELY OPAQUE AND OYSTERS PLUMP, ABOUT 3 MINUTES. SPOON RICE INTO SOUP BOWLS AND LADLE SOUP ON TOP. SERVES 4 TO 6

MARYLAND CRAB CAKES

1	EGG
¼	CUP MILK
3	TBLS. MAYONNAISE
1	TBL. ALL PURPOSE FLOUR
1	TBL. WORCESTERSHIRE SAUCE
1	TSP. PREPARED MUSTARD
1	TSP. SALT
¼	TSP. PEPPER
1	LB. COOKED CRAB MEAT OR 3 CANS (6 OZ. EACH), DRAINED, FLAKED & CARTILAGE REMOVED
½	CUP DRY BREAD CRUMBS
2	TBLS. BUTTER

IN A LARGE BOWL, WHISK TOGETHER THE FIRST 8 INGREDIENTS. FOLD IN CRAB. PLACE THE BREAD CRUMBS IN A SHALLOW DISH. DROP ⅓ CUP CRAB MIXTURE INTO CRUMBS. SHAPE INTO A ¾" PATTY. CAREFULLY TURN TO COAT. REPEAT WITH REMAINING CRAB MIXTURE.

IN A SKILLET, COOK PATTIES IN BUTTER FOR 3 MINUTES ON EACH SIDE OR UNTIL GOLDEN BROWN. YIELDS 6 PATTIES

MOM'S PAN-FRIED CATFISH

4	TO 6 SMALL CATFISH FILLETS
½	CUP FLOUR
1	TSP. SALT
¼	TSP. COARSE BLACK PEPPER
2	EGGS, SLIGHTLY BEATEN
2	TBLS. WATER
1	CUP CORNMEAL
	OIL FOR FRYING

RINSE THE CATFISH UNDER COLD WATER AND PAT DRY WITH PAPER TOWELS. MIX THE FLOUR, SALT AND PEPPER TOGETHER IN A PAPER SACK. ADD THE FISH AND SHAKE TO DUST EACH LIGHTLY WITH SEASONED FLOUR. SHAKE OFF THE EXCESS.

DIP THE FISH IN THE EGG BEATEN WITH THE WATER AND THEN ROLL IN CORNMEAL TO COAT. HEAT ¼" OF OIL IN A LARGE HEAVY SKILLET. ADD THE CATFISH AND BROWN NICELY ON BOTH SIDES. THIS WILL TAKE ONLY A MINUTE OR TWO ON EACH SIDE. REMOVE TO PAPER TOWELS TO DRAIN. SERVES 4 TO 6

OYSTER LOVER'S PIE

1	9" UNBAKED PIE CRUST
1	STICK BUTTER
¾	CUP FLOUR
1½	PINTS OYSTERS, DRAIN AND RESERVE LIQUOR
1	CLOVE GARLIC, CHOPPED
⅓	CUP CHOPPED CELERY
⅓	CUP CHOPPED PARSLEY
½	CUP CHOPPED GREEN ONIONS
	SALT, BLACK PEPPER AND RED PEPPER TO TASTE

MELT BUTTER IN SKILLET. ADD FLOUR TO THE BUTTER AND STIR CONSTANTLY UNTIL MIXTURE IS GOLDEN BROWN, ABOUT THE COLOR OF A PAPER SACK. ADD THE DRAINED OYSTERS, GARLIC, CELERY, PARSLEY AND GREEN ONIONS. SEASON TO TASTE. COOK ONLY ABOUT 5 MINUTES OR UNTIL EDGES OF OYSTERS CURL. REMOVE FROM HEAT AND STIR IN ABOUT ⅓ CUP OF THE OYSTER LIQUOR. IF TOO THICK, ADD A LITTLE MORE. AS THE PIE BAKES, THE OYSTERS THIN THE FILLING. CHECK FOR SEASONING. THIS NEEDS TO BE SPICY. POUR INTO UNBAKED PIE CRUST. BAKE IN 350° OVEN FOR 30 TO 40 MINUTES OR UNTIL CRUST IS GOLDEN BROWN.

Pasta & Rice

ITALIAN SAUSAGE PASTA SAUCE

1	LB. ITALIAN SAUSAGE, CASING REMOVED
½	CUP CHOPPED ONION
⅓	CUP CHOPPED ITALIAN PARSLEY
⅓	CUP CHOPPED BASIL
2	TBLS. GARLIC, MINCED
1	28 OZ. CAN CRUSHED TOMATOES
8	OZS. SLICED FRESH MUSHROOMS
1	TBL. SUGAR
	SALT AND PEPPER TO TASTE
	ROMANO OR PARMESAN CHEESE
	TO TASTE
	COOKED PASTA

IN LARGE SAUCEPAN, BROWN SAUSAGE. WHEN SAUSAGE IS ALMOST BROWNED, ADD THE ONION, PARSLEY, BASIL AND GARLIC. COOK UNTIL ONION IS TENDER. ADD TOMATOES, MUSHROOMS AND SUGAR. MIX WELL AND CONTINUE COOKING ABOUT 15 MINUTES OR UNTIL MUSHROOMS ARE COOKED. STIR OCCASIONALLY. CHECK SEASONING. SERVES 6

PASTA WITH EGGPLANT AND BASIL

1	EGGPLANT
1	CLOVE GARLIC
10	RIPE, PEELED AND SEEDED TOMATOES
1	LB. PENNE PASTA, BOILED
2	+1 OZS. GRATED AGED RICOTTA
10	BASIL LEAVES

         SALT AND PEPPER TO TASTE
7   TBLS. OLIVE OIL

CUT EGGPLANT INTO SLICES, SALT AND PLACE
UNDER A WEIGHTED OBJECT FOR ONE HOUR TO
ELIMINATE BITTER TASTE FROM EGGPLANT.

BROWN GARLIC IN 3 TBLS. OLIVE OIL, ADD
TOMATOES. BRING TO A SIMMER OVER MEDIUM
HEAT AND CONTINUE COOKING, STIRRING
OCCASIONALLY UNTIL TOMATOES HAVE
REDUCED BY ONE THIRD. ADD A PINCH OF SALT
AND PEPPER AND REMOVE FROM HEAT.

WASH AND PAT EGGPLANT DRY WITH PAPER
TOWEL. HEAT 4 TBLS. OLIVE OIL UNTIL HOT,
ADD EGGPLANT AND FRY UNTIL BROWN.
REMOVE AND PLACE ON TOWEL TO DRAIN. CHOP
EGGPLANT INTO CHUNKS.

COOK PASTA IN BOILING, SALTED WATER UNTIL
AL DENTE. STRAIN AND ADD HALF OF THE
TOMATO SAUCE AND ALL OF THE EGGPLANT,
PLUS 5 BASIL LEAVES. ADD PASTA TO SAUCE
POT AND HEAT. ADD MORE SALT AND PEPPER IF
NEEDED.

PLACE IN SERVING DISH AND ADD REMAINING
TOMATO SAUCE ON TOP. SPRINKLE RICOTTA
AND THE REMAINING BASIL ON TOP AND SERVE.

SPAGHETTI SAUCE

4	TBLS. OLIVE OIL
2	LARGE ONIONS, CHOPPED
2	GREEN ONIONS, CHOPPED
1	HEAD GARLIC, CHOPPED
2	STALKS CELERY, CHOPPED
1	SMALL BELL PEPPER, CHOPPED
1	LARGE FENNEL BULB, CHOPPED
1	LARGE CAN TOMATOES, CHOPPED
1	CAN RO-TEL TOMATOES
2	+1 SMALL CANS TOMATO PASTE
3	LARGE CANS TOMATO SAUCE
1	BAY LEAF
2	TBLS. FRESH BASIL
2	TSPS. DRIED OREGANO
3	+2 CUPS WATER
2	DOZEN EGGS
2	LBS. SPAGHETTI
1	CUP DRIED BREAD CRUMBS
½	CUP ROMANO CHEESE

SAUTE ONION, GREEN ONION, GARLIC, CELERY, BELL PEPPER AND FENNEL IN OLIVE OIL UNTIL SOFTENED. ADD TOMATOES, RO-TEL TOMATOES, TOMATO SAUCE AND TOMATO PASTE AND COOK FOR ABOUT 3 OR 4 MINUTES.

ADD WATER AND SEASONINGS AND COOK FOR
ABOUT 3 HOURS UNTIL THICK. BOIL EGGS, PEEL
AND ADD TO THE TOMATO GRAVY.
COOK SPAGHETTI, DRAIN AND SERVE WITH THE
TOMATO AND EGG GRAVY.

TOAST BREAD CRUMBS IN AN IRON SKILLET
UNTIL GOLDEN BROWN. MIX WITH ROMANO
CHEESE AND SERVE BREAD CRUMBS ON TOP OF
THE SPAGHETTI. SERVES 12

On this day celebrate the gifts within you.

TEX-MEX MACARONI & CHEESE

8	OZS. COOKED PENNE PASTA
1	CUP (4 OZ.) SHREDDED MONTERREY JACK CHEESE
$\frac{1}{2}$	CUP FINELY CHOPPED RED OR GREEN PEPPER
1	OR 2 JALAPENO PEPPERS, FINELY CHOPPED
$\frac{1}{2}$	CUP SOUR CREAM
$\frac{1}{2}$	CUP MILK
2	TSPS. FINELY MINCED ONION OR 1 TSP. ONION POWDER
$\frac{3}{4}$	TSP. GROUND CUMIN, DIVIDED
$\frac{1}{2}$	TSP. SALT
1	CUP CHOPPED, SEEDED, PLUM TOMATOES
$\frac{1}{2}$	CUP TOASTED WHEAT GERM
2	TBLS. DRY BREAD CRUMBS

| 3 | TBLS. VEGETABLE OIL SPREAD, MELTED |

HEAT OVEN TO 300°. LIGHTLY SPRAY 9" SQUARE BAKING DISH WITH NONSTICK VEGETABLE COOKING SPRAY.

IN LARGE BOWL, COMBINE DRAINED, COOKED PASTA, CHEESE, AND PEPPERS. SPOON INTO BAKING DISH.

IN SMALL BOWL, COMBINE SOUR CREAM, MILK, ONIONS OR ONION POWDER, ½ TSP. CUMIN AND SALT, MIX WELL. POUR SAUCE OVER PASTA MIXTURE. SPOON CHOPPED TOMATOES EVENLY OVER TOP. IN SMALL BOWL, COMBINE WHEAT GERM, BREAD CRUMBS, REMAINING ¼ TSP. CUMIN AND VEGETABLE OIL SPREAD. MIX WELL. SPRINKLE OVER TOMATOES. MAKES 5 SERVINGS

Carpe diem - Seize the day

TOSSED MUSHROOM LASAGNA

6	OZS. LASAGNA NOODLES, BROKEN INTO THIRDS (ABOUT 3½ CUPS)
2	TBLS. VEGETABLE OIL
1	LB. FRESH WHITE MUSHROOMS, SLICED
1½	TSPS. ITALIAN SEASONING
½	TSP. MINCED GARLIC
2	CUPS PREPARED SPAGHETTI SAUCE

1	16 OZ. PKG. FROZEN LARGE CUT MIXED VEGETABLES
$\frac{1}{4}$	CUP GRATED PARMESAN CHEESE
1	CUP SHREDDED MOZZARELLA CHEESE

PREPARE LASAGNA AS LABEL DIRECTS. DRAIN. PLACE IN A LARGE SERVING BOWL. COVER TO KEEP WARM.

MEANWHILE, IN A LARGE SKILLET OVER MEDIUM-HIGH HEAT, HEAT OIL UNTIL HOT. ADD MUSHROOMS, ITALIAN SEASONING AND GARLIC. COOK, STIRRING OCCASIONALLY, UNTIL MUSHROOMS ARE TENDER, ABOUT 6 MINUTES. STIR IN SPAGHETTI SAUCE AND FROZEN VEGETABLES. COOK UNCOVERED, OVER MEDIUM HEAT UNTIL MIXTURE IS HOT, ABOUT 5 MINUTES, STIRRING OCCASIONALLY. ADD MUSHROOM MIXTURE AND PARMESAN CHEESE TO LASAGNA IN SERVING BOWL. TOSS GENTLY. SPRINKLE WITH MOZZARELLA CHEESE. SERVE IMMEDIATELY. TOP EACH PORTION WITH A SPOONFUL OF RICOTTA CHEESE, IF DESIRED. MAKES 4 SERVINGS

AUTUMN PASTA WITH SMOKED CHEESE

1/4	CUP (1/2 STICK) BUTTER
1 1/2	CUPS BROCCOLI FLORETS
1	CUP FRESHLY SLICED MUSHROOMS
2/3	CUP JULIENNE-CUT RAW SWEET POTATO
3	TBLS. CHOPPED SHALLOTS
2	TBLS. CHOPPED FRESH OREGANO OR 1 TSP. DRIED OREGANO
1	CUP WHIPPING CREAM
1/8	TSP. PEPPER
8	OZ. FETTUCCINE OR WHOLE-WHEAT FETTUCCINE NOODLES
1/2	CUP ROASTED RED PEPPERS, CUT INTO STRIPS
1 1/2	CUPS (6 OZ.) SHREDDED SMOKED GOUDA CHEESE
1/4	CUP COARSELY CHOPPED WALNUTS

MELT BUTTER IN A LARGE SKILLET. ADD BROCCOLI, MUSHROOMS, SWEET POTATOES, SHALLOTS AND OREGANO. SAUTE UNTIL VEGETABLES ARE TENDER-CRISP, ABOUT 8 MINUTES. STIR IN CREAM AND PEPPER. BRING

TO A SIMMERING POINT. REDUCE CREAM
SLIGHTLY, STIRRING CONSTANTLY. (CREAM
SHOULD CLING TO VEGETABLES).

MEANWHILE, COOK PASTA ACCORDING TO
PACKAGE DIRECTIONS. RINSE AND DRAIN.
ADD COOKED PASTA TO VEGETABLE MIXTURE.
TOSS GENTLY TO COMBINE. STIR IN RED
PEPPERS. SPRINKLE CHEESE AND WALNUTS
OVER TOP.

GARLIC & BASIL "RAW" SAUCE

PASTA:

LINGUINE, FETTUCCINE OR PASTA OF
YOUR CHOICE ($\frac{3}{4}$ LB. DRIED OR 1 LB.
FRESH)

SAUCE:

2	ROMA TOMATOES, FINELY DICED
$\frac{1}{2}$	TSP. SALT, OR TO TASTE
20	TO 25 FRESH BASIL LEAVES, CHIFFONADE*
$1\frac{1}{2}$	TBLS. OLIVE OIL, DIVIDED
3	TO 4 CLOVES GARLIC, MINCED
$\frac{1}{4}$	CUP FRESHLY GRATED PARMESAN
2	TBLS. ROASTED PINE NUTS (OPTIONAL)

PREPARE TOMATOES AND BASIL AS SPECIFIED.
PLACE TOMATOES IN A BOWL. SALT TO TASTE.
ADD BASIL AND TOSS. DRIZZLE OVER $\frac{1}{2}$ TBL.

OLIVE OIL, TOSS GENTLY, COVER AND SET
ASIDE. INGREDIENTS MAY BE PREPARED UP TO 8
HOURS IN ADVANCE IF REFRIGERATED.

COOK PASTA IN PLENTLY OF RAPIDLY BOILING
SALTED WATER UNTIL AL DENTE. DRAIN AND
PLACE IN A LARGE, SHALLOW SERVING BOWL.
DRIZZLE 1 TBL. OLIVE OIL AND TOSS TO COAT
PASTA. ADD GARLIC AND TOSS TO EVENLY
DISTRIBUTE GARLIC. ADD TOMATO MIXTURE
AND TOSS AGAIN.

SERVE IMMEDIATELY, SPRINKLING A LITTLE
PARMESAN AND SOME PINE NUTS OVER EACH
DISH AT THE TABLE OR ALLOW TO COOL TO
ROOM TEMPERATURE AND SERVE AS A PASTA
SALAD OR AT A PICNIC. SERVES 4

*TO CUT BASIL LEAVES INTO CHIFFONADE
STRIPS, STACK THE LEAVES ON TOP OF EACH
OTHER, ROLL INTO A TIGHT "CIGAR" AND SLICE
INTO $\frac{1}{4}$" WIDE STRIPS WITH A SHARP KNIFE.

The heart is a wondrous and poetic spirit.

PENNE PASTA WITH SPINACH AND GARLIC

6	OZ. PENNE OR FLAVORED PENNE PASTA, UNCOOKED
2	TBLS. PINE NUTS
3	TBLS. BUTTER

½	CUP SLICED SHALLOTS OR LEEKS
4	CLOVES GARLIC, MINCED
½	CUP CANNED CHICKEN BROTH
¼	TSP. SALT
¼	TSP. FRESHLY GROUND BLACK PEPPER
5	CUPS PACKED FRESH SPINACH (6 OZ.)
¼	CUP FRESHLY GRATED PARMESAN OR ASIAGO CHEESE

PREHEAT OVEN TO 350°. COOK PASTA AL DENTE.

WHILE PASTA IS COOKING, TOAST PINE NUTS ON COOKIE SHEET IN PREHEATED OVEN FOR 5 TO 7 MINUTES. SET ASIDE.
MELT BUTTER IN LARGE SKILLET OVER MEDIUM HEAT. ADD SHALLOTS OR LEEKS AND COOK FOR 5 MINUTES, STIRRING OCCASIONALLY. ADD GARLIC. COOK 3 MORE MINUTES, STIRRING OCCASIONALLY. ADD BROTH, SALT AND PEPPER, SIMMER UNCOVERED FOR 5 MINUTES.

DISCARD STEMS FROM SPINACH. TEAR ANY LARGE LEAVES IN HALF. DRAIN PASTA AND RETURN TO POT. ADD SPINACH. TOSS WELL. ADD BUTTER MIXTURE. TOSS AGAIN.

TRANSFER TO TWO WARMED SERVING PLATES AND SPRINKLE WITH PINE NUTS. SPRINKLE WITH FRESHLY GRATED CHEESE, IF DESIRED. MAKES 2 SERVINGS

SUPER SHELLS

1	LB. LEAN GROUND BEEF
1	8 OZ. PKG. FROZEN CHOPPED SPINACH (THAWED)
1	16 OZ. CONTAINER LOW FAT COTTAGE CHEESE
1	EGG
1	TSP. CHOPPED GARLIC
20	JUMBO PASTA SHELLS
1	28 OZ. JAR OF YOUR FAVORITE SPAGHETTI SAUCE
6	OZS. SHREDDED MOZZARELLA CHEESE

PREHEAT OVEN TO 400°. COOK PASTA SHELLS IN BOILING WATER AS DIRECTED ON THE BOX. DRAIN AND RINSE WITH COLD WATER. BROWN GROUND BEEF AND DRAIN.

COMBINE HALF OF THE GROUND BEEF, SPINACH, COTTAGE CHEESE, EGG AND GARLIC IN A MIXING BOWL. USE THIS MIXTURE TO LIBERALLY STUFF THE PASTA SHELLS. PLACE THE STUFFED SHELLS IN A 13"x9" BAKING DISH.

COMBINE THE REMAINING GROUND BEEF AND SPAGHETTI SAUCE AND POUR OVER THE STUFFED SHELLS. SPRINKLE MOZZARELLA CHEESE OVER SHELLS. REMOVE COVER AND COOK FOR 8 TO 10 MINUTES UNTIL CHEESE IS LIGHTLY BROWNED.

TORTELLINI WITH MUSHROOM AND GARLIC SAUCE

2	9 OZ. PKGS. CHEESE-FILLED TORTELLINI
2	TBLS. OLIVE OIL
1	LB. FRESH WHITE MUSHROOMS, SLICED (ABOUT 5 CUPS)
1	TSP. MINCED GARLIC
1	10 OZ. PKG. FROZEN GREEN PEAS IN BUTTER SAUCE, SLIGHTLY DEFROSTED
1	7 OZ. JAR ROASTED RED PEPPERS, DICED
$\frac{3}{4}$	TSP. SALT
$\frac{1}{8}$	TSP. GROUND BLACK PEPPER

COOK TORTELLINI AL DENTE. DRAIN. PLACE IN A LARGE SERVING BOWL. COVER TO KEEP WARM.

MEANWHILE, IN A LARGE NON-STICK SKILLET HEAT OIL UNTIL HOT. ADD MUSHROOMS AND GARLIC. COOK STIRRING FREQUENTLY, UNTIL TENDER, ABOUT 6 MINUTES. ADD PEAS, ROASTED PEPPERS, SALT AND BLACK PEPPER. COOK, STIRRING OCCASIONALLY, UNTIL HEATED THROUGH, 2 TO 3 MINUTES. SPOON OVER HOT TORTELLINI. SPRINKLE WITH GRATED PARMESAN CHEESE, IF DESIRED. MAKES 6 SERVINGS

Cakes & Pies

CHESS SQUARES

1	BOX YELLOW CAKE MIX
1	EGG
1	STICK BUTTER
1	TBL. WATER

MIX TOGETHER AND PRESS INTO A WIDE, FLAT PAN.

1	8 OZ. PACKAGE CREAM CHEESE
2	EGGS
2	TBL. VANILLA
1	BOX POWDERED SUGAR

MIX CREAM CHEESE AND POWDERED SUGAR. ADD EGGS ONE AT A TIME. ADD VANILLA. POUR OVER CRUST. BAKE AT 350° FOR ABOUT 35 MINUTES.

Heaven smiles softly
and hears love's every wish.

ALMOND JOY CAKE

1	BOX DEVIL'S FOOD CAKE MIX WITH PUDDING
1	CUP PET MILK
1	CUP SUGAR
24	LARGE MARSHMALLOWS

14   OZS. FLAKED COCONUT
         SLICED ALMONDS
1½   CUPS SUGAR
½   CUP PET MILK
1   STICK BUTTER
1½   CUPS CHOCOLATE CHIPS

MIX CAKE ACCORDING TO PACKAGE DIRECTIONS.
POUR BATTER INTO A 10"x15" PAN SPRAYED
WITH PAM. BAKE IN A PREHEATED 400° OVEN
FOR 20 MINUTES.

MEANWHILE, MELT 1 CUP PET MILK, 1 CUP SUGAR
AND THE 24 MARSHMALLOWS IN A SAUCE PAN
OVER LOW HEAT UNTIL MELTED. REMOVE FROM
HEAT AND ADD THE COCONUT, MIX WELL AND
WHEN CAKE COMES OUT OF THE OVEN, POUR
MIXTURE OVER THE HOT CAKE. SPRINKLE
ALMONDS OVER COCONUT LAYER.

HEAT UNTIL MELTED 1½ CUPS SUGAR, ½ CUP PET
MILK AND 1 STICK BUTTER. ADD THE 1½ CUPS
CHOCOLATE CHIPS, STIR UNTIL WELL BLENDED,
THEN POUR OVER ALMONDS. COOL BEFORE
SLICING.

ALMOND SOUR CREAM CAKE

2	EGGS
2/3	CUP LIGHT SOUR CREAM
1	TSP. ALMOND EXTRACT
$\frac{1}{4}$	TSP. VANILLA EXTRACT
1 2/3	CUPS CAKE FLOUR, SIFTED
1	CUP SUGAR
$\frac{1}{2}$	TSP. BAKING POWDER
$\frac{1}{2}$	TSP. BAKING SODA
1/3	CUP SLICED ALMONDS
$\frac{1}{2}$	TSP. SALT
$\frac{3}{4}$	CUP UNSALTED BUTTER, SOFTENED
1	LB. SWEETENED FROZEN RASBERRIES, THAWED

PREHEAT OVEN TO 350°. BUTTER AND FLOUR AN 8" BAKING PAN. LINE BOTTOM WITH WAX PAPER AND SET ASIDE. COMBINE EGGS, 3 TBLS. SOUR CREAM, ALMOND EXTRACT, AND VANILLA IN A MIXING BOWL. BEAT WITH AN ELECTRIC MIXER UNTIL MIXED THOROUGHLY. SET ASIDE.

COMBINE NEXT 6 INGREDIENTS IN ANOTHER BOWL. BEAT WITH AN ELECTRIC MIXER AT LOW SPEED. ADD BUTTER AND REMAINING SOUR CREAM. BEAT UNTIL DRY INGREDIENTS ARE MOISTENED. INCREASE SPEED TO MEDIUM AND BEAT 1$\frac{1}{2}$ MINUTES. GRADUALLY ADD EGG MIXTURE, ONE THIRD AT A TIME. MIX THOROUGHLY. TRANSFER BATTER TO BAKING

PAN. SMOOTH SURFACE WITH A SPATULA. BAKE
35 TO 40 MINUTES OR UNTIL A TESTER COMES
OUT CLEAN WHEN INSERTED IN CENTER. COOL
CAKE ON A WIRE RACK 10 MINUTES. LOOSEN
EDGES OF CAKE WITH A KNIFE. TRANSFER CAKE
TO A PLATTER. SERVE WITH RASBERRIES.

*When we believe in ourselves we can make
anything happen.*

APPLE UPSIDE-DOWN CAKE

¼	CUP BUTTER
3	CUPS PEELED APPLE SLICES, GRANNY SMITH OR GOLDEN DELICIOUS
½	CUP BROWN SUGAR
1½	CUPS SELF-RISING FLOUR
½	CUP GRANULATED SUGAR
½	CUP MELTED BUTTER
1	EGG, BEATEN
½	CUP MILK
1	TSP. VANILLA

HEAT OVEN TO 375°. MELT ¼ CUP BUTTER IN 10"
CAST IRON SKILLET OVER MEDIUM HEAT. STIR
IN APPLES AND COOK JUST UNTIL TENDER,
ABOUT 5 MINUTES. DO NOT OVERCOOK. STIR
IN BROWN SUGAR AND SET ASIDE.

IN MEDIUM BOWL, COMBINE FLOUR AND SUGAR.
STIR IN ½ CUP MELTED BUTTER, EGG, MILK AND
VANILLA, BLEND UNTIL SMOOTH.

POUR BATTER OVER APPLES IN SKILLET,
SPREADING BATTER EVENLY TO THE EDGES.
BAKE AT 375° FOR 20 TO 25 MINUTES OR UNTIL
GOLDEN BROWN. REMOVE FROM OVEN AND
COOL 2 TO 3 MINUTES, TURN OUT ONTO
PLATTER. SERVE WARM OR AT ROOM
TEMPERATURE. SERVES 8

Some people move our souls to dance.

BANANAS FOSTER BREAD PUDDING

BREAD PUDDING:

15	EGGS
2	QTS. HEAVY CREAM
2	LBS. SUGAR
	STALE BREAD, ENOUGH TO FILL A 6"x12" PAN
2	BANANAS
$\frac{1}{2}$	LB. BROWN SUGAR
$\frac{1}{4}$	LB. WHITE SUGAR
$\frac{1}{2}$	LB. UNSALTED BUTTER, SOFTENED

MIX EGGS, HEAVY CREAM AND SUGAR WELL AND
SET ASIDE. PEEL AND SLICE BANANAS INTO
THE PAN WITH BREAD. POUR EGG MIXTURE
OVER STALE BREAD. PRESS DOWN BREAD SO ALL
OF BREAD IS COMPLETELY SATURATED. COVER

ENTIRE TOP WITH MIXTURE OF BROWN AND
WHITE SUGARS. BREAK UP BUTTER INTO SMALL
CHUNKS AND SCATTER OVER SUGAR. BAKE
UNCOVERED AT 250° UNTIL CENTER IS FIRM.
SERVE WITH SAUCE.

SAUCE:

1	QT. CREAM
$\frac{1}{2}$	CUP SUGAR
15	EGG YOLKS
1	VANILLA BEAN, SPLIT LENGTHWISE
	RUM

SCALD CREAM AND $\frac{1}{4}$ CUP OF THE SUGAR WITH
VANILLA BEAN. BEAT REMAINING SUGAR AND
EGG YOLKS TO RIBBON STAGE (PALE AND
FOAMY). WHILE WHISKING, TEMPER EGGS BY
SLOWLY ADDING HALF OF THE SCALDED CREAM.

RETURN EGG/CREAM MIXTURE TO PAN WITH
HOT CREAM. COOK UNTIL DESIRED
CONSISTENCY OVER LOW HEAT. PULL OFF HEAT
AND POUR INTO SHALLOW PAN TO COOL. WHEN
COOL, ADD RUM TO TASTE. SERVES 8 TO 10

The world needs the gifts you bring.

BLACK WALNUT CAKE

½	CUP BUTTER, SOFTENED
½	CUP SHORTENING
2	CUPS SUGAR
5	EGGS, SEPARATED
1	CUP BUTTERMILK
1	TSP. SODA
2	CUPS ALL PURPOSE FLOUR
1	TSP. VANILLA EXTRACT
1½	CUPS CHOPPED BLACK WALNUTS
1	3 OZ. CAN FLAKED COCONUT
½	TSP. CREAM OF TARTAR
	CREAM CHEESE FROSTING
	CHOPPED BLACK WALNUTS, FOR GARNISH

CREAM BUTTER AND SHORTENING. GRADUALLY ADD SUGAR, BEATING UNTIL LIGHT AND FLUFFY UNTIL SUGAR IS DISSOLVED. ADD EGG YOLKS, BEATING WELL.

COMBINE BUTTERMILK AND SODA. STIR UNTIL SODA DISSOLVES. ADD FLOUR TO CREAMED MIXTURE ALTERNATIVELY WITH BUTTERMILK MIXTURE, BEGINNING AND ENDING WITH FLOUR. STIR IN VANILLA. ADD 1½ CUPS WALNUTS AND COCONUT, STIRRING WELL.

BEAT EGG WHITES (AT ROOM TEMPERATURE)
WITH CREAM OF TARTAR UNTIL STIFF PEAKS
FORM. FOLD EGG WHITES INTO BATTER.
POUR BATTER INTO 3 GREASED AND FLOURED 9"
ROUND CAKE PANS. BAKE AT 350° FOR 30
MINUTES OR UNTIL CAKE TESTS DONE. COOL
LAYERS IN PANS 10 MINUTES. REMOVE FROM
PANS, AND COOL COMPLETELY. FROST WITH
CREAM CHEESE FROSTING. SPRINKLE
REMAINING WALNUTS ON TOP OF CAKE. MAKES
ONE 9" LAYER CAKE.

Spring is a time of beginnings, a time of celebration and joy, a time of love and miracles.

CREAM CHEESE FROSTING

$\frac{3}{4}$	CUP BUTTER, SOFTENED
1	8 OZ. PKG. CREAM CHEESE, SOFTENED
1	3 OZ. PKG. CREAM CHEESE, SOFTENED
$6\frac{3}{4}$	CUPS SIFTED POWDERED SUGAR
$1\frac{1}{2}$	TSPS. VANILLA EXTRACT

CREAM BUTTER AND CREAM CHEESE, GRADUALLY
ADD SUGAR, BEATING UNTIL LIGHT AND FLUFFY.
STIR IN VANILLA. MAKES ENOUGH FOR ONE
CAKE.

BREAD PUDDING

12	SLICES BREAD
2	TBLS. BUTTER
3	EGGS
$2\frac{1}{4}$	CUPS MILK
2	TBLS. CINNAMON
2	CUPS SUGAR
2	TBLS. VANILLA
$\frac{1}{2}$	CUP RAISINS
1	8 OZ. CAN FRUIT COCKTAIL, DRAINED

SET OVEN AT 250°. PLACE BREAD SLICES ON
SHEET PAN AND TOAST IN OVEN UNTIL THE
BREAD TURNS LIGHT BROWN. TURN BREAD AND
TOAST OTHER SIDE. LEAVE OVEN AT 250°. USE
A KNIFE TO CUT TOASTED BREAD INTO
QUARTERS. SET ASIDE.

IN A LARGE, STAINLESS STEEL BOWL, MIX 2
CUPS SUGAR AND $1\frac{1}{2}$ TBLS. CINNAMON.

IN A SMALL BOWL, SLIGHTLY BEAT 3 EGGS
WITH A WIRE WHIP. ADD $2\frac{1}{4}$ CUPS MILK AND
BEAT UNTIL FOAMY. BLEND IN $1\frac{1}{2}$ TBLS.
VANILLA EXTRACT AND IN A LARGE BOWL, ADD
EGG MIXTURE TO SUGAR. ADD TOASTED BREAD
QUARTERS TO MIXTURE AND ALLOW TO SOAK 5

MINUTES. ADD DRAINED FRUIT COCKTAIL AND
RAISINS. MIX WELL.

PUT $\frac{3}{4}$ TBLS. OF MELTED BUTTER INTO A
SPRINGFORM PAN AND SPREAD THE BOTTOM
AND SIDES WITH PASTRY BRUSH. POUR BREAD
MIXTURE INTO THE SPRINGFORM PAN. PAT
DOWN ANY RAISINS OR FRUIT COCKTAIL,
MAKING SURE THAT BOTH ARE PRESSED INTO
THE PUDDING. PLACE THE PUDDING IN THE
OVEN SET AT 250°. BAKE $1\frac{3}{4}$ TO 2 HOURS OR
UNTIL THE MIDDLE OF THE BREAD PUDDING
HAS RISEN. ALLOW 5" CLEARANCE ABOVE PAN
TO RACK ABOVE. REMOVE FROM OVEN. USE A
PASTRY BRUSH TO TOP WITH $\frac{3}{4}$ TBLS. BUTTER.
ALLOW TO COOL. SERVES 8

BREAD PUDDING WITH RUM SAUCE

1	QT. MILK
3	CUPS SUGAR (2 CUPS CAN BE USED)
4	EGGS, SLIGHTLY BEATEN
$\frac{1}{4}$	CUP VANILLA EXTRACT
1	STICK BUTTER, MELTED
1	LOAF FRENCH BREAD
	(DAY OLD BREAD PREFERABLE)

MIX FIRST 5 INGREDIENTS TOGETHER.

BREAK BREAD INTO 2" PIECES, PLACE INTO
LIQUID MIXTURE AND MIX UNTIL ALL PIECES

OF BREAD ARE COATED. POUR INTO UNGREASED 9"x13" OVEN PROOF GLASS BAKING DISH. BAKE AT 300° FOR ABOUT 45 MINUTES OR UNTIL GOLDEN BROWN.

To believe is to know that every
day is a new beginning.

RUM SAUCE

1	16 OZ. CONTAINER COOL WHIP
1	CUP SUGAR
1	STICK BUTTER, MELTED
½	CUP RUM OR 2 TBLS. RUM EXTRACT

SPOON OUT COOL WHIP INTO MIXING BOWL AND PLACE IN MICROWAVE FOR ABOUT 1 MINUTE, 30 SECONDS. MIX IN OTHER INGREDIENTS AND RETURN TO MICROWAVE FOR ABOUT ANOTHER 90 SECONDS. REMOVE FROM MICROWAVE. SPOON HOT SAUCE OVER PUDDING SERVINGS. MAKES 8 TO 10 SERVINGS

In every ordinary day
there are a thousand miracles.

BREAD PUDDING WITH RAISINS

1	CUP "BROWNULATED" BROWN SUGAR
2	SLICES WHITE BREAD
2	TBLS. BUTTER
⅓	CUP RAISINS
3	EGGS
2	CUPS MILK
$\frac{1}{8}$	TSP. SALT
1	TSP. VANILLA

PUT BROWN SUGAR IN TOP OF DOUBLE BOILER.

BUTTER BREAD (USING THE 2 TBLS. OF BUTTER).
DICE BREAD AND SPRINKLE MORE BROWN SUGAR
OVER THE BREAD. ADD RAISINS.
BEAT TOGETHER EGGS, MILK, SALT AND
VANILLA AND POUR OVER BREAD. DO NOT STIR.

PLACE OVER SIMMERING WATER AND COOK FOR
1 HOUR WITH TIGHT LID ON IT. (THE BROWN
SUGAR WILL FORM A SAUCE.)

Blessed are they who believe
and see through the eyes of a child.

HONEY CAKE

½	CUP GOLDEN RAISINS
2	TBLS. ORANGE JUICE
2½	CUPS ALL PURPOSE FLOUR
1	TSP. BAKING POWDER
1	TSP. BAKING SODA
½	TSP. GROUND CINNAMON
¼	TSP. GROUND GINGER
	PINCH GROUND CLOVES
2	EGGS
1	CUP SUGAR
½	CUP BUCKWHEAT OR WILDFLOWER HONEY
½	CUP UNSWEETENED APPLESAUCE
	JUICE OF 1 ORANGE, ½ CUP
¼	CUP BLACK COFFEE
1	TSP. GRATED ZEST FROM THE ORANGE
½	CUP CHOPPED WALNUTS

PREHEAT THE OVEN TO 350°. SPRAY TWO 6 CUP LOAF PANS WITH COOKING SPRAY.

IN A SMALL BOWL, PLUMP THE RAISINS IN THE ORANGE JUICE FOR 20 MINUTES. DRAIN WELL.

IN A LARGE BOWL, SIFT THE FLOUR WITH THE BAKING POWDER, BAKING SODA, CINNAMON, GINGER, AND CLOVES.
IN A MEDIUM BOWL, BEAT THE EGGS WITH THE SUGAR UNTIL FOAMY. ADD THE HONEY,

APPLESAUCE, ORANGE JUICE, ZEST, AND COFFEE
AND BLEND WELL. ADD THE HONEY MIXTURE TO
THE DRY INGREDIENTS, MIXING UNTIL THEY
ARE JUST BLENDED. STIR IN THE RAISINS AND
NUTS.

DIVIDE THE BATTER EVENLY BETWEEN THE 2
PREPARED PANS. PLACE THE PANS ON A RACK IN
THE CENTER OF THE OVEN AND BAKE 45
MINUTES, UNTIL A TOOTHPICK INSERTED IN
THE CENTER OF THE CAKE COMES OUT CLEAN.
DO NOT WORRY IF THE LOAVES ARE VERY
BROWN ON THE OUTSIDE.

COOL ON A RACK FOR 10 MINUTES. REMOVE THE
CAKES FROM THE PAN AND COOL COMPLETELY.

WRAP TIGHTLY IN PLASTIC WRAP AND STORE
AT ROOM TEMPERATURE 2 TO 3 DAYS BEFORE
SERVING.

*Every child born on earth has the right to be
loved, to be nurtured, and to reach for a dream.*

PISTACHIO PIE

1¾	CUPS PLAIN FLOUR
1	CUP CHOPPED PECANS
1¾	STICKS MELTED BUTTER
1	8 OZ. PKG. CREAM CHEESE
1¼	CUPS POWDERED SUGAR
2	3 OZ. PKGS. INSTANT PISTACHIO PUDDING MIX
3	CUPS MILK
1	CONTAINER WHIPPED TOPPING

MIX FLOUR AND PECANS. ADD BUTTER. SPREAD AND PRESS IN 9"x12" PAN. BAKE AT 350° 20 TO 25 MINUTES. COOL COMPLETELY.

WHIP CREAM CHEESE, POWDERED SUGAR AND 1 CUP WHIPPED TOPPING. SPREAD CAREFULLY OVER COOLED CRUST.

MIX PUDDING MIX WITH MILK UNTIL BLENDED. SPREAD AS NEXT LAYER. CHILL 30 MINUTES. TOP WITH REMAINING WHIPPED TOPPING AND SERVE.

7-UP CAKE

5	EGGS
3	CUPS CAKE FLOUR
3	CUPS SUGAR
3	STICKS BUTTER
1	TSP. BUTTER FLAVORING
2	TBLS. LEMON EXTRACT
$\frac{3}{4}$	CUP 7-UP
1	TSP. LEMON ZEST (OPTIONAL)
	BAKER'S JOY (SHORTENING AND FLOUR COOKING SPRAY)
	POWDERED SUGAR FOR DUSTING

CREAM BUTTER AND SUGAR TOGETHER, ADD EGGS ONE AT A TIME, BEAT WELL AFTER EACH ADDITION. FOLD SIFTED FLOUR INTO BUTTER AND EGG MIXTURE. GRADUALLY ADD 7-UP, BUTTER FLAVORING, LEMON EXTRACT AND LEMON ZEST. POUR INTO BUNDT PAN SPRAYED WITH BAKER'S JOY. BAKE AT 325° FOR AN HOUR.

COOL 10 MINUTES IN PAN, REMOVE TO WIRE RACK UNTIL COMPLETELY COOL. DUST WITH POWDERED SUGAR.

FRESH APPLE CAKE

2	CUPS SIFTED FLOUR
1	TSP. SALT
1	TSP. SODA
2	TSPS. CINNAMON
1	CUP OIL
2	TSPS. VANILLA
3	EGGS
2	CUPS SUGAR
1	CUP CHOPPED PECANS
3	CUPS FINELY CHOPPED FIRM GRANNY SMITH APPLES (3 LARGE)

SIFT FLOUR, SALT, SODA AND CINNAMON TOGETHER INTO A LARGE MIXING BOWL. ADD THE OIL AND VANILLA. BEAT UNTIL SMOOTH.

IN A SEPARATE BOWL, BEAT EGGS UNTIL THICK AND FOAMY. GRADUALLY ADD SUGAR UNTIL WELL BLENDED.

COMBINE EGG AND FLOUR MIXTURE. FOLD IN PECANS AND APPLES. POUR INTO A GREASED AND FLOURED BUNDT OR TUBE PAN. BAKE AT 350° FOR 1 HOUR. COOL IN PAN 15 MINUTES.

IMPOSSIBLE FRENCH APPLE PIE

6	CUPS SLICED, PARED, TART APPLES
1¼	TSPS. GROUND CINNAMON
¼	TSP. GROUND NUTMEG
1	CUP SUGAR
¾	CUP MILK
½	CUP BISQUICK BAKING MIX
2	EGGS
3	TBLS. BUTTER, SOFTENED
	STREUSEL

HEAT OVEN TO 325°. GREASE 10" x 1½" PIE PLATE. MIX APPLES AND SPICES; TURN INTO PLATE. BEAT REMAINING INGREDIENTS EXCEPT STREUSEL UNTIL SMOOTH, 15 SECONDS IN BLENDER ON HIGH OR 1 MINUTE WITH HAND BEATER. POUR INTO PLATE. SPRINKLE WITH STREUSEL. BAKE UNTIL KNIFE INSERTED COMES OUT CLEAN, 55 TO 60 MINUTES.

STREUSEL:

MIX 1 CUP BISQUICK BAKING MIX, ½ CUP CHOPPED NUTS, ⅓ CUP PACKED BROWN SUGAR AND 3 TBLS. FIRM BUTTER UNTIL CRUMBLY.

PEAR AND APPLE CRISP

FOR THE TOPPING:

¾	CUP ALL PURPOSE FLOUR
¾	CUP FIRMLY PACKED
	LIGHT BROWN SUGAR
¾	TSP. CINNAMON
½	TSP. NUTMEG
6	TBLS. BUTTER
2/3	CUP COARSELY CRUSHED
	TOASTED ALMOND

FOR THE FRUIT:

6	MEDIUM SIZE COOKING APPLES
6	MEDIUM SIZE PEARS
3	TBLS. FIRMLY PACKED
	LIGHT BROWN SUGAR
2	TBLS. FRESH LEMON JUICE
	VANILLA YOGURT

FOR THE TOPPING:

COMBINE THE FLOUR, SUGAR AND SPICES IN A
MIXING BOWL. CUT IN BUTTER UNTIL MIXTURE

RESEMBLES FINE CRUMBS. STIR IN TOASTED
ALMONDS. SET ASIDE.

PREHEAT OVEN TO 400°. PEEL FRUIT. THINLY
SLICE. TOSS FRUIT WITH SUGAR AND LEMON
JUICE.

PLACE IN A 2½ QT. BAKING DISH. SPRINKLE
TOPPING OVER FRUIT. BAKE IN PREHEATED 400°
OVEN FOR 30 MINUTES, OR UNTIL FRUIT IS
TENDER WHEN PIERCED WITH A FORK. SERVE
WARM OR COLD, TOPPING EACH WITH VANILLA
YOGURT.

*Under paper-star nights,
we hold the hands of our children, listen quietly
with them to the sound of crickets, and let our
hearts fill with the tender moment.*

RETIREMENT CAKE

2	CUPS FLOUR
1½	CUPS SUGAR
2	TSPS. SODA
2	EGGS
1	16 OZ. CAN FRUIT COCKTAIL

MIX INGREDIENTS WELL.

POUR INTO A 9"x13" GREASED AND FLOURED
PAN. BAKE AT 300° FOR ABOUT 45 MINUTES OR

UNTIL A TOOTHPICK INSERTED IN CENTER
COMES OUT CLEAN.

TOPPING:

½   CUP BUTTER
1   CUP SUGAR
1   TSP. VANILLA
½   CUP EVAPORATED MILK
1   CUP COCONUT
1   CUP CHOPPED PECANS

MIX WELL AND LET COME TO A BOIL. LET BOIL
FOR 2 MINUTES. SPREAD ON CAKE WHILE HOT.

*The break of dawn,
the twinkling of stars, the glow of moonlight are
each, within themselves, a miracle on earth.*

LEMON GLAZED CHEESECAKE

CRUST:

2   CUPS GRAHAM CRACKER CRUMBS
¼   CUP SUGAR
7   TBLS. MELTED BUTTER

COMBINE CRUMBS AND SUGAR. STIR IN BUTTER
WELL. QUICKLY PRESS MIXTURE FIRMLY AND
EVENLY ONTO SIDES (½" FROM TOP) AND

BOTTOM OF 9"x3" SPRINGFORM PAN. BAKE AT
350°.

FRESH LEMON FILLING:

2   PKGS. (8 OZ. EACH) NON-FAT CREAM
         CHEESE, SOFTENED
1   8 OZ. PKG. REDUCED-FAT CREAM CHEESE,
         SOFTENED
3   +1 EGGS
⅓   CUP SUGAR
         JUICE OF 1 LEMON
1   TSP. VANILLA EXTRACT
         GRATED PEEL OF ½ LEMON

IN LARGE BOWL, WITH ELECTRIC MIXER, BEAT
SOFTENED CREAM CHEESE AT MEDIUM SPEED
UNTIL COMPLETELY SMOOTH, ABOUT 2
MINUTES. ADD EGGS, ONE AT A TIME, BEATING
UNTIL SMOOTH. CONTINUE BEATING
GRADUALLY, ADDING ⅓ CUP SUGAR, THEN
LEMON JUICE AND VANILLA. STIR IN LEMON
PEEL. POUR INTO CRUST (FILLING WILL NOT
YET COME UP TO TOP OF CRUST). BAKE AT 350°
FOR 55 MINUTES. TOP WITH 1 CUP SOUR CREAM.

*Be careful not to confuse the limits of your own
field of vision with the limits of the world.*

VERY BERRY PIE

CRUST:

½	RECIPE BASIC FLAKY PIE CRUST, IF USING THE CRUMB TOPPING (RECIPE FOLLOWS) OR
1	RECIPE BASIC FLAKY PIE CRUST (IF MAKING A LATTICE OR SOLID TOP CRUST)

FOLLOW DIRECTIONS FOR BASIC FLAKY PIE CRUST USING A 9" DEEP DISH PIE PAN. REFRIGERATE THE UNBAKED CRUST UNTIL READY TO USE.

PREHEAT THE OVEN TO 350°. BAKE PIE CRUST ON CENTER RACK IN OVEN FOR APPROXIMATELY 10 MINUTES OR UNTIL SLIGHTLY BROWN. LET THE CRUST COOL COMPLETELY BEFORE FILLING.

FILLING:

1	TBL. CORNSTARCH
1	TBL. LEMON JUICE
1	CUP GRANULATED SUGAR
2	+1 CUPS FRESH ASSORTED BERRIES
3	CUPS SLICED STRAWBERRIES

IN A LARGE BOWL, BLEND CORNSTARCH AND LEMON JUICE UNTIL SMOOTH. ADD SUGAR AND MIX UNTIL BLENDED. TOSS FRUIT INTO THE

CORNSTARCH/SUGAR MIXTURE AND LET THE
MIXTURE SIT FOR 15 TO 20 MINUTES. TOSS
AGAIN AND DRAIN OFF THE EXCESS LIQUID.

POUR THE FRUIT MIXTURE INTO THE BAKED PIE
CRUST. TOP WITH THE CRUMB TOPPING
MIXTURE OR WITH A LATTICE OR SOLID TOP
CRUST.

CRUMB TOPPING:

2/3	CUP ALL PURPOSE FLOUR
1/3	CUP GRANULATED SUGAR
1/3	CUP LIGHT BROWN SUGAR, PACKED
1/8	STICK UNSALTED BUTTER, COLD

USING AN ELECTRIC MIXER ON LOW SPEED,
COMBINE FLOUR AND SUGARS. CUT BUTTER
INTO $\frac{1}{2}$" PIECES AND ADD TO THE FLOUR/SUGAR
MIXTURE. MIX UNTIL IT RESEMBLES COARSE
MEAL. SPRINKLE CRUMB TOPPING OVER THE
FRUIT. BAKE THE PIE ON CENTER RACK IN OVEN
FOR 1 TO $1\frac{1}{4}$ HOURS OR UNTIL THE CRUST OR
TOPPING IS GOLDEN BROWN. COOL COMPLETELY
ON A WIRE RACK.

IF PIE IS MADE IN ADVANCE, REFRIGERATE PIE,
BUT BRING IT TO ROOM TEMPERATURE OR HEAT
BEFORE SERVING. SERVES 6 TO 8

BASIC FLAKY PIE CRUST

THIS RECIPE MAKES ENOUGH DOUGH FOR
EITHER TWO 9" DEEP DISH BOTTOM CRUSTS OR
ONE BOTTOM AND ONE TOP (SOLID OR LATTICE)
CRUST.

$2\frac{1}{2}$	CUPS ALL PURPOSE FLOUR
$\frac{1}{2}$	TSP. SALT
$\frac{1}{4}$	LB. (1 STICK) UNSALTED BUTTER, VERY COLD AND CUT INTO $\frac{1}{2}$" PIECES
1	TBL. GRANULATED SUGAR
$\frac{1}{4}$	CUP BUTTER FLAVORED VEGETABLE SHORTENING
4	TO 5 TBLS. ICE WATER

USING A FOOD PROCESSOR FITTED WITH A
METAL BLADE, COMBINE FLOUR, SALT AND
SUGAR. ADD BUTTER AND SHORTENING ALL AT
ONCE, AND "PULSE" THE PROCESSOR ON AND
OFF UNTIL THE MIXTURE RESEMBLES COARSE
MEAL. WITH THE MACHINE RUNNING, ADD ICE
WATER, 1 TBL. AT A TIME UNTIL THE MIXTURE
BEGINS TO HOLD TOGETHER. (STOP
PROCESSING BEFORE THE DOUGH FORMS A
BALL).

GATHER THE DOUGH INTO A BALL WITH YOUR HANDS AND DIVIDE IN HALF. FLATTEN EACH HALF INTO AN 8" DISC AND WRAP IN WAXED PAPER. REFRIGERATE AT LEAST 8 HOURS BEFORE HANDLING. (THE DOUGH MAY ALSO BE FROZEN AT THIS POINT AND KEPT FOR LATER USE. IF FROZEN, DEFROST THE DOUGH IN THE REFRIGERATOR BEFORE USING). REMOVE THE DOUGH FROM THE REFRIGERATOR 20 TO 30 MINUTES BEFORE ROLLING.

PREHEAT THE OVEN TO 350°.

SPRINKLE A FLAT SURFACE WITH FLOUR AND, USING A FLOURED ROLLING PIN, ROLL OUT ONE DISC INTO A 15" CIRCLE. CAREFULLY TRANSFER THE DOUGH INTO THE 9" DEEP DISH PIE PAN. TRIM THE DOUGH, LEAVING ENOUGH TO ALLOW FOR SHRINKAGE AND TO FINISH THE EDGE DECORATIVELY. PRICK THE CRUST WITH A FORK SEVERAL TIMES BEFORE BAKING.

BAKE ON CENTER RACK IN OVEN FOR 15 TO 20 MINUTES OR UNTIL LIGHTLY BROWNED. COOL THE CRUST COMPLETELY.

IF YOU ARE USING EITHER A LATTICE OR SOLID TOP CRUST, LIGHTLY BRUSH THE DOUGH BEFORE BAKING, WITH A MIXTURE OF 1 EGG BEATEN WITH 1 TBL. OF WATER. YOU MIGHT ALSO WANT TO LIGHTLY SPRINKLE THE CRUST WITH GRANULATED SUGAR. IF YOU OPT FOR THE

SOLID TOP CRUST, DON'T FORGET TO MAKE
SEVERAL SLITS IN THE TOP BEFORE BAKING THE
PIE.

278

Cookies & Treats

FORGOTTEN COOKIES

PREHEAT OVEN TO 350°

BEAT 2 EGG WHITES (AT ROOM TEMPERATURE) UNTIL STIFF AND GLOSSY. SLOWLY ADD 2/3 CUP SUGAR UNTIL DISSOLVED. MIX 1 CUP PECANS IN BY HAND. MIX IN 1 PACK SEMI-SWEET CHOCOLATE CHIPS BY HAND. LINE COOKIE SHEET WITH ALUMINUM FOIL. DROP BY SPOONFULS. TURN OFF OVEN. BAKE 20 MINUTES.

May this day bring miracles and dreams.

BANANA-PECAN MUFFINS

$4\frac{1}{2}$	CUPS ALL PURPOSE FLOUR
$1\frac{3}{4}$	CUPS SUGAR
5	TSPS. BAKING POWDER
$1\frac{3}{4}$	TSPS. SALT
$1\frac{3}{4}$	CUPS MASHED RIPE BANANAS
$\frac{1}{4}$	CUP CANOLA OIL
2	LARGE EGGS
$1\frac{1}{3}$	CUPS NON-FAT MILK
$1\frac{3}{4}$	CUPS PECAN HALVES, DO NOT CHOP

PREHEAT OVEN TO 350°. LINE 2 (12 CUP) MUFFIN TINS WITH PAPER LINERS.

IN A LARGE BOWL, MIX TOGETHER THE FLOUR, SUGAR, BAKING POWDER AND SALT. SET ASIDE.

IN ANOTHER LARGE BOWL, MIX TOGETHER THE
BANANA, CANOLA OIL AND EGGS. GRADUALLY
ADD DRY INGREDIENTS TO BANANA MIXTURE,
ALTERNATING WITH THE MILK, ADDING DRY
INGREDIENTS LAST. STIR IN NUTS.

MEASURE OUT BATTER EVENLY INTO LINED
MUFFIN CUPS, FILLING CUPS 7/8 FULL. BAKE 25
MINUTES, UNTIL MUFFINS ARE PUFFED AND
GOLDEN BROWN. CHECK WITH TOOTHPICK FOR
DONENESS. SERVE WARM, OR COOL MUFFINS
ON RACKS. FREEZE FOR LONGER STORAGE.

*Every heart has its passion, doing what you love
gives your spirit wings.*

CHOCOLATE MINT BROWNIES

BROWNIE LAYER:

2	BEATEN EGGS
$\frac{1}{2}$	CUP MELTED BUTTER
1	CUP SUGAR
2	SQUARES MELTED UNSWEETENED CHOCOLATE
$\frac{1}{2}$	TSP. PEPPERMINT FLAVORING
$\frac{1}{2}$	CUP FLOUR
$\frac{1}{2}$	CUP CHOPPED PECANS

COMBINE THE EGGS, BUTTER AND SUGAR. BEAT
WELL. ADD THE CHOCOLATE AND PEPPERMINT
FLAVORING AND STIR UNTIL THOROUGHLY
BLENDED. ADD THE FLOUR AND NUTS AND MIX
WELL. POUR INTO A GREASED 9" SQUARE PAN.
BAKE AT 350° FOR 25 TO 30 MINUTES.

MINT LAYER:

2   TBLS. MELTED BUTTER
1   TBL. MILK
1   CUP SIFTED CONFECTIONERS SUGAR
1   TSP. PEPPERMINT FLAVORING
        GREEN FOOD COLORING

COMBINE MINT LAYER INGREDIENTS AND
SPREAD OVER COOLED BAKED BROWNIE LAYER.
PLACE IN REFRIGERATOR UNTIL FIRM.

FROSTING:

1   SQUARE MELTED UNSWEETENED
        CHOCOLATE
1   TBL. BUTTER

COMBINE THE CHOCOLATE AND BUTTER AND
SPREAD OVER THE FIRM MINT LAYER.
RETURN TO REFRIGERATOR UNTIL FIRM. CUT
INTO STRIPS. MAKES 48 STRIPS

FUDGE MUFFINS

MELT TOGETHER:

2	STICKS BUTTER
4	1 OZ. SQUARES OF SEMI-SWEET CHOCOLATE (OR WHITE CHOCOLATE) (DO NOT BEAT)

ADD:

$1\frac{3}{4}$	CUPS SUGAR
1	CUP FLOUR
4	EGGS
1	TSP. VANILLA
1	CUP CHOPPED PECANS

SPRAY MUFFINS TINS WITH PAM. FILL MUFFIN TINS $\frac{1}{2}$ FULL. BAKE 25 TO 30 MINUTES AT 325°. MAKES 26 MUFFINS

LEMON OAT SHORTBREAD

2	CUPS (4 STICKS) BUTTER, SOFTENED
1 ⅓	CUPS POWDERED SUGAR
3	+1 TSPS. FINELY GRATED LEMON PEEL (FIRMLY PACKED)
2½	CUPS ALL-PURPOSE FLOUR
2	CUPS OATS (QUICK OR OLD-FASHIONED, UNCOOKED)*
½	TSP. BAKING POWDER
½	TSP. SALT (OPTIONAL)

*IF USING OLD-FASHIONED OATS, INCREASE THE FLOUR TO 2¾ CUPS.

IN LARGE BOWL, BEAT BUTTER, SUGAR AND LEMON PEEL WITH ELECTRIC MIXER UNTIL CREAMY. GRADUALLY ADD COMBINED FLOUR, OATS, BAKING POWDER AND SALT. MIX WELL. DIVIDE DOUGH IN HALF. WRAP EACH HALF IN PLASTIC WRAP. CHILL 1 HOUR OR UNTIL FIRM.

HEAT OVEN TO 325°. REMOVE ONE PORTION OF DOUGH FROM REFRIGERATOR.

ON LIGHTLY FLOURED SURFACE, ROLL DOUGH INTO 10" SQUARE. WITH SHARP KNIFE, CUT INTO 30 RECTANGLES (EACH ABOUT 3" LONG AND 1" WIDE). TRANSFER RECTANGLES TO UNGREASED COOKIE SHEETS. PRICK EACH

RECTANGLE THREE TIMES WITH A FORK.
REPEAT WITH REMAINING DOUGH.

BAKE 18 TO 20 MINUTES OR UNTIL LIGHTLY
BROWNED. COOL 1 MINUTE ON COOKIE SHEETS.
REMOVE TO WIRE RACK. COOL COMPLETELY.
STORE TIGHTLY COVERED. MAKES 5 DOZEN

It is not always the understanding of life that is important, but rather the believing in the wonder of it.

MINI-CHOCOLATE CHEESECAKES

18	OREO COOKIES
2	8 OZ. PKGS. CREAM CHEESE
2	EGGS
$\frac{1}{2}$	CUP SUGAR
1	CUP MILK CHOCOLATE CHIPS, MELTED (CAN SUBSTITUTE WHITE CHOCOLATE OR VANILLA CHIPS)

TOPPING:

WHIPPING CREAM OR WHIPPED TOPPING
CHOCOLATE CURLS OR CHERRIES

PUT 1 COOKIE IN EACH PAPER-LINED MUFFIN
TIN.

COMBINE CREAM CHEESE AND SUGAR. MIX AT
MEDIUM SPEED UNTIL WELL BLENDED. ADD
EGGS, ONE AT A TIME. BLEND IN MELTED
CHOCOLATE. POUR INTO MUFFIN TINS
(ALMOST FULL).

BAKE AT 325° FOR 25 MINUTES. SERVE TOPPED
WITH WHIPPED CREAM AND CHOCOLATE CURLS
OR CHERRIES.

Our days belong to those who believe in miracles
and wonder, and know in their hearts what a
rare, rare, world it is.

PROMISE OF CHOCOLATE COOKIES

1	CUP BUTTER, ROOM TEMPERATURE
1	CUP DARK BROWN SUGAR
1	CUP GRANULATED SUGAR
2	EGGS, ROOM TEMPERATURE
1	TSP. VANILLA
1	TSP. CINNAMON
½	TSP. LEMON JUICE
1	TBL. HONEY
2½	CUPS OATMEAL
2	CUPS FLOUR
½	TSP. SALT
1	TSP. BAKING POWDER
1	TSP. BAKING SODA
12	OZS. CHOCOLATE CHIPS
1½	CUPS CHOPPED PECANS

10   DOVE MILK CHOCOLATE PROMISES,
           FINELY GRATED

CREAM TOGETHER THE BUTTER AND SUGARS UNTIL LIGHT AND FLUFFY. ADD IN THE EGGS, VANILLA, CINNAMON, LEMON JUICE AND HONEY. SET ASIDE.

IN A BLENDER OR FOOD PROCESSOR, PROCESS THE OATMEAL INTO A FINE POWDER. ADD IN THE FLOUR, SALT, BAKING POWDER AND BAKING SODA. BLEND TOGETHER BRIEFLY, THEN STIR INTO THE BUTTER AND SUGAR MIXTURE. FOLD IN THE CHOCOLATE CHIPS, PECANS AND GRATED DOVE MILK CHOCOLATE PROMISES.

SHAPE DOUGH INTO GOLF BALL SIZE BALLS AND DROP ONTO GREASED COOKIE SHEETS 2" APART. BAKE IN A PREHEATED 350° OVEN FOR 14 TO 16 MINUTES. LET SET 1 MINUTE, THEN REMOVE FROM COOKIE SHEETS TO BAKING RACKS TO FINISH COOLING. MAKES 6 DOZEN COOKIES

Love exists in many forms and weaves its golden thread into the fabric of our living.

COOKIES 'N' CRÈME MOUSSE

1   7 OZ. HERSHEY'S COOKIES 'N' CRÈME BAR
       OR
       21 COOKIES 'N' CRÈME NUGGETS

1	CUP MINIATURE MARSHMALLOWS
2	CUPS (1 PT.) COLD WHIPPING CREAM, DIVIDED
3	TBLS. POWDERED SUGAR

REMOVE WRAPPERS FROM CANDY, BREAK INTO PIECES. IN SMALL SAUCEPAN, STIR TOGETHER MARSHMALLOWS AND $\frac{1}{2}$ CUP WHIPPING CREAM. COOK OVER MEDIUM HEAT, STIRRING CONSTANTLY, UNTIL MARSHMALLOWS ARE MELTED. REMOVE FROM HEAT, STIR IN CANDY PIECES. STIR UNTIL MELTED, TRANSFER TO LARGE BOWL. COOL COMPLETELY.

IN SMALL MIXER BOWL, BEAT REMAINING $1\frac{1}{2}$ CUPS WHIPPING CREAM AND POWDERED SUGAR UNTIL STIFF. GRADUALLY FOLD INTO COOLED CANDY MIXTURE. SPOON INTO INDIVIDUAL DESSERT DISHES. COVER, REFRIGERATE UNTIL READY TO SERVE. REFRIGERATE LEFTOVER MOUSSE. MAKE 8 ($\frac{1}{2}$ CUP) SERVINGS

Seedlings, with their quiet strength, break through the ground, and just like the morning, reach for the sun.

EASY CHERRY RUM BALLS

2	CUPS CRUSHED VANILLA WAFERS, (40 TO 45 WAFERS)
1	CUP POWDERED SUGAR
$\frac{1}{2}$	CUP FINELY CHOPPED CANDIED RED AND/OR GREEN CHERRIES
$\frac{1}{2}$	CUP FINELY CHOPPED PECANS OR WALNUTS
$\frac{1}{4}$	CUP RUM
3	TBLS. CORN SYRUP
2	TBLS. BUTTER, MELTED
$\frac{1}{4}$	CUP POWDERED SUGAR

IN MEDIUM BOWL, COMBINE VANILLA WAFERS, ONE CUP POWDERED SUGAR, CHERRIES AND PECANS. MIX WELL. ADD RUM, CORN SYRUP AND BUTTER. MIX WELL.

SHAPE MIXTURE INTO 1" BALLS. ROLL IN $\frac{1}{4}$ CUP POWDERED SUGAR. COVER TIGHTLY. LET STAND FOR 24 HOURS TO BLEND FLAVORS. MAKES 3 DOZEN COOKIES

Love is the passion of the soul
and the strength of the spirit.

GISELE'S COOKIES

1½	CUPS BUTTER, SOFTENED
1¼	CUPS GRANULATED SUGAR
1¼	CUPS BROWN SUGAR
1	TBL. VANILLA
½	TSP. ALMOND EXTRACT
2	EGGS
4	CUPS ALL PURPOSE FLOUR
2	TSPS. BAKING SODA
1	TSP. SALT
3	+1 CUPS GUITTARD MILK CHOCOLATE CHIPS
2	CUPS CHOPPED PECANS

MIX BUTTER, SUGARS, VANILLA, ALMOND
EXTRACT AND EGGS IN LARGE BOWL. STIR IN
FLOUR, BAKING SODA AND SALT. STIR IN
CHOCOLATE CHIPS AND PECANS.

DROP DOUGH BY TABLESPOONFULS ONTO A
BUTTER-GREASED COOKIE SHEET. BAKE AT 300°
FOR 12 TO 15 MINUTES. MAKES 3½ DOZEN

*Understand that it is not necessary
to understand.*

BETTY'S LEMON CRUNCH

$\frac{1}{2}$	CUP (1 STICK) FIRM BUTTER
$\frac{1}{4}$	CUP PACKED BROWN SUGAR
1	CUP ALL PURPOSE FLOUR
$\frac{1}{2}$	CUP CHOPPED PECANS
1	13 OZ. CAN EVAPORATED MILK, CHILLED
1	6 OZ. CAN FROZEN LEMONADE CONCENTRATE PARTIALLY THAWED
5	DROPS YELLOW FOOD COLOR, IF DESIRED

HEAT OVEN TO 400°. CUT BUTTER INTO BROWN SUGAR AND FLOUR UNTIL EVENLY MIXED. STIR IN PECANS. PRESS MIXTURE EVENLY IN UNGREASED SQUARE PAN, 9"x9"x2". BAKE ABOUT 12 MINUTES OR UNTIL LIGHT BROWN. STIR TO BREAK UP. COOL. RESERVE $\frac{1}{4}$ CUP CRUMB MIXTURE. PRESS REMAINING CRUMBS IN PAN.

BEAT MILK IN CHILLED MEDIUM BOWL UNTIL STIFF. STIR IN REMAINING INGREDIENTS. POUR INTO PAN. SPRINKLE RESERVED CRUMB MIXTURE OVER TOP. COVER AND FREEZE 8 HOURS OR UNTIL FIRM. REMOVE FROM FREEZER 10 MINUTES BEFORE SERVING. FREEZE ANY REMAINING DESSERT.

MICROWAVE PECAN PRALINES

1	1 LB. BOX LIGHT BROWN SUGAR
1	SMALL CARTON WHIPPING CREAM
2	CUPS PECANS
3	TBLS. BUTTER

MIX SUGAR AND CREAM IN A MICROWAVE-SAFE
DISH. COOK IN MICROWAVE FOR 3 MINUTES.

ADD NUTS AND BUTTER. STIR. DROP ONTO
WAXED PAPER.

MONSTER CHOCOLATE CHIP
COOKIES

$2\frac{1}{4}$	CUPS FLOUR
$\frac{1}{2}$	CUP SUGAR
1	CUP BROWN SUGAR
2	TSPS. VANILLA

1	TSP. SALT
1	TSP. BAKING POWDER
2	EGGS
1	CUP BUTTER
2	CUPS OATMEAL
3	CUPS CHOCOLATE CHIPS
1	CUP BUTTERSCOTCH CHIPS
2	CUPS PECANS AND WALNUTS

MIX TOGETHER SOFTENED BUTTER, SUGARS, VANILLA AND EGGS. ADD IN SALT, BAKING POWDER AND FLOUR. STIR MIXTURE TOGETHER AND ADD IN OATMEAL, NUTS, CHOCOLATE AND BUTTERSCOTCH CHIPS. MIX WELL AND DROP ONTO GREASED COOKIE SHEET. BAKE AT 350° FOR 12 MINUTES. MAKES 1½ DOZEN

Lucky is the world to have you in it.

PECAN PRALINES

1	CUP BROWN SUGAR
1	CUP WHITE SUGAR
1	CUP CREAM
1	TBL. BUTTER
1	TSP. VANILLA
1	CUP PECANS

MIX ALL INGREDIENTS, EXCEPT PECANS TOGETHER IN A SAUCEPAN. BOIL UNTIL IT REACHES THE SOFT BALL STAGE. REMOVE FROM

HEAT AND ADD NUTS. STIR UNTIL MIXTURE
BEGINS TO THICKEN. DROP QUICKLY BY
SPOONFULS ONTO WAX PAPER TO HARDEN.

TRIPLE CHIP CHOCOLATE COOKIES

1	CUP BUTTER, SOFTENED
½	CUP BUTTER-FLAVORED CRISCO
1	CUP GRANULATED SUGAR
1¼	CUPS BROWN SUGAR, PACKED
2	EGGS
2	TSPS. VANILLA
⅓	CUP COCOA
3	CUPS ALL PURPOSE FLOUR
1	TSP. SODA
1	HEAPING TSP. SALT
12	OZS. WHITE CHOCOLATE CHIPS
6	OZS. SEMI-SWEET CHOCOLATE CHIPS
7	OZS. NESTLE CRUNCH BAKING PIECES

MIX BUTTER, CRISCO, SUGAR AND BROWN
SUGAR UNTIL FLUFFY AND LIGHTER IN COLOR.
ADD IN EGGS, VANILLA AND COCOA AND MIX
TOGETHER.

MIX TOGETHER FLOUR, SODA AND SALT AND
ADD TO MIXTURE.

FOLD IN WHITE CHOCOLATE CHIPS, SEMI-
SWEET CHOCOLATE CHIPS AND NESTLE CRUNCH
BAKING PIECES AND USING SMALL ICE CREAM
SCOOP, SCOOP UP DOUGH, SCRAPING ON EDGE
OF BOWL SO DOUGH IS NO HIGHER THAN EDGE
OF SCOOP, PLACE ON UNGREASED COOKIE
SHEETS. BAKE AT 375° FOR 11 MINUTES.

Give yourself time
for your heart to find its pleasure,
for life should not all labor be.

CARRIE'S COOKIES

1	BOX LEMON CAKE MIX WITH PUDDING
1	STICK BUTTER
1	EGG
1	CUP RICE KRISPIES

MIX ALL INGREDIENTS. SHAPE INTO 1" BALLS.
GREASE COOKIE SHEET. BAKE IN A 350° OVEN
FOR 15 MINUTES OR UNTIL LIGHTLY BROWN.

We spend time wishing we had forever, and
overlook the golden moments
we hold in our hands.

EASY LEMON SOURS

1	(1 LB., 2.5 OZ.) PKG. YELLOW CAKE MIX
2	CUPS CRUSHED CORNFLAKES
½	CUP PACKED BROWN SUGAR
⅓	CUP CHOPPED NUTS
½	CUP BUTTER, SOFTENED
1	(3 OZ.) PKG. LEMON PUDDING MIX (NOT INSTANT)
1	14 OZ. CAN SWEETENED CONDENSED MILK
1	TSP. LEMON EXTRACT, DIVIDED
1	CUP POWDERED SUGAR, SIFTED
2	TO 5 TSPS. WATER

HEAT OVEN TO 350°. GENEROUSLY GREASE BOTTOM AND SIDES OF A (15"x10"x1") PAN.

IN A LARGE BOWL, COMBINE CAKE MIX, CORNFLAKES, BROWN SUGAR, NUTS AND BUTTER. RESERVE 1½ CUPS OF THE MIXTURE FOR THE TOPPING. PRESS THE REMAINING MIXTURE INTO BOTTOM OF PAN.

IN A SMALL BOWL, COMBINE PUDDING MIX, CONDENSED MILK AND ¾ TSP. LEMON EXTRACT. MIX WELL. POUR EVENLY OVER MIXTURE PRESSED IN BOTTOM OF PAN. SPREAD GENTLY. SPRINKLE WITH MIXTURE RESERVED FOR TOPPING.

BAKE IN 350° OVEN FOR 20 TO 30 MINUTES.
LOOSEN EDGES WITH KNIFE.

COMBINE POWDERED SUGAR AND ¼ TSP. LEMON
EXTRACT. ADD ENOUGH WATER FOR DESIRED
DRIZZLING CONSISTENCY. BLEND UNTIL
SMOOTH. DRIZZLE OVER WARM BARS. COOL
COMPLETELY. CUT INTO BARS. MAKES 48 BARS

ITALIAN FIG COOKIES

DOUGH:

2	STICKS BUTTER
1	CUP GRANULATED SUGAR
2	EGGS, BEATEN
6	CUPS ALL PURPOSE FLOUR, SIFTED
3	TSPS. BAKING POWDER
2	TSPS. VANILLA
½	CUP MILK

IN LARGE BOWL, CREAM BUTTER WITH SUGAR.
ADD EGGS AND VANILLA AND MIX WELL.
SIFT FLOUR AND BAKING POWDER TOGETHER.
ADD TO EGG MIXTURE.

WORKING WITH FLOURED HANDS, ADD ENOUGH
MILK TO HOLD DOUGH TOGETHER SO IT CAN BE
ROLLED. PINCH OFF A SMALL AMOUNT AND
ROLL OUT ON FLOURED SURFACE ABOUT 3"
WIDE AND 12" LONG AND 3/16" THICK.

SPREAD DATE FILLING ALONG HALF OF THE
LENGTH OF DOUGH. LAP THE DOUGH OVER THE
FILLING AND PRESS TO SEAL. CUT INTO ABOUT
1½" SQUARES. YOU CAN ALSO NOTCH DOUGH
FOR A FANCY LOOK.

BAKE ON LIGHTLY GREASED COOKIE SHEET AT
350° ABOUT 15 TO 20 MINUTES OR UNTIL
LIGHTLY BROWNED. COOL ON WIRE RACK
THOROUGHLY BEFORE ADDING ICING.

DATE FILLING:

3	PACKS DRIED FIGS
	WITH STEMS REMOVED
1	TO 2 CUPS CHOPPED PECANS
1	BOX RAISINS
	JUICE FROM 1 ORANGE AND
	ABOUT 1 TSP. GRATED ORANGE RIND
½	TO 1 PINT FIG PRESERVES
1	TSP. CINNAMON
1	TSP. ALLSPICE
½	CUP GRANULATED SUGAR
	ABOUT ⅓ CUP WARM WATER,
	TO MAKE MIXTURE MANAGEABLE
1	LB. DATES

GRIND FIGS, PECANS, RAISINS AND DATES IN
FOOD PROCESSOR. ADD PRESERVES, SPICES AND
ORANGE RIND AND JUICE.

DISSOLVE SUGAR IN WATER AND ADD TO FRUIT
MIXTURE, BLENDING WELL. FILLING NEEDS TO
BE SOFT ENOUGH TO SPREAD.

RUM BALLS

3	CUPS VANILLA WAFER CRUMBS, FINELY CHOPPED (MEASURE AFTER CHOPPING)
1	CUP POWDERED SUGAR
1	CUP PECANS, CHOPPED FINE
2	+1 JIGGERS RUM

MIX ABOVE INGREDIENTS TOGETHER IN LARGE
BOWL (MAY NEED TO USE HANDS FOR THIS -
NOT AN ELECTRIC MIXER).

SHAPE INTO SMALL BALLS, THEN ROLL IN
POWDERED SUGAR TO COAT. STORE IN COVERED
CONTAINER. MAKES ABOUT 4 DOZEN

*Beyond the clouds, behind the rain,
there are a thousand rainbows.*

TOFFEE CRUNCH BROWNIES

1	1 LB., 5.2 OZ. PKG. FUDGE BROWNIE MIX
1	CUP CRISP RICE CEREAL

½   CUP ENGLISH TOFFEE BITS
         HEAVY DUTY ALUMINUM FOIL

PREHEAT OVEN TO 350°. LINE A 13"x9"x2"
BAKING PAN WITH HEAVY DUTY ALUMINUM
FOIL. SPRAY WITH NONSTICK COOKING SPRAY
AND SET ASIDE.

FOLLOW PACKAGE DIRECTIONS TO PREPARE
BROWNIE MIX. SPREAD BATTER EVENLY IN
FOIL-LINED PAN. SPRINKLE CEREAL EVENLY
OVER BATTER. PRESS LIGHTLY. SPRINKLE
TOFFEE BITS EVENLY OVER CEREAL.

BAKE UNTIL BROWNIES ARE SET, 30 TO 35
MINUTES. COOK IN PAN ON WIRE RACK.

LIFT FOIL TO REMOVE BROWNIES FROM PAN TO
CUTTING BOARD. FOLD FOIL BACK TO CUT
BROWNIES.

*May your dreams sail high and wide and may
the child in your heart stay forever.*

BLONDIE SWIRLS

½   CUP BUTTER
1½   CUPS FIRMLY PACKED BROWN SUGAR
2   EGGS
1   TSP. VANILLA EXTRACT
1½   CUPS ALL PURPOSE FLOUR

2	TSPS. BAKING POWDER
$\frac{1}{2}$	TSP. SALT
$\frac{1}{2}$	CUP CHOPPED WALNUTS
1	6 OZ. PKG. SEMISWEET CHOCOLATE MORSELS, DIVIDED

MELT BUTTER IN A HEAVY SAUCEPAN. ADD
BROWN SUGAR, AND STIR UNTIL COMBINED.
REMOVE FROM HEAT AND COOL. ADD EGGS, ONE
AT A TIME, BEATING AFTER EACH ADDITION.
STIR IN VANILLA.

COMBINE FLOUR, BAKING POWDER AND SALT.
ADD TO SUGAR MIXTURE, STIRRING WELL. STIR
IN WALNUTS AND $\frac{1}{4}$ CUP CHOCOLATE MORSELS.

SPREAD BATTER IN A GREASED AND FLOURED
13"x9"x2" BAKING PAN. SPRINKLE WITH
REMAINING CHOCOLATE MORSELS. BAKE AT
350° FOR 3 MINUTES. REMOVE FROM OVEN AND
GENTLY SWIRL BATTER WITH A KNIFE. RETURN
TO OVEN AND BAKE AN ADDITIONAL 20
MINUTES. COOL AND CUT INTO BARS. MAKES
ABOUT 2$\frac{1}{2}$ DOZEN

Love is the real gift and the magic that will abundantly fill our hearts, if only we let it in.

BUTTERMINT COOKIES

12	TBLS. UNSALTED BUTTER, SOFTENED
2/3	CUP SUGAR
1	LARGE EGG
$\frac{1}{2}$	TSP. VANILLA EXTRACT
$\frac{1}{2}$	TSP. PEPPERMINT EXTRACT, OPTIONAL
2	CUPS UNBLEACHED WHITE FLOUR, SIFTED
2	TBLS. MINCED PEPPERMINT OR ORANGE MINT LEAVES
	PINCH OF SALT

CREAM THE BUTTER AND SUGAR. BEAT IN THE
EGG AND THE EXTRACTS. GRADUALLY MIX IN
THE FLOUR AND STIR IN THE MINCED
PEPPERMINT AND A PINCH OF SALT. THE DOUGH
WILL BE SOFT.

DIVIDE THE DOUGH INTO 3 PARTS. USING
PLASTIC WRAP TO SHAPE THE DOUGH, ROLL
EACH PART INTO A CYLINDER ABOUT $1\frac{1}{4}$" IN
DIAMETER. CHILL THE ROLLS FOR AN HOUR, OR
PLACE IN THE FREEZER FOR 20 MINUTES.

PREHEAT THE OVEN TO 350°. REMOVE THE
PLASTIC WRAP AND SLICE THE DOUGH $\frac{1}{4}$" THICK.
PLACE THE SLICES ON UNGREASED BAKING
SHEETS AND BAKE FOR ABOUT 10 MINUTES,
UNTIL THEY ARE A LIGHT GOLDEN BROWN.

IMMEDIATELY TRANSFER THE COOKIES TO
RACKS TO COOL. YIELDS 4 DOZEN COOKIES

May you fill this day with wonder,
and live the magic of your forgotten dreams.

ITALIAN SPICE COOKIES

7	CUPS ALL PURPOSE FLOUR
3	TBLS. BAKING POWDER
1	TBL. VANILLA EXTRACT
1	LB. BUTTER
1	CUP COCOA
1	TBL. CINNAMON
1	TSP. NUTMEG
1	TSP. ALLSPICE
2	CUPS GRANULATED SUGAR
3	EGGS
1	CUP MILK
1	CUP CHOPPED PECANS

IN LARGE BOWL, BEAT EGGS, SUGAR AND
BUTTER UNTIL BLENDED. STIR IN VANILLA AND
SET ASIDE.

SIFT FLOUR, BAKING POWDER, COCOA AND
SPICES. ADD TO EGG MIXTURE AND BEAT UNTIL
BLENDED. STIR IN MILK AND PECANS.

ROLL INTO SMALL BALLS. PLACE ON LIGHTLY
GREASED COOKIE SHEET AND BAKE AT 350°
ABOUT 10 TO 15 MINUTES OR UNTIL THE

BOTTOM LOOKS LIGHTLY BROWNED. FROST
WITH THE FOLLOWNG ICING. MAKES 7 DOZEN

Spend your summer days like shiny dimes.

ICING FOR SPICE COOKIES

$\frac{1}{2}$ CUP EVAPORATED MILK
1   TSP. VANILLA
1   CUP SIFTED POWDERED SUGAR

IN BOWL, COMBINE ALL INGREDIENTS AND MIX
WELL.

PLACE COOKIES IN A LARGE BOWL, A FEW AT A
TIME, AND ADD SOME OF THE ICING. GENTLY
MIX UNTIL COOKIES ARE COATED. BE CAREFUL
AS COOKIES WILL CRUMBLE. REMOVE AND
PLACE ON WAXED PAPER. REPEAT UNTIL ALL
COOKIES ARE COATED.

ALLOW TO DRY AND STORE IN AIRTIGHT
CONTAINER. (YOU MAY NEED TO MAKE MORE
ICING FOR THIS RECIPE).

*Childhood is the world where make-believe lives
and dreams are kept in a jar.*

OLD ENGLISH CARAMEL APPLES

½	CUP SUGAR
½	CUP FIRMLY PACKED BROWN SUGAR
1	TBL. CORNSTARCH
½	CUP HALF AND HALF
½	CUP SWEET CREAM BUTTER
¼	CUP CHOPPED PECANS, TOASTED
½	TSP. VANILLA
3	MEDIUM APPLES

IN 2 QT. SAUCEPAN, COMBINE SUGARS AND CORNSTARCH. STIR IN HALF AND HALF. ADD BUTTER. COOK OVER MEDIUM HEAT, STIRRING CONSTANTLY, UNTIL MIXTURE COMES TO A FULL BOIL (6 TO 10 MINUTES). BOIL 1 MINUTE. STIR IN PECANS AND VANILLA. LET COOK 15 MINUTES.

MEANWHILE, CORE AND CHUNK APPLES AND PLACE IN 6 INDIVIDUAL BOWLS.

SERVE ABOUT ⅓ CUP WARM SAUCE OVER EACH SERVING OF APPLES. SERVES 6

SUGAR COCOONS

4½	CUPS ALL PURPOSE FLOUR
1	LB. BUTTER
8	HEAPING TBLS. POWDERED SUGAR
1	TSP. WATER
2	TSPS. VANILLA
3	CUPS PECANS, CHOPPED FINE

MIX BUTTER AND POWDERED SUGAR TOGETHER WITH ELECTRIC MIXER. ADD REST OF INGREDIENTS, EXCEPT PECANS. MIX WELL, THEN STIR IN PECANS. ROLL INTO BALLS OR CRESCENTS.

BAKE ON UNGREASED COOKIE SHEETS AT 325° ABOUT 15 MINUTES OR UNTIL VERY LIGHTLY BROWNED. DO NOT LET COOKIES GET TOO BROWN.

REMOVE FROM COOKIE SHEET AND ROLL GENTLY IN POWDERED SUGAR. LET COOKIES COOL, THEN ROLL AGAIN IN POWDERED SUGAR.
MAKES ABOUT 5 TO 6 DOZEN

THE ULTIMATE BROWNIE

2/3	CUP BUTTER
2½	BARS (5 OZS.) UNSWEETENED BAKING CHOCOLATE
1¾	CUPS SUGAR
2	TSPS. VANILLA
3	EGGS
1	CUP ALL PURPOSE FLOUR
1	CUP CHOPPED NUTS
1	6 OZ. PKG. SEMI-SWEET CHOCOLATE MORSELS (1 CUP) CHOCOLATE FROSTING, IF DESIRED

HEAT OVEN TO 350°. GREASE A SQUARE PAN, 9"x9"x2". HEAT BUTTER AND CHOCOLATE OVER LOW HEAT, STIRRING OCCASIONALLY, UNTIL MELTED. REMOVE FROM HEAT. COOL SLIGHTLY.

BEAT SUGAR, VANILLA AND EGGS IN LARGE BOWL ON HIGH SPEED 5 MINUTES. BEAT IN CHOCOLATE MIXTURE ON LOW SPEED. BEAT IN FLOUR ON LOW SPEED JUST UNTIL BLENDED. STIR IN NUTS AND CHOCOLATE CHIPS. SPREAD IN PAN.

BAKE 40 TO 45 MINUTES OR JUST UNTIL BROWNIES BEGIN TO PULL AWAY FROM SIDES

OF PAN. COOK COMPLETELY. SPREAD WITH
CHOCOLATE FROSTING. CUT INTO BARS.
MAKES 2 DOZEN BROWNIES

CHOCOLATE FROSTING:

1	2 OZ. BAR UNSWEETENED BAKING CHOCOLATE
2	TBLS. BUTTER
2	CUPS POWDERED SUGAR
3	TBLS. HOT WATER

HEAT CHOCOLATE AND BUTTER IN 2 QT.
SAUCEPAN OVER LOW HEAT, STIRRING
OCCASIONALLY, UNTIL MELTED. REMOVE FROM
HEAT.

STIR IN POWDERED SUGAR AND WATER UNTIL
SMOOTH. (IF FROSTING IS TOO THICK, ADD
MORE WATER. IF FROSTING IS TOO THIN, ADD
MORE POWDERED SUGAR.)

Because we are friends, blessed am I.

POP-POURRI

2	CUPS SUGAR OR 2 CUPS FIRMLY PACKED LIGHT BROWN SUGAR
1	CUP BUTTER
$\frac{1}{2}$	CUP LIGHT CORN SYRUP
1	TSP. SALT
1	TSP. VANILLA

$\frac{1}{2}$ TSP. BAKING SODA
5   QTS. POPPED CORN
10   OZ. WHOLE ALMONDS
10   OZ. PECAN HALVES (OR WALNUTS)

PREHEAT OVEN TO 250°. BRING SUGAR, BUTTER,
CORN SYRUP AND SALT TO BOIL IN A HEAVY
SAUCEPAN, STIRRING CONSTANTLY. BOIL
WITHOUT STIRRING 5 MINUTES. REMOVE FROM
HEAT. STIR IN VANILLA AND BAKING SODA.
POUR MIXTURE OVER POPPED CORN AND NUTS
IN A VERY LARGE MIXING BOWL. MIX UNTIL
WELL COATED.

POUR INTO TWO 9"x13" PANS. BAKE AT 250°
FOR 1 TO 1$\frac{1}{2}$ HOURS OR UNTIL DRY. STIR EVERY
20 MINUTES. REMOVE FROM OVEN AND COOL.
STORE IN AIRTIGHT CONTAINERS. MAKES 5$\frac{1}{2}$
QUARTS

The garden of life offers a thousand miracles,
and the promise of tomorrow is born of the seeds
of faith we plant today.

WHEAT THIN SURPRISE

1   BOX WHEAT THINS
       (REGULAR OR AIR CRISP)
       CREAMY PEANUT BUTTER
1   1 LB. PKG. WHITE ALMOND BARK

SPREAD ONE SIDE OF WHEAT THINS WITH
PEANUT BUTTER. TOP WITH ANOTHER WHEAT
THIN. REPEAT UNTIL ENTIRE BOX OF CRACKERS
IS USED.

FOLLOW PACKAGE DIRECTIONS AND MELT
ALMOND BARK. WITH TONGS, DIP EACH WHEAT
THIN "SANDWICH" INTO BARK AND MAKE SURE
IT IS COMPLETELY COATED. PLACE ON WAXED
PAPER AND LET HARDEN. STORE IN AIR TIGHT
CONTAINER.

YOU NEED TO KEEP WORKING FAST. I DROP
ABOUT 4 OR 5 IN MELTED BARK AT ONE TIME,
THEN REMOVE ONE AT A TIME WITH TONGS
AND PLACE ON WAXED PAPER. THESE TASTE
LIKE BUTTERFINGERS.

True love is a gift from God.
It is the silent link between the heart and mind,
the silver thread that ties two souls together.

CANDIED ORANGE RIND

1	LARGE ORANGE
1/3	CUP WATER
2/3	CUP SUGAR

CUT ORANGE RIND INTO 24 3" STRIPS, USING
CITRUS PEELER OR SHARP PARING KNIFE.

HEAT WATER, ⅓ CUP SUGAR AND ORANGE RIND
TO BOILING IN SMALL SAUCEPAN. REDUCE
HEAT AND SIMMER UNCOVERED 10 MINUTES.
STRAIN MIXTURE TO REMOVE ORANGE RIND.
DRAIN BRIEFLY ON PAPER TOWELS.

PLACE ⅓ CUP SUGAR AND THE RIND IN PLASTIC
STORAGE BAG. SEAL BAG AND SHAKE TO COAT
RIND. TIE EACH PIECE OF RIND INTO A TWIST
OR KNOT. LET STAND ON WIRE RACK UNTIL
DRY.

*Hope is the tiny song that clings to our hearts
and never stops singing.*

BUTTERSCOTCH POPCORN CRUNCHIES

12	CUPS POPPED POPCORN
1	12 OZ. CAN COCKTAIL PEANUTS
1	12 OZ. PKG. (2 CUPS) BUTTERSCOTCH-FLAVORED MORSELS
1	CUP CORN SYRUP
¼	CUP (1/2 STICK) BUTTER

PREHEAT OVEN TO 300°. PLACE POPCORN AND
NUTS IN LARGE, GREASED ROASTING PAN. SET
ASIDE.

IN HEAVY 3 QT. SAUCEPAN, COMBINE
BUTTERSCOTCH-FLAVORED MORSELS, CORN

SYRUP AND BUTTER. COOK OVER MEDIUM HEAT,
STIRRING CONSTANTLY, UNTIL MIXTURE
BOILS.

POUR BUTTERSCOTCH MIXTURE OVER POPCORN.
STIR TO COAT WELL. BAKE 45 MINUTES,
STIRRING FREQUENTLY.

REMOVE FROM OVEN. STIR EVERY 10 MINUTES
UNTIL SLIGHTLY COOLED. COOL. STORE IN
TIGHTLY COVERED CONTAINER. MAKES ABOUT
3½ QUARTS

Strength cannot be hidden, that which we endure shows our courage.

PEANUT BUTTER BALLS

2	STICKS SOFTENED BUTTER
1	JAR CREAMY PEANUT BUTTER (18 OZ.)
1	LB. POWDERED SUGAR, SIFTED
1	(1 LB.) PKG. CHOCOLATE ALMOND BARK, MELTED ACCORDING TO PACKAGE DIRECTIONS

MIX PEANUT BUTTER AND BUTTER WITH
ELECTRIC MIXER. ADD POWDERED SUGAR AND
MIX WELL. ROLL INTO LITTLE BALLS AND CHILL
AT LEAST 2 HOURS.

WHEN READY TO COVER WITH CHOCOLATE,
MELT THE ALMOND BARK AND DIP PEANUT

BUTTER BALLS IN IT. REMOVE AND LET HARDEN
ON WAXED PAPER.

CAN STORE IN SEALED CONTAINER IN
REFRIGERATOR.

LACE COOKIES

$\frac{3}{4}$	CUP (1$\frac{1}{2}$ STICKS) UNSALTED BUTTER
1	CUP GRANULATED SUGAR
$\frac{1}{4}$	CUP MOLASSES
1	EGG, LIGHTLY BEATEN
2	CUPS ALL PURPOSE FLOUR
2	TSPS. BAKING SODA
$\frac{1}{2}$	TSP. FRESHLY GROUND CLOVES
$\frac{1}{2}$	TSP. GROUND GINGER
1	TSP. FRESHLY GROUND CINNAMON
$\frac{1}{4}$	TSP. SALT

PREHEAT OVEN TO 375°. IN A SAUCEPAN, MELT
THE BUTTER OVER MEDIUM HEAT, STIRRING
FREQUENTLY, 3 TO 4 MINUTES, REMOVE AND
LET COOL TO ROOM TEMPERATURE. POUR IT
INTO A LARGE BOWL AND STIR IN $\frac{3}{4}$ CUP OF
SUGAR, MOLASSES, AND EGG UNTIL WELL
BLENDED. STIR IN THE FLOUR, BAKING SODA,
CLOVES, GINGER, CINNAMON, AND SALT AND

MIX WELL. COVER AND REFRIGERATE FOR 30
MINUTES.

SPRINKLE A SHEET OF WAXED PAPER WITH THE
REMAINING ¼ CUP SUGAR. TEAR OFF PIECES OF
DOUGH ABOUT THE SIZE OF WALNUTS AND
FORM THEM INTO 1" BALLS. ROLL THE BALLS IN
THE SUGAR AND PLACE THEM ABOUT 1½" APART
ON A BAKING SHEET. BAKE FOR 10 MINUTES, OR
UNTIL THE COOKIES PUFF UP, THEN SETTLE
BACK DOWN. TRANSFER THE COOKIES TO A
WIRE RACK AND LET COOL. TO STORE, PLACE IN
SINGLE LAYERS, SEPARATED BY WAXED PAPER
IN AN AIR-TIGHT CONTAINER. MAKES ABOUT 48
COOKIES.

The songs of the wind float soft and silently on the air, like faraway glimpses of forgotten dreams.

CARLA'S PEANUT BUTTER COOKIES

1	EGG
1	CUP PEANUT BUTTER
1	CUP SUGAR

MIX INGREDIENTS AND FORM INTO SMALL
BALLS. BAKE AT 325° TO 350° UNTIL DONE.

If we cling too long to the memory of yesterday,
we will never take notice of the
glory that is today.

SAM'S CHIPS

¾	CUP BROWN SUGAR
¾	CUP SUGAR
1	CUP BUTTER, (SOFTENED)
2	EGGS
1	TSP. VANILLA
1½	CUPS FLOUR
1	TSP. BAKING SODA
½	TSP. BAKING POWDER
½	TSP. SALT
2	CUPS QUICK OATMEAL
1	16 OZ. BAG CHOCOLATE CHIPS (FROZEN)
1	CUP PECANS

COMBINE SUGARS AND BUTTER. ADD EGGS AND VANILLA. COMBINE FLOUR, BAKING SODA, BAKING POWDER AND SALT. ADD TO SUGAR MIXTURE. ADD OTHER INGREDIENTS. BAKE AT 350° TO 375° FOR 10 TO 12 MINUTES.

If we cling too long to the memory of yesterday,
we will never take notice of
the glory that is today.

Breakfast

PAIN PERDU (LOST BREAD)

3	EGGS
¾	CUP MILK
1	TSP. GROUND CINNAMON
½	TSP. GRATED NUTMEG
2	TBLS. SUGAR
½	TSP. VANILLA EXTRACT
1	STICK BUTTER
8	SLICES FRENCH BREAD (DAY OLD)
	POWDERED SUGAR

WHISK IN A LARGE MIXING BOWL, EGGS, MILK, CINNAMON, NUTMEG, SUGAR AND VANILLA UNTIL THE SUGAR IS DISSOLVED.

HEAT 2 TBLS. BUTTER IN A NONSTICK SKILLET OVER MEDIUM HEAT. DIP 2 SLICES OF THE FRENCH BREAD INTO THE EGG MIXTURE, COATING EVENLY. BROWN IN SKILLET UNTIL GOLDEN BROWN, 2 TO 3 MINUTES ON EACH SIDE. REMOVE FROM PAN AND PLACE ON PLATE.

SPRINKLE WITH POWDERED SUGAR OR COVER WITH CANE SYRUP OR A WARM FRUIT COMPOTE. CONTINUE PROCESS WITH REMAINING SLICES OF BREAD.

FRENCH BREAKFAST PUFFS

$\frac{1}{2}$	CUP SUGAR
$\frac{1}{3}$	CUP SHORTENING
1	EGG
$1\frac{1}{2}$	CUPS SIFTED ALL PURPOSE FLOUR
$1\frac{1}{2}$	TSPS. BAKING POWDER
$\frac{1}{2}$	TSP. SALT
$\frac{1}{4}$	TSP. GROUND NUTMEG
$\frac{1}{2}$	CUP MILK
$\frac{1}{2}$	CUP SUGAR
1	TSP. GROUND CINNAMON
6	TBLS. BUTTER, MELTED

IN MIXER BOWL, CREAM TOGETHER THE FIRST $\frac{1}{2}$ CUP SUGAR, THE SHORTENING AND THE EGG.

SIFT TOGETHER FLOUR, BAKING POWDER, SALT AND NUTMEG. ADD TO CREAMED MIXTURE ALTERNATELY WITH MILK. BEAT WELL AFTER EACH ADDITION.

FILL GREASED MUFFIN PAN CUPS 2/3 FULL AND BAKE IN 350° OVEN FOR 20 TO 25 MINUTES.

COMBINE THE REMAINING SUGAR AND CINNAMON. REMOVE MUFFINS FROM OVEN AND IMMEDIATELY DIP MUFFIN TOPS IN MELTED BUTTER, THEN IN THE CINNAMON-SUGAR MIXTURE UNTIL COATED. SERVE WARM.

OVEN-BAKED NUTMEG FRENCH TOAST

8	SLICES ITALIAN OR FRENCH BREAD, CUT ¾" THICK
4	EGGS
1	CUP MILK OR HALF AND HALF
2	TBLS. SUGAR
2	TBLS. ORANGE-FLAVORED LIQUEUR OR ORANGE JUICE
½	TSP. VANILLA
½	TSP. NUTMEG
½	TSP. SALT
⅓	CUP BUTTER
½	CUP CHOPPED PECANS
¼	CUP FIRMLY PACKED LIGHT BROWN SUGAR
1	TBL. BUTTER, MELTED

PLACE BREAD IN SINGLE LAYER IN 13"x9"x2" BAKING DISH. WHISK EGGS, MILK OR HALF AND HALF, SUGAR, LIQUEUR OR ORANGE JUICE, VANILLA, NUTMEG AND SALT. POUR OVER BREAD, TURNING ONCE TO COAT EVENLY.

REFRIGERATE, COVERED, SEVERAL HOURS OR OVERNIGHT.

PLACE ⅓CUP BUTTER IN 15"x10" JELLY ROLL PAN, PLACE IN 400° OVEN TO MELT BUTTER.

REMOVE FROM OVEN, TILT PAN TO COAT EVENLY
WITH BUTTER. ARRANGE BREAD IN SINGLE
LAYER IN PREPARED PAN. BAKE, UNCOVERED,
ABOUT 25 MINUTES OR UNTIL FIRM AND
GOLDEN BROWN. COMBINE PECANS, BROWN
SUGAR AND 1 TBL. BUTTER. SPRINKLE OVER
BAKED FRENCH TOAST. BROIL, ABOUT 5" FROM
HEAT, WATCH CAREFULLY, ABOUT 1 MINUTE OR
UNTIL TOPPING BEGINS TO BUBBLE. SERVES 4

*Our days belong to those who hold
the warmth of days in a golden cup, and the
wonder of evenings in a silver box.*